T0215484

Artificial Intelligence Technology

Huawei Technologies Co., Ltd.

Artificial Intelligence Technology

 Springer

 人民邮电出版社
POSTS & TELECOM PRESS

Huawei Technologies Co., Ltd.
Hangzhou, China

ISBN 978-981-19-2878-9   ISBN 978-981-19-2879-6 (eBook)
https://doi.org/10.1007/978-981-19-2879-6

This Springer imprint is published by the registered company Springer Nature Singapore Pte Ltd.
The registered company address is: 152 Beach Road, #21-01/04 Gateway East, Singapore 189721, Singapore

Preface

The rapid development of information technology in China since the twenty-first century has completely changed the way people study, work, and live. As a key research topic in information science, artificial intelligence, also known as AI, has gone through tumultuously good and hard times ever since the concept was coined half a century ago. It is inspiring to see that AI has achieved a tremendous progress and has been applied in a wide range of fields over the past several years, as a result of the advancements in computing power and big data technology. Today, AI is developing at an exponential rate, and its fruits will be continuously consolidated and deepened.

Despite its drawbacks, the future of AI is believed to be promising. As China has put AI on its national agenda, the interests of almost all the industries have been triggered, and the relevant practitioners are eager to know the status quo and research hotspots of AI, as well as its basic principles and research methodologies.

Although a bulk of AI themed books have been published both in China and the world, providing insightful and precise analysis covering almost all the topics of almost the entire AI sub-disciplines, we have to admit that they could be esoteric for beginners. Artificial Intelligence is a typical interdisciplinary science concerned with wide-ranging aspects and a subject unlikely to be exhausted by only one or two monographs. Therefore, this book aims at presenting our readers fundamental AI knowledge through a streamlined structure and thought-provoking cases. As a Chinese saying goes, "the teacher can teach you the skills, but it depends on yourself to master them." We expect our readers could find the topics they are interested in after reading this book and press ahead with more in-depth studies.

Since intelligence is a very complicated subject, different people could generate distinctive understanding and simulation of intelligence from different perspectives and viewpoints. Therefore, this book explores AI from diversified perspectives in the eight chapters. Chapter 1 is the general introduction, which introduces the origin, technology, fields of application, and trend of the development of AI, as well as Huawei's AI development strategy. Chapter 2 focuses on the machine learning, illustrating the types, overall process, and the popular algorithms of machine learning, such as the decision trees, support vector machine, and clustering algorithms commonly in use today. Chapter 3 gives an overview to the deep learning by reviewing its evolement, and elaborating on its training rules, activation functions, regularization, and optimizers on the basis of neural networks, a widely adopted approach in deep learning. Chapter 4 is about the deep learning frameworks, exemplified by TensorFlow 2.0 as one of the three mainstream frameworks. Chapter 5 brings up the topic of MindSpore, centering on the AI development framework of Huawei and MindSpore's development and application. Chapter 6 is about Huawei Atlas AI computing solution, with the discussion revolving around the software and hardware architecture of Ascend AI processor, Atlas AI computing platform, and its industrial applications. Chapter 7 introduces Huawei's smart terminal AI open platform known as the HUAWEI HiAI platform and the apps developed on it. Chapter 8 looks at the enterprise intelligence application platform Huawei CLOUD by taking Huawei CLOUD EI and ModelArts as major examples. In terms of the narrative style, each chapter has the theories and methods thoroughly expounded, characterized by relatively independent and integral contents. Meanwhile, the chapters are presented in a progressive order to offer asystematic reading experience. Our readers can either read the book chapter by chapter or just jump to certain chapters to have a detailed reading. The chapters are written in concise languages while dealing with profound theories, with part of the derivations of formulas and theorems provided and palpable examples quoted to help beginners to master the basic knowledge, grasp the essence, and put it into practice flexibly. For those abstruse theories, this book only gives a brief overview without any further discussions.

The book is edited by Huawei Technologies Co. Ltd, with LvYunxiang, Wang Luting, Gong Xiaogang, and Chen Miaoran working as the specific editors. Zeng Hongli also contributed to the compilation of several chapters and prepared materials and relevant supporting resources for writing.

Although we worked as careful and prudent as possible during the editing, the inadequacy is inevitable due to our limitations. Therefore, any comments and corrections from our readers are most welcome. In the meantime, we also invite you to share your feedbacks regarding reading this book with us (yunxianglu@hotmail.com).

Hangzhou, China   Huawei Technologies Co., Ltd.
December 2021

Contents

About the Author

Huawei Technologies Co., Ltd. Founded in 1987, Huawei is a leading global provider of information and communications technology (ICT) infrastructure and smart devices. We have approximately 197,000 employees and we operate in over 170 countries and regions, serving more than three billion people around the world.

Huawei's mission is to bring digital to every person, home and organization for a fully connected, intelligent world. To this end, we will: drive ubiquitous connectivity and promote equal access to networks to lay the foundation for the intelligent world; provide the ultimate computing power to deliver ubiquitous cloud and intelligence; build powerful digital platforms to help all industries and organizations become more agile, efficient, and dynamic; redefine user experience with AI, offering consumers more personalized and intelligent experiences across all scenarios, including home, travel, office, entertainment, and fitness & health.

Chapter 1
A General Introduction to Artificial Intelligence

The emergence and rise of artificial intelligence undoubtedly played an important role during the development of the Internet. Over the past decade, with extensive applications in the society, artificial intelligence has become more relevant to people's daily life. This chapter introduces the concept of artificial intelligence, the related technologies, and the existing controversies over the topic.

1.1 The Concept of Artificial Intelligence

1.1.1 What Is Artificial Intelligence?

Currently, people mainly learn about artificial intelligence (AI) through news, movies, and the applications in daily life, as shown by Fig. 1.1.

A rather widely accepted definition of AI, also a relatively early one, was proposed by John McCarthy at the 1956 Dartmouth Conference, which outlined that artificial intelligence is about letting a machine simulate the intelligent behavior of humans as precisely as it can be. However, this definition seemingly ignores the possibility of strong artificial intelligence (which means the machine that has the ability or intelligence to solve problems by reasoning).

Before explaining what "artificial intelligence" is, we had better clarify the concept of "intelligence" first.

According to the theory of multiple intelligences, human intelligence can be categorized into seven types: Linguistic, Logical-Mathematical, Spatial Bodily-Kinesthetic, Musical, Interpersonal and Intrapersonal intelligence.

1. Linguistic Intelligence

   Linguistic intelligence refers to the ability to effectively express one's thoughts in spoken or written language, understand others' words or texts, flexibly master the phonology, semantics, and grammar of a language, manage

Huawei Technologies Co., Ltd., *Artificial Intelligence Technology*,
https://doi.org/10.1007/978-981-19-2879-6_1

Haidian Park, the World's First AI Park! AI Program Defeated Top Human Players at StarCraft II, AlphaStar Gained Fame! Portrait by AI Program Portrait of Edmond Belamy Sells for $430,000 AI Programmer Demand Skyrocketed 35 Times! Salary Ranked No.1! 50% of the Jobs Will be Replaced by AI in the Future The Winter is Coming? AI Faces Big Challenges	The Terminator 2001: A Space Odyssey The Matrix I, Robot Blade Runner Her Bicentennial Man	Self-service security screening Speaking skills assessment Movie and music recommendation Smart loudspeaker Robot vacuums Bank self-service terminal Smart service Siri ......
News	Movies	Daily Application
Application of AI Industry trends and outlook for AI Challenges of AI	AI controls humans Fall in love with AI Self-consciousness of AI	Security & protection Entertainment Smart home Finance ......

Fig. 1.1 Social cognition of AI

verbal thinking, and convey or decode the connotation of linguistic expressions through the verbal thinking. For the people with strong linguistic intelligence, the ideal career choices could be politician-activist, host, attorney, public speaker, editor, writer, journalist, teacher, etc.

2. Logical-Mathematical Intelligence

Logical-mathematical intelligence designates the capability to calculate, quantify, reason, summarize and classify effectively, and to carry out complicated mathematical operations. This capability is characterized by the sensitivity to abstract concepts, such as logical patterns and relationships, statements and claims, and functions. People who are strong in logic-mathematical intelligence are more suitable to work as scientists, accountants, statisticians, engineers, computer software developers, etc.

3. Spatial Intelligence

Spatial intelligence features the potential to accurately recognize the visual space and things around it, and to represent what they perceived visually in paintings and graphs. People with strong spatial intelligence are very sensitive to spatial relationships such as color, line, shape, and form. The jobs suitable for them are interior designer, architect, photographer, painter, pilot and so on.

4. Bodily-Kinesthetic Intelligence

Bodily-kinesthetic intelligence indicates the capacity to use one's whole body to express thoughts and emotions, and to use hands and other tools to fashion products or manipulate objects. This intelligence demonstrates a variety of particular physical skills such as balance, coordination, agility, strength, suppleness and speed, and tactile abilities. Potential careers for people with strong body-kinesthetic intelligence include athlete, actor, dancer, surgeon, jeweler, mechanic and so on.

5. Musical Intelligence

Musical intelligence is the ability to discern pitch, tone, melody, rhythm, and timbre. People having relatively high musical intelligence are particularly sensitive to pitch, tone, melody, rhythm or timbre, and are more competitive in

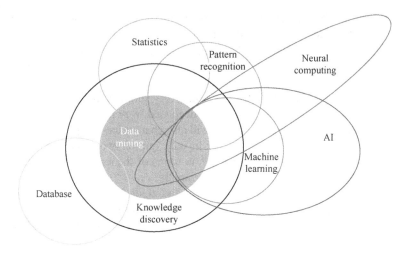

Fig. 1.2 Fields covered by artificial intelligence

performing, creating and reflecting on music. Their recommended professions include singer, composer, conductor, music critic, the piano tuner and so on.

6. Interpersonal Intelligence

   Interpersonal intelligence is the capability to understand and interact effectively with others. People with strong interpersonal intelligence can better recognize the moods and temperaments of others, empathize with their feelings and emotions, notice the hidden information of different interpersonal relationships, and respond appropriately. The professions suitable for them include politician, diplomat, leader, psychologist, PR officer, salesmen, and so on.

7. Intrapersonal Intelligence

   Intrapersonal intelligence is about self-recognition, which means the capability to understand oneself and then act accordingly based on such knowledge. People with strong intrapersonal intelligence are able to discern their strengths and weaknesses, recognize their inner hobbies, moods, intentions, temperaments and self-esteem, and they like to think independently. Their suitable professions include philosopher, politician, thinker, psychologist and so on.

8. Naturalist Intelligence

   Naturalist intelligence refers to the ability to observe the various forms of nature, identify and classify the objects, and discriminate the natural and artificial systems.

However, AI is a new type of technological science that investigates and develops the theories, methods, technologies and application systems to simulate, improve and upgrade the human intelligence. The AI is created to enable machines to reason like human being and to endow them with intelligence. Today, the connotation of AI has been greatly broadened, making it an interdisciplinary subject, as shown by Fig. 1.2.

Machine learning (ML) is apparently one of the major focuses of this interdisciplinary subject. According to the definition by Tom Mitchell, the so-called "the godfather of global ML", machine learning is described as: with respect to certain type of tasks T and performance P, if the performance of a computer program at tasks in T improves with experience E as measured by P, then the computer program is deemed to learn from experience E. It is a relatively simple and abstract definition. However, as our perception on the concept deepened, we may find that the connotation and denotation of machine learning will also change accordingly. It is not easy to define machine learning that precisely in only one or two sentences, not only because that it covers a wide span of fields in terms of theory and application, but also it is developing and transforming quite rapidly.

Generally speaking, the processing system and algorithms of machine learning make predictions mainly by identifying the hidden patterns from data. It is an important sub-field of AI, and AI is intertwined with data mining (DM) and knowledge discovery in database (KDD) in a broader sense.

1.1.2 The Relationship Between AI, Machine Learning, and Deep Learning

The study of machine learning aims at enabling computers to simulate or perform human learning ability and acquire new knowledge and skills. Deep learning (DL) derives from the study of artificial neural networks (ANN). As a new subfield of machine learning, it focuses on mimicking the mechanisms of human brain in interpreting data like images, sound, and text.

The relationship between AI, machine learning, and deep learning is shown in Fig. 1.3.

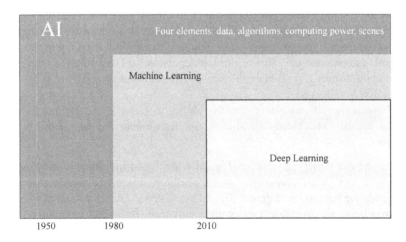

Fig. 1.3 The relationship between artificial intelligence, machine learning, and deep learning

Among the three concepts, machine learning is an approach or a subset of AI, and deep learning is one of ML's special forms. If we take AI as the brain, then machine learning is the process of the acquisition of cognitive abilities, and deep learning is a highly efficient self-training system that dominates this process. Artificial intelligence is the target and result while deep learning and machine learning are methods and tools.

1.1.3 Types of AI

AI can be divided into two types: strong artificial intelligence and weak artificial intelligence.

Strong artificial intelligence is about the possibility to create the intelligent machines that can accomplish reasoning problem-solving tasks. The machines of this kind are believed to have consciousness and self-awareness and be able to think independently and come up with the best solutions to the problems. Strong AI also has its distinctive values and worldview, and is endowed with instincts, such as the needs of survival and safety, just like all the living beings. In a certain sense, strong AI is a new civilization.

Weak artificial intelligence depicts the circumstance when it is not able to make machines that can truly accomplish reasoning and problem-solving. These machines may look smart, but they do not really have intelligence or self-awareness.

We are currently in the era of weak artificial intelligence. The introduction of weak artificial intelligence reduces the burden of intellectual work by functioning in a way similar to the advanced bionics. Whether it is AlphaGo, or the robot who writes news report and novels, they all belong to weak artificial intelligence and outperform humans in only certain fields. In the era of weak artificial intelligence, it is undeniable that data and computing power are both crucial, as they can facilitate the commercialization of AI. In the coming age of strong artificial intelligence, these two factors will still be two decisive elements. Meanwhile, the exploration on quantum computing by companies like Google and IBM also lays the foundation for the advent of the strong artificial intelligence era.

1.1.4 The History of AI

Figure 1.4 presents us a brief history of AI.

The official origin of modern AI can be traced back to the Turing Test proposed by Alan M. Turing, known as "the Father of Artificial Intelligence", in 1950. According to his assumption, if a computer can engage in dialogue with humans without being detected as a computer, then it is deemed as having intelligence. In the same year he proposed this assumption, Turing boldly predicted that creating the

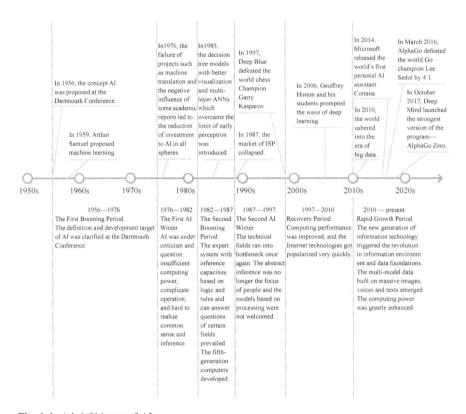

Fig. 1.4 A brief history of AI

machines with real human intelligence was possible in the future. But up to now, none of the computers has ever passed the Turing Test.

Although AI is a concept with a history of only a few decades, the theoretical foundation and supporting technology behind it have developed for a time-honored period. The current prosperity of AI is a result of the advancement of all related disciplines and the collective efforts of the scientists of all generations.

1. Precursors and Initiation Period (before 1956)

The theoretical foundation for the birth of AI can date back to as early as the fourth century BC, when the famous ancient Greek philosopher and scientist Aristotle invented the concept of formal logic. In fact, his theory of syllogism is still working as an indispensable and decisive cornerstone for the deductive reasoning today. In the seventeenth century, the German mathematician Gottfried Leibniz advanced universal notation and some revolutionary ideas on reasoning and calculation, which laid the foundation for the establishment and development of mathematical logic. In the nineteenth century, the British mathematician George Boole developed Boolean algebra, which is the bedrock of the operation of modern computers, and its introduction makes the invention of computer possible. During the same period, the British inventor Charles Babbage created the Difference Engine, the first computer capable of solving quadratic polynomial equations in the world. Although it only had limited functions, this computer reduced the burden of human brain in calculation per se for the first time. The machines were endowed with computational intelligence ever since.

In 1945, John Mauchly and J. Presper Eckert from a team at Moore School designed the Electronic Numerical Integrator and Calculator (ENIAC), the world's first general-purpose digital electronic computer. As an epoch-making achievement, ENIAC still had its fatal deficiencies, such as its enormous size, excessive power consumption, and reliance on manual operation to input and adjust commands. In 1947, John von Neumann, the father of modern computers, modified and upgraded on the basis of ENIAC and created the modern electronic computer in the real sense: Mathematical Analyzer Numerical Integrator and Automatic Computer (MANIAC).

In 1946, the American physiologist Warren McCulloch established the first model of neural network. His research on artificial intelligence at microscopic level laid an important foundation for the development of neural networks. In 1949, Donald O. Hebb proposed Hebbian theory, a neuropsychological learning paradigm, which states the basic principles of synaptic plasticity, namely, the efficacy of synaptic transmission will arise greatly with the repeated and persistent stimulation from a presynaptic neuron to a postsynaptic neuron. This theory is fundamental to the modelling of neural networks. In 1948, Claude E. Shannon, the founder of information theory, introduced the concept of information entropy by borrowing the term from thermodynamics, and defined information entropy as the average amount of information after the redundancy has being removed. The impact of this theory is quite far-reaching as it played an important role in fields such as non-deterministic inference and machine learning.

2. The First Booming Period (1956–1976)

Finally, in 1956, John McCarthy officially introduced AI as a new discipline at the 2-month long Dartmouth Conference, which marks the birth of AI. A number of AI research groups were formed in the United States ever since, such as the Carnegie-RAND group formed by Allen Newell and Herbert Alexander Simon, the research group the Massachusetts Institute of Technology (MIT) by Marvin Lee Minsky and John McCarthy, and Arthur Samuel's IBM engineering research group, etc.

In the following two decades, AI was developing rapidly in a wide range of fields, and thanks to the great enthusiasm of researchers, the AI technologies and applications have kept expanding.

(a) Machine Learning

In 1956, Arthur Samuel of IBM wrote the famous checkers-playing program, which was able to learn an implicit model by observing the positions on checkerboard to instruct moves for the latter cases. After played against the program for several rounds, Arthur Samuel concluded that the program could reach a very high level of performance during the course of learning. With this program, Samuel confuted the notion that computers cannot go beyond the written codes and learn patterns like human beings. Since then, he coined and defined a new term—machine learning.

(b) Pattern Recognition

In 1957, C.K. Chow proposed to adopt statistical decision theory to tackle pattern recognition, which stimulated the rapid development of pattern recognition research since the late 1950s. In the same year, Frank Rosenblatt proposed a simplified mathematical model that imitated the recognition pattern of human brain—the perceptron, the first machine that could possibly train the recognition system by the sample of each given category, so that the system was able to correctly classify patterns of other unknown categories after learning.

(c) Pattern Matching

In 1966, ELIZA, the first conversation program in the world was invented, which was written by the MIT Artificial Intelligence Laboratory. The program was able to perform pattern matching on the basis of the set rules and user's questions, so as to give appropriate replies by choosing from the pre-written answer archives. This is also the first program try to have passed the Turing Test. ELIZA once masqueraded as a psychotherapist to talk to patients, and many of them failed to recognize it as a robot when it was firstly applied. "Conversation is pattern matching", thus this unveiled the computer natural language conversation technology.

In addition, during the first development period of AI, John McCarthy developed the LISP, which became the dominant programming language for AI IN the following decades. Marvin Minsky launched a more in-depth study of neural networks and discovered the disadvantages of simple neural networks. In order to overcome these limitations, the scientists started to introduce multilayer neural networks and Back Propagation (BP) algorithms. Meanwhile, the expert system (ES) also emerged. During this period the first industrial robot was applied on the production line of General Motors, and the world also witnessed the birth of the first mobile robot which was capable of actioning autonomously.

The advancement of relevant disciplines also contributed to the great strides of AI. The emergence of bionics in the 1950s ignited the research enthusiasm of scientists, which led to the invention of simulated annealing algorithm. It is a type of heuristic algorithm, and is the foundation for the searching algorithms, such as the ant colony optimization (ACO) algorithm which is quite popular in recent years.

3. The First AI Winter (1976–1982)

However, the AI manic did not last too long, as the over-optimistic projections failed to be fulfilled as promised, and thus incurred the doubt and suspicion on AI technology globally.

The perceptron, once a sensation in the academic world, had a hard time in 1969 when Marvin Minsky and the rest scientists advanced the famous logical operation exclusive OR (XOR), demonstrating the limitation of the perceptron in terms of the linear inseparable data similar to the XOR problem. For the academic world, the XOR problem became an almost undefeatable challenge.

In 1973, AI was under strict questioning by the scientific community. Many scientists believed that those seemingly ambitious goals of AI were just some unfulfilled illusions, and the relevant research had been proved complete failures. Due to the increasing suspicion and doubts, AI suffered from severe criticism, and its actual value was also under question. As a consequence, the governments and research institutions all over the world withdrew or reduced funding on AI, and the industry encountered its first winter of development in the 1970s.

The setback in 1970s was no coincidence. Due to the limitation of computing power at that time, although many problems were solved theoretically, they cannot be put into practice at all. Meanwhile, there were many other obstacles, such as it was difficult for the expert system to acquire knowledge, leaving lots of projects ended in failure. The study on machine vision took off in the 1960s. And the edge detection and contour composition methods proposed by the American scientist L.R. Roberts are not only time-tested, but also still widely used today. However, having a theoretical basis does not mean actual yield. In the last 1970s, there were scientists concluded that to let a computer to imitate human retinal vision, it would need to execute at least one billion instructions. However, the calculation speed of the world's fastest supercomputer Cray-1 in 1976 (which costed millions of US dollars to make) could only register no more than 100 million times per second, and the speed of an ordinary computer could meet even no more than one million times per second. The hardware limited the development of AI. In addition, another major basis for the progress of AI is the data base. At that time, computers and the Internet were not as popular as today, so there were nowhere for the developers to capture massive data.

During this period, artificial intelligence developed slowly. Although the concept of BP had been proposed by Juhani Linnainmaa in the "automatic differential flip mode" in the 1970s, it was not until 1981 that it was applied to the multilayer perceptron by Paul J. Werbos. The invention of multilayer perceptron and BP algorithm contributed to the second leap-frogging of neural networks. In 1986, David E. Rumelhart and other scholars developed an effective BP algorithm to successfully train multilayer perceptron, which exerted a profound impact.

4. The Second Booming Period (1982–1987)

In 1980, XCON, a complete expert system developed by the Carnegie Mello University (CMU) was officially put into use. The system contained more than 2500 set rules, and processed more than 80,000 orders featuring an accuracy of over 95% in the following years. This is considered a milestone that heralds a new era, when the expert system begun to showcase its potential in specific fields, which lifted AI technology to a completely new level of booming development.

An expert system normally attends to one specific professional field. By mimicking the thinking of human experts, it attempts to answer questions or provide knowledge to help with the decision-making by practitioners. Focusing on only a narrow domain, the expert system avoids the challenges related to artificial general intelligence (AGI) and is able to make full use of the knowledge and experience of existing experts to solve problems of the specific domains.

The big commercial success of XCON encouraged 60% of Fortune 500 companies to embark on the development and deployment of expert systems in their respective fields in the 1980s. According to the statistics, from 1980 to 1985, more than 1 billion US dollars was invested in AI, with a majority went to the internal AI departments of those enterprises, and the market witnessed a surge in AI software and hardware companies.

In 1986, the Bundeswehr University in Munich equipped a Mercedes-Benz van with a computer and several sensors, which enabled an automatic control of the steering wheel, accelerator and brake. The installation was called VaMoRs, which proved to be the first self-driving car in the real sense in the world.

LISP was the mainstream programming language used for AI development at that time. In order to enhance the operating efficiency of LISP programs, many agencies turned to develop computer chips and storage devices designed specifically to executive LISP programs. Although LISP machines had made some progress, personal computers (PCs) were also on the rise. IBM and Apple quickly expanded the market presence in the entire computer marketplace. With a steady increase of CPU frequency and speed, the PCs were becoming even more powerful than the costly LISP machines.

5. The Second AI Winter (1987–1997)

In 1987, along with the crash of sales market of LISP machine hardware, the AI industry once again fell into another winter. The second AI trough period lasted for years as the hardware market collapsed and governments and institutions all over the world stopped investing in AI research. But during this period, the researchers still made some important achievements. In 1988, the American scientist Judea Pearl championed the probabilistic approach to AI inference, which made a crucial contribution to the future development of AI technology.

In the almost 20 years after the advent of the second AI winter, the AI technology became gradually and deeply integrated with computer and software technologies, while the research on artificial intelligence algorithm theory had a slow progress. The research results of many researchers were only something based on the old theories, and the computer hardware that was more powerful and faster.

6. Recovery Period (1997–2010)

In 1995, Richard S. Wallace was inspired by ELIZA and developed a new chatbot program named A.L.I.C.E. (the Artificial Linguistic Internet Computer Entity). The robot was able to optimize the contents and enrich its datasets automatically through the Internet.

In 1996, the IBM supercomputer Deep Blue played a chess game against the world chess champion Gary Kasparov and was defeated. Gary Kasparov believed that it was impossible for computers to defeat human in chess games ever. After the match, IBM upgraded Deep Blue. The new Deep Blue was enhanced with 480 specialized CPUs and a doubled calculation speed up to 200 million times per second, enabling it to predict the next 8 or more moves on the chessboard. In the later rematch, the computer defeated Gary Kasparov successfully. However, this landmark event actually only marks a victory of computer over human in a game with clear rules by relying on its calculation speed and enumeration. This is not real AI.

In 2006, as Geoffrey Hinton published a paper in *Science Magazine*, AI industry entered the era of deep learning.

7. Rapid Growth Period (2010–present)

In 2011, the Watson system, also a program from IBM, participated the quiz show *Jeopardy*, competing with human players. The Watson system defeated two human champions with its outstanding natural language processing capabilities and powerful knowledge database. This time, computers can already comprehend human language, which is a big advancement in AI.

In the twenty-first century, with the widespread application of PCs and the burst of mobile Internet and cloud computing technology, the institutions are able to capture and accumulate an unimaginably huge mass of data, providing sufficient material and impetus for the ongoing development of AI. Deep learning became a mainstream of AI technology, exemplified by the famous Google Brain project, which enhanced the recognition rate of the ImageNet dataset to 84% by a large margin.

In 2011, the concept semantic network was proposed. The concept steams from the World Wide Web. It is essentially a large-scale distributed database that centers on Web data and connects Web data in the method of machine understanding and processing. The emergence of the semantic network greatly promoted the progress of technology of knowledge representation. A year later, Google first announced the concept of knowledge graph and launched a knowledge-graph-based searching service.

In 2016 and 2017, Google launched two Go competitions between human and mechanical players that shocked the world. Its AI program AlphaGo defeated two Go world champions, first Lee Sedol of South Korea and then Ke Jie of China.

Today, AI can be found in almost all aspects of people's life. For instance, the voice assistant, such as the most typical Siri of Apple, is based on the natural language processing (NLP) technology. With the support of NLP, computers can process human language and match it with the commands and responses in line with human expectation more and more naturally. When users are browsing e-commerce websites, they could possibly receive product recommendation feeds generated by a recommendation algorithm. The recommendation algorithm can predict the products that the users might want to buy by reviewing and analyzing the historical data of the users' recent purchases and preferences.

1.1.5 The Three Main Schools of AI

Currently, symbolism, connectionism, and behaviorism constitute the three main schools of AI. The following passages will introduce them in detail.

1. Symbolism

    The basic theory of symbolism believes that, the cognitive process of human being consists of the inference and processing of symbols. Human is an example of physical symbol system, and so does the computer. Therefore, computers should be able to simulate human intelligent activities. And knowledge representation, knowledge reasoning, and knowledge application are three crucial to artificial intelligence. Symbolism argues that knowledge and concepts can be represented by symbols, thus cognition is a process of processing the symbols, and reasoning is a process of solving problems with heuristic knowledge. The core of symbolism lies in reasoning, namely the symbolic reasoning and machine reasoning.

2. Connectionism

    The foundation of connectionism is that the nature of human logical thinking is neurons, rather than a process of symbol processing. Connectionism believes that the human brain is different from computers, and put forward a connectionist model imitating brain work to replace the computer working model operated by symbols. Connectionism is believed to stem from bionics, especially in the study of human brain models. In connectionism, a concept is represented by a set of numbers, vectors, matrices, or tensors, namely, by the specific activation mode of the entire network. Each node (neuron) in the network has no specific meaning, but every node all participates in the expression of overall concept. For example, in symbolism, the concept of a cat can be represented by a "cat node" or a group of nodes that feature the attributes of a cat (e.g., the one with "two eyes", "four legs" or "fluffy"). However, connectionism believes that each node does not have a specific meaning, so it is impossible to search for a "cat node" or "eye neuron". The core connectionism lies in neuron networks and deep learning.

3. Behaviorism

    The fundamental theory of behaviorism believes that intelligence depends on perception and behavior. Behaviorism introduces a "perception-action" model for intelligent activities. Behaviorism believes that intelligence has nothing to do with knowledge, representation, or reasoning. AI can evolve gradually like human intelligence, and intelligent activities can only be manifested through human's ongoing interactions with the surrounding environment in the real world. Behaviorism emphasizes application and practices and constantly learning from the environment to modify the activities. The core behaviorism lies in behavior control, adaptation and evolutionary computing.

1.2   AI-Related Technologies

AI technology is multi-layered, running through technical levels such as applications, algorithms, chips, devices, and processes, as shown in Fig. 1.5.

AI technology has achieved the following developments at all technical levels.

1. Application Level

   Video and image: face recognition, target detection, image generation, image retouching, search image by image, video analysis, video review, and augmented reality (AR).

   Speech and voice: speech recognition, speech synthesis, voice wake-up, voiceprint recognition, and music generation.

   Text: text analysis, machine translation, human-machine dialogue, reading comprehension and recommender system.

   Control: autonomous driving, drones, robots, industrial automation.

2. Algorithm Level

   Machine learning algorithms: neural network, support vector machine (SVM), K-nearest neighbor algorithm (KNN), Bayesian algorithm, decision tree, hidden Markov model (HMM), ensemble learning, etc.

   Common optimization algorithms for machine learning: gradient descent, Newton's method, quasi-Newton method, conjugate gradient, spiking timing dependent plasticity (STDP), etc.

   Deep learning is one of the most essential technologies for machine learning. The deep neural network (DNN) is a hotspot of research in this field in recent years, consisting of multilayer perceptron (MLP) and convolutional neural network (CNN), recurrent neural network (RNN), spiking neural network (SNN) and other types. While the relatively popular CNNs include AlexNet, ResNet amd VGGNet, and the popular RNNs include long short-term memory (LSTM)

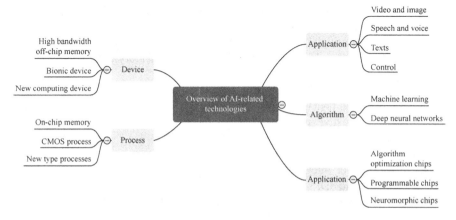

Fig. 1.5 Overview of AI-related technologies

networks and Neural Turing Machine (NTM). For instance, Google's BERT (Bidirectional Encoder Representation from Transformers) is a natural language processing pre-training technology developed on the basis of neural networks.

In addition to deep learning, transfer learning, reinforcement learning, one-shot learning and adversarial machine learning are also the important technologies to realize machine learning, and the solutions to some of the difficulties faced by deep learning.

3. Chip Level

Algorithm optimization chips: performance optimization, low power consumption optimization, high-speed optimization, and flexibility optimization-such as deep learning accelerator and face recognition chip.

Neuromorphic chips: bionic brain, biological brain-inspired intelligence, imitation of brain mechanism.

Programmable chips: taking flexibility, programmability, algorithm compatibility, and general software compatibility into consideration, such as digital signal processing (DSP) chips, graphics processing units (GPUs), field programmable gates array (FPGA).

Structure of system on chip: multi-core, many-core, single instruction, multiple data (SIMD), array structure of operation, memory architecture, on-chip network structure, multi-chip interconnection structure, memory interface, communication structure, multi-level cache.

Development toolchain: connection between deep learning frameworks (TensorFlow, Caffe, MindSpore), compiler, simulator, optimizer (quantization and clipping), atomic operation (network) library.

4. Device Level

High-bandwidth off-chip memory: high-bandwidth memory (HBM), dynamic random-access memory (DRAM), high-speed graphics double data rate memory (GDDR), low power double data rate (LPDDR SDRAN), spin-transfer torque magnetic random-access memory (STT-MRAM).

High-speed interconnection devices: serializer/deserializer (SerDes), optical interconnection communication.

Bionic devices (artificial synapses, artificial neurons): memristor.

New type computing devices: analog computing, in-memory computing (IMC).

5. Process Level

On-chip memory (synaptic array): distributed static random-access memory (SRAM), Resistive random-access memory (ReRAM), and phase change random-access memory (PCRAM).

CMOS process: technology node (16 nm, 7 nm).

CMOS multi-layer integration: 2.5D IC/SiP technology, 3D-Stack technology and Monolithic 3D.

New type processes: 3D NAND, Flash Tunneling FETs, FeFET, FinFET.

1.2.1 Deep Learning Framework

The introduction of deep learning frameworks has made deep learning easier to build. With the deep learning framework, we do not need to firstly code complex neural networks with backpropagation algorithms, but can just configure the model hyperparameters according to our demands, and the model parameters can be learned automatically from training. We can also add a custom layer for the existing model, or choose the classifier and optimization algorithm we need at the top.

We can consider a deep learning framework as a set of building blocks. Each block, or component of the set is a model or algorithm, and we can assemble the components into an architecture that meets the demands.

The current mainstream deep learning frameworks include: TensorFlow, Caffe, PyTorch and so on.

1.2.2 An Overview of AI Processor

In the four key elements of AI technology (data, algorithms, computing power, and scenarios), computing power is the one most reliant on AI processor. Also known as AI accelerator, an AI processor is a specialized functional module to tackle the large-scale computing tasks in AI applications.

1. Types of AI Processors

   AI processors can be classified into different categories from different perspectives, and here we will take the perspectives of technical architecture and functions.

   In terms of the technical architecture, AI processors can be roughly classified into four types.

   (a) CPU

   Central processing unit (CPU) is a large-scale integration circuit, which is the core of computing and control of a computer. The main function of CPU is to interpret program instructions and process data in software that it receives from the computer.

   (b) GPU

   Graphics processing unit (GPU), also known as display core (DC), visual processing unit (VPU) and display chip, is a specialized microprocessor dealing with image processing in personal computers, workstations, game consoles and some mobile devices (such as tablets and smartphones).

   (c) ASIC

   Application specific integrated circuit (ASIC) is designed for the integrated circuit product customized for a particular use.

   (d) FPGA

Field programmable gate array (FPGA) is designed to build reconfigurable semi-custom chips, which means the hardware structure can be adjusted and re-configured flexibly real-time as required.

In terms of the functions, AI processors can be classified into two types: training processors and inference processors.

(a) In order to train a complex deep neural network model, the AI training usually entails the input of a large amount of data and learning methods such as reinforcement learning. Training is a compute-intensive process. The large-scale training data and the complex deep neural network structure that the training involves put up a huge challenge to the speed, accuracy, and scalability of the processor. The popular training processors include NVIDIA GPU, Google's tensor processing unit (TPU), and Huawei's neural-network processing unit (NPU).

(b) Inference here means inferring various conclusions with new data obtained on the basis of the trained model. For instance, the video monitor can distinguish whether a captured face is the specific target by making use of the backend deep neural network model. Although inference entails much less computation than training, it still involves lots of matrix operations. GPU, FPGA and NPU are commonly used in inference processors.

2. Current Status of AI Processor

(a) CPU

The improvement of CPU performance in the early days mainly relied on the progress made by the underlying hardware technology in line with Moore's Law. In recent years, as Moore's Law seems gradually losing its effectiveness, the development of integrated circuits is slowing down, and the hardware technology has faced physical bottlenecks. The limitation of heat dissipation and power consumption restricted the CPU performance and serial program efficiency under the traditional architecture from making much progress.

The status quo of the industry prompted researchers to keep on looking for CPU architectures and the relevant software frameworks that can better adapted to the post-Moore Era. As a result, the multi-core processor came into being, which allows higher CPU performance with more cores. Multi-core processors can better meet the demands of software on hardware. For example, Intel Core i7 processors adopt instruction-level parallel processors with multiple independent kernels on the x86 instruction set, which improves the performance considerably, but also leads to higher power consumption and cost. Since the number of cores cannot be increased indefinitely, and most traditional programs are written in serial programming, this approach has limited improvements in CPU performance and program efficiency.

In addition, AI performance can be improved by adding instruction set. For example, adding instruction sets like AVX512 to the x86 complex instruction set computer (CISC), architecture, adding the fused-multiply-add (FMA) instruction set to the arithmetic logic unit (ALU) module, and adding instruction set to the ARM reduced instruction set computer (RISC) architecture.

The CPU performance can also be improved by increasing the frequency, but there is a limit, and the high frequency will cause excessive power consumption and high temperature.

(b) GPU

GPU is very competitive in matrix computing and parallel computing and serves as the engine of heterogeneous computing. It was first introduced into the field of AI as an accelerator to facilitate deep learning and now has formed an established ecology.

With regard to the GPUs in the field of deep learning, NVIDIA made efforts mainly in the following three aspects:

- Enrich ecology: NVINIA launches the NVIDIA CUDA deep neural network horary (CUDNN), the GPU-accelerated library customized for deep learning, which optimizes the underlying architecture of GPU and ensures an easier application of GPU in deep learning.
- Improve customization: embracing multiple data types (no longer insisting on float32, and adopting int8, etc.).
- Add module specialized for deep learning (e.g., NVIDIA V100 Tensor Core GPU adopts the improved Volta architecture introducing and equipped with tensor cores).

   The main challenges of current GPUs are high cost, low energy consumption ratio, and high input and output latency.

(c) TPU

Since 2016, Google has been committed to applying the concept of application-specific integrated circuits (ASIC) to the study of neural networks. In 2016, it launched the AI custom-developed processor TPU which supports the open-source deep learning framework TensorFlow. By combining large-scale systolic arrays and high-capacity on-chip memory, TPU manages to efficiently accelerate the convolutional operations that are most common in deep neural networks: systolic arrays can optimize matrix multiplication and convolutional operations, so as to increase computing power and reduce energy consumption.

(d) FPGA

FPGA uses a programmable hardware description language (HDL), which is flexible, reconfigurable, and can be deeply customized. It can load DNN model on the chips to perform low-latency operation by incorporating multiple FPGAs, contributing to a computing performance higher than GPU. But as it has to take account the constant erasing process, the performance of FPGA cannot reach the optimal. As FPGA is reconfigurable, its risk of supply and R&D is relatively low. The cost of hardware is decided by the amount of

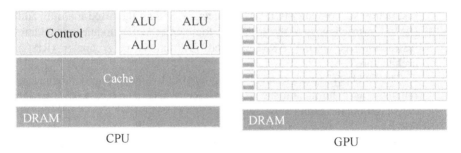

Fig. 1.6 CPU and GPU architecture

hardware purchased, so it is easy to control the cost. However, the design of FPGA and the tape-out process are decoupled, so the development cycle is long, which usually takes half a year, and has high standards.

3. Comparison Between the Design of GPU and CPU

The GPU is generally designed to tackle large-scale data that are highly unified in type and independent from each other, and deal with a pure computing environment without interruption. The CPU is designed more general-purpose, so as to process different types of data, and perform logical decisions at the same time, and it also needs to introduce a large number of branch-jump instructions and interrupt processing. The comparison between CPU and GPU architecture is shown in Fig. 1.6.

The GPU has numerous massively parallel computing architectures composed by thousands of much smaller cores (designed for simultaneous processing of multiple tasks). The CPU consists of several cores optimized for serial processing.

(a) The GPU works with many ALUs and little cache memory. Unlike the CPU, cache of the GPU serves for threads merely and plays the role of data forwarding. When multiple threads need to access the same data, the cache will coalesce these accesses, then access the DRAM, and forward the data to each thread after obtaining them, which will cause latency. However, as the large number of ALUs ensure the threads run in parallel, the latency is eased. In addition, the control units of GPUs can coalesce access.

(b) The CPU has powerful ALUs, which can complete computation in a very short clock cycle. The CPU has a large number of caches to reduce latency, and the complicated control units that can perform branch prediction and data forwarding: when a program has multiple branches, the control units will reduce latency through branch prediction; for the instructions that depend on the results of previous instructions, the control units must determine the positions of these instructions in the pipeline and forward the result of the previous instruction as quickly as they can.

Table 1.1 The relevant parameters of Ascend 310 and Ascend 910

Ascend 310	Ascend 910
Chip: Ascend-Mini	Chip: Ascend-Max
Architecture: Da Vinci	Architecture: Da Vinci
16-bit floating point precision (FP16) performance: 8 TFLOPS	16-bit floating point precision (FP16) performance: 256 TFLOPS
8-bit integer precision (INT8) performance: 16 TOPS	8-bit integer precision (INT8) performance: 512 TOPS
16 channel full HD video decoder – H.264/265	128 channel full HD video decoder – H.264/265
1 channel full HD video encoder – H.264/265	Maximum power consumption: 350 W Process: 7 nm
Maximum power consumption: 8 W	
Process: 12 nm FFC	

GPUs are good at dealing with operations that are intensive and easy to be run in parallel, while CPUs excel at logic control and serial operations.

The difference in architecture between GPU and CPU is because that they have different emphasis. The GPU has an outstanding advantage in processing the parallel computing of large-scale intensive data, while CPU more stresses the logic control while executing the instructions. In order to optimize a program, it often needs to coordinate both CPU and GPU at the same time to give a full play to their capabilities.

4. Huawei Ascend AI Processor

NPU refers to the processor carrying out the optimization design specialized for neural network computing, whose performance of neural network tasks processing is much higher than that of CPU and GPU.

The NPU mimics human neurons and synapses on the circuitry, and directly processes large scale neurons and synapses through deep learning processor instruction set. In NPUs, the processing of a group of neurons will take only one instruction. Currently, the typical examples of NPU include Huawei Ascend AI processor, the Cambrian chip and IBM's TrueNorth chip.

There are two kinds of Huawei Ascend AI processor: Ascend 310 and Ascend 910.

Ascend 910 is mainly applied to training scenarios, mostly deployed in the data center. While Ascend 310 is mainly designed for reasoning scenarios, whose deployment covers the device, edge and cloud full scenarios.

Ascend 910 is currently the AI processor with the strongest computing power and fastest training speed in the world, its computing power is twice that of the international top AI processor, equivalent to 50 latest and strongest CPUs today.

The relevant parameters of Ascend 310 and Ascend 910 are shown in Table 1.1.

1.2.3 Ecosystem of AI Industry

Over the past half a century, the world has witnessed three waves of AI. And these three waves are exemplified and unveiled by human-computer matches. The first was in 1962, when the checkers-playing program developed by Arthur Samuel from IBM defeated the world's best checkers player in the United States. The second time was in 1997, when IBM's supercomputer Deep Blue defeated the human chess world champion Garry Kasparov by 3.5:2.5. And the third wave of AI came in 2016 when the Go AI AlphaGo developed by DeepMind, a subsidiary of Google, defeated the Go world champion and nine-dan player from the South Korean, Lee Sedol.

In the future, AI will be embedded in every walk of life, from automobiles, finance, consumer goods to retail, healthcare, education, manufacturing, communications, energy, tourism, culture and entertainment, transportation, logistics, real estate and environmental protection, etc.

For example, in the automobile industry, the intelligent driving technologies such as assisted driving, assisted decision-making, and fully automated driving are all realized with the help of AI. As a huge market, the intelligent driving can also support technical research in AI in return, thus form a virtuous circle, and become a solid foundation to the AI development.

As for the financial industry, with the huge amount of data accumulated, AI can help with intelligent asset management, robo-advisor, and making more sensible financial decisions. AI can also play a part in combat financial fraud and be adopted in anti-fraud and anti-money laundering campaigns, as the related AI program can infer the reliability of a transaction by analyzing data and materials of all kinds, to predict where the funds will flow to, and identify the cycles of the financial market.

AI can also be widely used in the healthcare industry. For instance, it can assist doctors to diagnose and treat diseases by identifying problems reflected by the X-ray images, after being trained to interpret images at geometric level. AI can distinguish cancer cells from normal cells after training on classification tasks.

The related research data show that by 2025, the size of AI market will exceed 3 trillion US dollars, as shown in Fig. 1.7.

As can be inferred from Fig. 1.7, the AI market has a huge potential. It is known that AI has three pillars, namely, data, algorithms and computing power. But to apply AI in real life, these three pillars are far from enough, because we also need to take scenarios into consideration. Data, algorithms, and computing power can prompt the evolvement of AI technically, but without application scenarios, the technological development is merely about data. We need to integrate AI with cloud computing, big data and the Internet of Things (IoT) so as to make the application of AI in real life possible, which is the foundation of the platform architecture for AI application, as shown in Fig. 1.8.

The infrastructure includes smart sensors and smart chips, which reinforces the computing power for AI industry, and guarantees its development. AI technological service is mainly about building up an AI technological platform and providing solutions and services to external users. The manufacturers of these AI technologies

Fig. 1.7 AI market size forecast

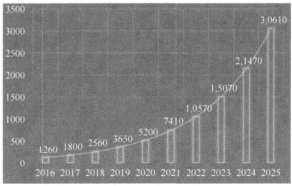

(Unit: 10 million USD)

are critical in the AI industry chain, as they provide key technological platforms, solutions and services to all kinds of AI applications thanks to strong infrastructure and massive data that they acquire. With the acceleration of the campaign of building a competitive China by developing manufacturing, Internet, and digital industry, the demand for AI in manufacturing, houseware, finance, education, transportation, security, medical care, logistics and other fields will be further released, and the AI products will have more and more diversified forms and categories. Only when the infrastructure, the four major elements of AI and AI technical services converge, can the architecture fully buttress the upper-layer application of the AI industrial ecosystem.

Although the AI technology can be applied in a wide range of fields, its development and application are facing challenges as well: the unbalance between the limited AI development and the huge market demands. Currently, the development and application of AI needs to deal with the following three problems.

1. High occupational standards: To get engaged in AI industry, it is a prerequisite for a person to have considerable knowledge in machine learning, deep learning, statistics, linear algebra and calculus.
2. Low efficiency. Training a model will take a long working cycle, which consists of data collection, data cleaning, model training and tuning, and optimization of visualization experience.
3. Fragmented capabilities and experiences: to apply a same AI model in other scenarios requires will need to repeat data collection, data cleaning, model training and tuning, and experience optimization, and the capabilities of the AI model cannot be directly passed to the next scenario.
4. Difficult capacity upgrading and improvement: the model upgrading and effective data capturing are difficult tasks.

Currently, the smartphone-centered on-device AI has become a consensus of the industry. More and more smartphones will boast AI capabilities. As several consulting agencies in the UK and the USA estimated, about 80% of the world's smartphones will have AI capabilities by 2022 or 2023. To meet the market outlook and tackle the challenges of AI, HUAWEI launched its open AI capability platform

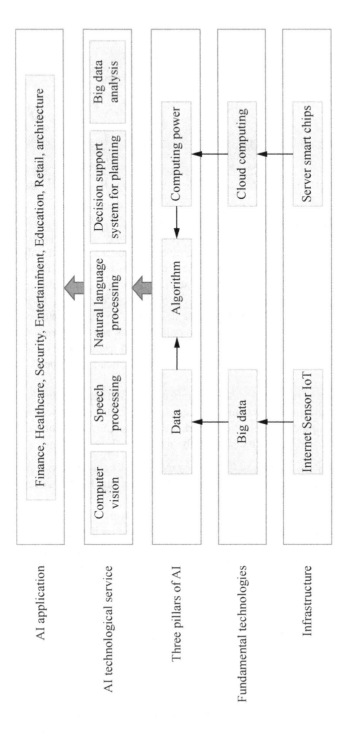

Fig. 1.8 Platform architecture for AI application

for smart devices, namely, HUAWEI HiAI. With a mission of "providing developers with convenience while connecting unlimited possibilities through AI", HUAWEI HiAI enables developers to provide users with a better experience of smart application by swiftly making use of Huawei's powerful AI processing capabilities.

1.2.4 Huawei CLOUD Enterprise Intelligence Application Platform

1. An Overview of Huawei CLOUD Enterprise Intelligence Application Platform
   Huawei CLOUD Enterprise Intelligence (EI) application platform is an enabler of enterprise intelligence that aims at providing open, credible and smart platforms based on AI and big data technologies and in the form of cloud service (including public cloud and customized cloud, etc.), By combining the industrial scenarios, the enterprise application systems created with Huawei CLOUD are visualized, audible and can express themselves, featuring the capabilities to analyze and interpret images, videos, languages and texts and easier access to AI and big data services. Huawei CLOUD can help the enterprises to speed up business development and benefit the society.
2. Features of Huawei CLOUD EI
   Huawei CLOUD EI has four remarkable features.

   (a) Industrial wisdom: Huawei CLOUD has a deep understanding of the industry, the industrial know-how, and the major industrial deficiencies. It searches solutions to the problems in the AI technologies and navigate the implementation of AI.
   (b) Industrial data: It enables the companies to utilize their own data to create massive value through data processing and data mining.
   (c) Algorithms: It provides enterprises with extensive algorithm libraries and model libraries, and solutions to corporate problems through general AI services and one-stop development platform.
   (d) Computing power: Based on Huawei's 30 years of experiences in ICT, the full-stack AI development platform can provide enterprises with the strongest and most economical AI computing power for fusion and changes.

3. The History of Huawei CLOUD EI
   The evolvement of Huawei CLOUD EI is shown in Fig. 1.9.
   The evolvement of Huawei CLOUD EI is as follows.

   (a) In 2002, Huawei began to develop products of data governance and analysis targeting the traditional Business Intelligence (BI) operations in the field of telecommunication.
   (b) In 2007, Huawei initiated the Hadoop technology research project, mapping out big data-related strategies, and building a pool of relevant professionals and technology patents.

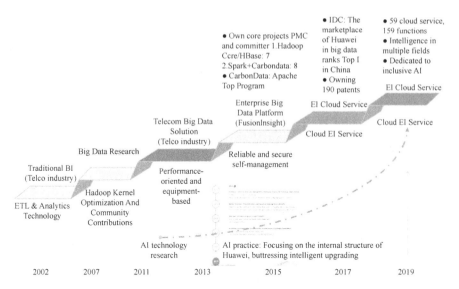

Fig. 1.9 The history of Huawei CLOUD EI

(c) In 2011, Huawei tried to apply the big data technology in telecom big data solutions to deal with the network diagnosis and analysis, network planning, and network tuning.

(d) In 2013, some large companies such as China Merchants Bank and Industrial and Commercial Bank exchanged views with Huawei regarding their big data-related demands and kicked off technical cooperation. In September of the same year, Huawei launched its enterprise-grade big data analysis platform FusionInsight at the Huawei Cloud Congress (HCC), which has been adopted by a wide range of industries.

(e) In 2012, Huawei officially stepped into AI industry and productized the research outcomes successively since 2014. By the end of 2015, the products developed for finance, supply chain, acceptance of engineering work, and e-commerce began to put into use internally, with the following achievements accomplished.

- Optical character recognition (OCR) for customs declaration documents recognition: The import efficiency was enhanced by 10 times.
- Delivery route planning: Additional fees were reduced by 30%.
- Intelligent auditing: The efficiency was increased by 6 times.
- Intelligent recommendation for e-commerce users: Application conversion rate was increased by 71%.

(f) In 2017, Huawei officially engaged in EI services in the form of cloud service and cooperated with more partners to provide more diversified AI services to the external users.

(g) In 2019, Huawei CLOUD EI started to emphasize the inclusive AI, in the hope of making AI affordable and accessible, and safe to use. Based on the self-developed chip Ascend, it provided 59 cloud services (21 platform services, 22 vision services, 12 language services and 4 decision-making services) and developed 159 functions (52 platform functions, 99 application programming interface [API] functions and 8 pre-integrated solutions).

Thousands of developers of Huawei were engaged in the technology R&D projects mentioned above (including the research and development of product technology, and the cutting-edge technologies such as analysis algorithms, machine learning algorithms, and natural language processing), while Huawei also actively shared the outcomes with the Huawei AI research community in return.

1.3 The Technologies and Applications of AI

1.3.1 The Technologies of AI

As shown by Fig. 1.10, the AI technologies mainly include three types of applicational technologies of computer vision, speech processing and natural language processing.

1. Computer Vision

   Computer vision is a science that explores how to make computers "see" things, and the most established technology among the three genres of AI application technologies. The subjects that computer vision mainly deals with include image classification, object detection, image segmentation, visual tracking, text recognition and facial recognition. Currently, computer vision is generally used in electronic attendance tracking, identity verification, image recognition and image search, as shown in Figs. 1.11, 1.12, 1.13 and 1.14. In the future, computer vision will be upgraded to a more advanced level that it is capable to interpret, analyze images and make decisions autonomously, thus truly endow machines with the capability to "see", and play a greater role in scenarios such as unmanned vehicles and smart homes.

2. Speech Processing

   Speech processing is the study of the statistical characteristics of speech signals and voice production. The processing technologies such as speech recognition, speech synthesis and speech wake-up can collectively be addressed as "speech processing". The sub-domains of speech processing research majorly include speech recognition, speech synthesis, voice wake-up, voiceprint recognition and sound event detection. And the most mature sub-domain is the speech recognition, which can achieve an accuracy rate of 96% premised on a quiet indoor environment and near-field recognition. At present, the speech recognition technology is mainly used in intelligent question answering and intelligent navigation, as shown in Figs. 1.15 and 1.16.

3. Natural Language Processing (NLP)

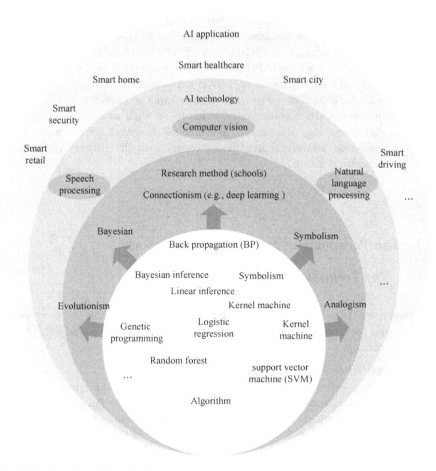

Fig. 1.10 The technologies of AI

Fig. 1.11 Electronic attendance

Fig. 1.12 Identity verification

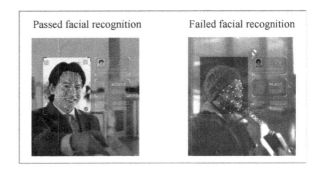

Passed facial recognition   Failed facial recognition

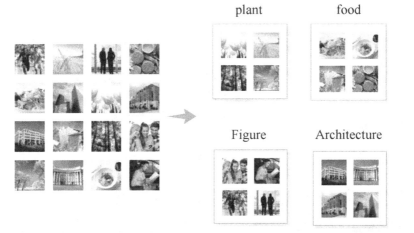

plant   food

Figure   Architecture

Fig. 1.13 Image recognition

Fig. 1.14 Image search

Fig. 1.15 Intelligent Q&A

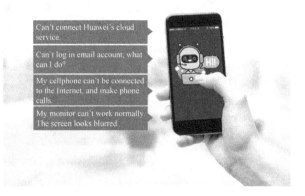

Fig. 1.16 Intelligent navigation

Natural language processing is a technology aiming at interpreting and utiliz-
ing natural language through computer technologies. The subjects of NLP
include machine translation, text mining and sentiment analysis. Faced with a
number of technical challenges, NLP is not yet a very mature technology
currently. Due to the high complexity of semantics, it is impossible for AI to
rival human in understanding semantics only by the deep learning based on big
data and parallel computing. In the future, AI is excepted to develop to a stage that
it can automatically extract features and understand deep semantics from the
current status that can only understand shallow semantics to, and to upgrade from
single intelligence (machine learning) to hybrid intelligence (machine learning,
deep learning and reinforcement learning). The NLP technology is now widely

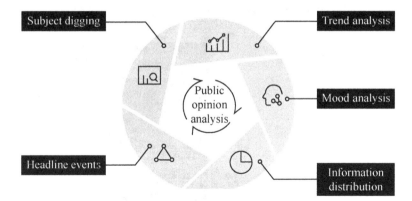

Fig. 1.17 Public opinion analysis

Fig. 1.18 Comment analysis

applied in the fields such as public opinion analysis, comment analysis and machine translation, as shown in Figs. 1.17, 1.18 and 1.19.

1.3.2 The Applications of AI

The applications of AI are as follows.

1. Smart City

Fig. 1.19 Machine translation

Social management	Public service	Industry operation	Personal application
AI+security	AI+healthcare	AI+agriculture	AI+life and entertainment
AI+transportation	AI+governance	AI+building	AI+education
AI+energy	AI+service robot	AI+retail	

Fig. 1.20 Smart city

A smart city is to use ICT technologies to sense, analyze, and integrate the key information of the core urban operation system, so as to intelligently respond to the city's demands in people's livelihood, environmental protection, public safety, urban services, and industrial and commercial activities. The nature of smart city is to realize an intelligent management and operation of the city through advanced information technology, thereby improving the living standards of the citizens, and promoting a harmonious and sustainable development for the city. In a smart city, AI is mainly exemplified as smart environment, smart economy, smart life, smart information, smart supply chain and smart government. To put it more specifically, AI technologies are adopted by traffic monitoring logistics, and facial recognition for security and protection. Figure 1.20 shows the structure of a smart city.

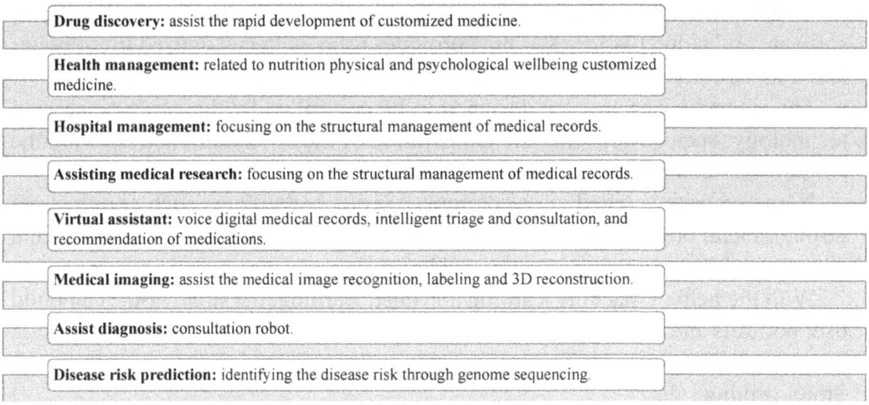

Drug discovery: assist the rapid development of customized medicine.

Health management: related to nutrition physical and psychological wellbeing customized medicine.

Hospital management: focusing on the structural management of medical records.

Assisting medical research: focusing on the structural management of medical records.

Virtual assistant: voice digital medical records, intelligent triage and consultation, and recommendation of medications.

Medical imaging: assist the medical image recognition, labeling and 3D reconstruction.

Assist diagnosis: consultation robot.

Disease risk prediction: identifying the disease risk through genome sequencing.

Fig. 1.21 Smart healthcare

2. Smart healthcare

We can enable AI to "learn" professional medical knowledge, to "memorize" loads of health records, and to analyze medical images with computer vision, so as to provide doctors with reliable and efficient assistance, as shown in Fig. 1.21. For example, for the medical imaging widely used today, AI can build models based on historical data to analyze the medical images and quickly detect the lesions, thus improving the efficiency of consultation.

3. Smart Retail

AI will also revolutionize the retail industry. A typical case is the unmanned supermarket. Amazon's unmanned supermarket Amazon Go adopts sensors, cameras, computer vision, and deep learning algorithms and cancels the traditional check-out, so that customers can just walk in the store, grab the products they need and go.

One of the major challenges faced by unmanned supermarket is how to charge the customers correctly. Up to now Amazon Go is the only successful case, but it is also achieved with many preconditions. For instance, Amazon Go is only open to Amazon's Prime members. Other companies will need to build their own membership system first if they want to follow Amazon's model.

4. Smart security

It is easier for AI to be implemented in the field of security, and the development of AI in this field is relatively mature. The excessive security-related image and video data have provided a good foundation for the training of AI algorithms and models. In the security domain, the application of AI technology can be classified as for civilian-use and for police-use.

For civilian use: facial recognition, early warning of potential dangers, home defense, and so on. For police-use: identification of suspicious targets, vehicle analysis, tracking suspects, searching and comparing criminal suspects, entrance guard of the key supervised areas, etc.

5. Smart home

Smart home refers to a IoT technology-based home ecosystem of hardware, software and cloud platforms, which provides users with customized life services and a more convenient, comfortable and safe living environment a home.

The smart housewares are designed to be controlled by the voice processing technology, such as adjusting the temperature of the air conditioner, opening the curtains and controlling the lighting system.

Home security is relied on the computer vision technology, such as unlocking through facial or fingerprint recognition, real-time smart camera monitoring, and detection of illegal intrusion to the residence.

With the help of machine learning and deep learning, the smart home can build user portraits and make recommendations based on the historical records stored in smart speakers and smart TVs.

6. Smart driving

The Society of Automotive Engineers (SAE) defines six levels for autonomous driving from L0 to L5 based on the degree of dependence the vehicle has on the driving system. The L0-level vehicles need to reply on driver's operation completely, and the vehicles at level L3 and above allow the hands-off driving under certain circumstances, while the L5-level vehicles are completely operated by the driving system without a driver in all scenarios.

Currently only a handful of models of commercial passenger vehicle manufacturers such as Audi A8, Tesla and Cadillac are equipped with L2 and L3 Advanced Driving Assistance System (ADAS). With the further enhancement of sensors and on-board processors, the year 2020 witnessed the emergence of more L3 models. The vehicles with L4 and L5 autonomous driving system are expected to be firstly used in the commercial vehicle platforms in the enclosed industry parks. But for the high-level autonomous driving on passenger vehicle platforms, it will require further optimization in technology, relevant policies and infrastructure construction. It is estimated that such passenger vehicles will not be put in use on the common roads until 2025.

1.3.3 The Current Status of AI

As shown in Fig. 1.22, the AI development has undergone three stages and now AI is still in the stage of perceptual intelligence.

1.4 Huawei's AI Development Strategy

1.4.1 Full-Stack All-Scenario AI Solutions

In the first quarter of 2020, Huawei's all-scenario AI computing framework MindSpore was released to the open-source community. Later Huawei released the GaussDB OLTP stand-alone database to the open-source community in June 2020,

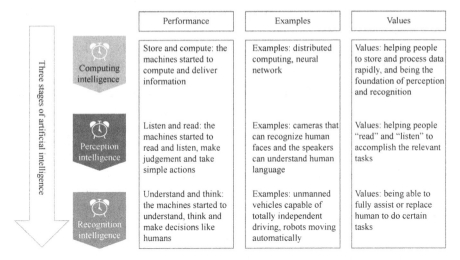

Fig. 1.22 The three stages of artificial intelligence

and released the server operating system to the open-source community on 31 December 2020.

Full-stack refers to a full-stack solution including chip, chip enable, training and reasoning framework and application enable.

All-scenario refers to an all-scenario deployment environment including public cloud, private cloud, all kinds of edge computing, IoT terminals and consumer terminals.

As the bedrock of Huawei's full-stack all-scenario AI solution, the Atlas artificial intelligence computing solution, based on the Ascend AI processor, provides products in different forms, including modules, circuit boards and servers to meet the all-scenario demands for computing power by customers.

1.4.2 Directions of Huawei Full-Stack AI

1. Huawei's one-stop AI development platform—ModelArts
   ModelArts is a one-stop development platform that Huawei designed for AI developers. It supports large-scale data preprocessing, semi-automatic labeling, distributed training, automated model building and on-demand model deployment on end, edge and cloud, to help developers quickly build and deploy models and manage the full AI development lifecycle. ModelArts features characteristics as follows.

   (a) Automatic learning: With the automatic learning function, ModelArts can automatically design models, adjust parameters, train, compress and deploy models based on the labeled data, thus the developers do not need to have experience in coding or model development.

The automatic learning of Model Arts is mainly realized through ModelArts Pro, a professional development kit designed for enterprise-grade AI. Based on the advanced algorithms and rapid training capability of HUAWEI CLOUD, ModelArts Pro provides the pre-installed workflows and models to improve the efficiency and reduce the difficulty of AI application development by the enterprises. It supports the users to recreate workflow independently and the real-time development, sharing and launching of applications, conducive to building an open ecosystem through joint efforts, and the implementation of AI in industries that benefit the general public. The toolkit of ModelArts Pro includes the kit of natural language processing, text recognition, computer vision, etc., which will enable it to quickly respond to the demands of different industries and scenarios on AI implementation.

(b) Device-edge-cloud: Device, edge, and cloud refer to end-device, Huawei intelligent edge device, and Huawei CLOUD respectively.

(c) Support online inference: Online inference is an online service (Web service) that generates the real-time predictions upon each request.

(d) Support batch inference: batch inference is to generate a batch of predictions on a batch of data.

(e) Ascend AI processor: Ascend AI processor is an AI chip featuring high computing power and low power consumption designed by Huawei.

(f) High efficiency of data preparation: ModelArts has a built-in AI data framework, which can enhance the efficiency of data preparation through the convergence of automatic pre-labeling and hard example dataset labeling.

(g) Reduced training time: ModelArts is installed with Huawei's self-developed high-performance distributed framework MoXing, using core technologies including cascaded hybrid parallelism, gradient compression, and convolution acceleration to speed up the model training by a large margin.

(h) ModelArts supports one-click deployment of models: ModelArts supports the deployment of models to end, edge, and cloud devices and scenarios by only one click, which can meet multiple requirements such as high concurrency and lightweight devices at the same time.

(i) Full-process management: ModelArts provides visual workflow management of data, training, models and inference (covering the entire AI development cycle), and enables training auto-restart after power outage, training result comparison, and traceable management of models.

(j) Active AI market: ModelArts supports data and model sharing, which can help companies improve the efficiency of internal AI development activities and can also let developers transform their knowledge into value.

2. MindSpore, All-Scenario AI Computing Framework

Although the application of AI services to the device, edge and cloud scenarios is thriving in this intelligent age, AI technology still faces huge challenges including the high technological standards, soaring development costs and long deployment cycles. These challenges are a brake on the development of AI ecosystem for developer in all-industry. Consequently, the all-scenario AI computing framework MindSpore was introduced. It was designed based on three principles: development-friendly, efficient execution and flexible deployment.

In today's world of deep learning frameworks, if we call Google's TensorFlow, Amazon's MXNet, Facebook's PyTorch and Microsoft's CNTK as the "four giants", then Huawei's MindSpore is the strongest competitor.

Thanks to the automatic parallelization provided by MindSpore, the senior data scientists and algorithm engineers dedicated to data modeling and problem solving can send an algorithm to visit dozens or even thousands of AI processing nodes with just several lines of code.

MindSpore supports architectures of different sizes and types, adaptable to all-scenario independent deployment, Ascend AI processor, and other processors such as GPUs and CPUs.

3. CANN

Compute Architecture for Neural Networks (CANN) is a chip enablement layer Huawei built for deep neural networks and Ascend AI processors. It consists of the following four major function modules.

(a) Fusion Engine: The operator-level fusion engine is mainly used to perform operator fusion to reduce the memory movement among operators and improve performance by 50%.

(b) CCE operator library: It is a deeply optimized common operator library of Huawei that can meet most of the needs of the mainstream computer vision and NLP neural network.

Certainly, it is inevitable for some clients and partners to ask for custom operators out of timeliness, privacy or doing research. This will entail the third function module of CANN.

(c) Tensor Boost Engine (TBE). It is an efficient and high-performance custom operator development tool, which makes abstraction of hardware resources into application programming interfaces (API). The clients can quickly build the operators they need.

(d) The last module is the compiler at the bottom. It provides ultimate optimization of performance to support Ascend AI processor in all scenarios.

4. Ascend AI processor

Given the rising demands for AI, the AI processor market is currently monopolized by a few companies, leading to high prices, long supply cycles and weak local service support. The demands for AI in many industries have not been met effectively.

At the HUAWEI CONNECT conference in October 2018, Huawei released Ascend 310 and Ascend 910 processors specialized for AI inference and training scenarios. The unique Da Vinci 3D Cube architecture of Ascend AI processors

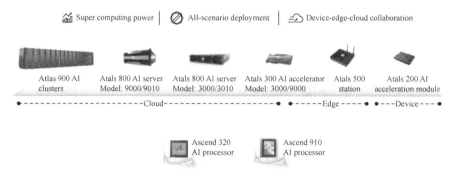

Fig. 1.23 A panorama of atlas artificial intelligence computing platform

makes the series quite competitive in computing power, energy efficiency and scalability.

Ascend 310 is a highly efficient AI system-on-chip (SoC) designed for the edge intelligent scenarios of inference. It uses a 12 nm chip and delivers a computing power of up to 16 TOPS (tera operations per second) with a consumption of only 8 W, highly suitable for the edge intelligence scenarios requiring low power consumption.

Ascend 910 is currently the single chip with the greatest computing density, suitable for AI training. It adopts a 7 nm chip and provides a computer power of up to 512 TOPS with a maximum power consumption of 350 W.

5. Atlas artificial intelligence computing solutions

Huawei Atlas artificial intelligence computing solution is based on the Huawei Ascend AI processors to build an all-scenario AI infrastructure solution for device, edge and cloud scenarios through a wide range of products including modules, circuit boards, edge stations, servers and clusters, etc., as shown in the Fig. 1.23. As a crucial section of Huawei's full-stack all-scenario AI solution, Atlas launched its inference products in 2019 and brought the industry a complete AI computing solution by complementing the training products in 2020. Meanwhile, Huawei created a device-edge-cloud collaboration platform through all-scenario deployment, letting AI to empower every link in the industry.

1.5   The Controversy of AI

1.5.1   Algorithmic Bias

The algorithmic bias is mainly cause by the biased data.

While we are making decisions with the help of AI, the algorithms may learn to discriminate against a certain group of individuals as trained on the collected data. For instance, the algorithms could make discriminatory-prone decisions based on race, gender or other factors. Even if we exclude the factors such as race or gender from the data, the algorithms could still make discriminatory decisions based on the personal information such as the name or address of a person.

Here is an example. If you search with a name sounding like an African-American, you may get an advertisement for a tool of criminal records inquiry, which is unlikely to happen if you search with other styles of names. Online advertisers tend to feed advertisements of a product with lower price to female viewers. Google' image app once mistakenly tagged a photo of black people as "gorillas."

1.5.2 Privacy Issues

Currently, the existing AI algorithms are all data-driven, as the training of models require massive data. While enjoying the convenience brought by AI, people are also threatened by the risk of privacy leakage. For instance, the huge amount of user data that collected by some technology company may put us into the risk of full exposure of our daily life if these data are leaked.

When people are online, technically the technology companies can record every click, every page scroll, the viewing time spent for any content, and browsing history of the users.

These technology companies can also know the location of the users, where they have been, what they have done, and their education background, purchasing power, preferences and other personal privacy according to the users' records of rides and purchases every day.

1.5.3 The Contradiction Between Technology and Ethics

Along with the development of computer vision, it is more and more difficult to judge the credibility of images. People can produce fake or manipulated images through image processors (e.g., Photoshop, PS), generative adversarial networks (GAN) and other techniques, making it really difficult to tell whether they are fake or real.

Let's take GAN as an example. This concept was introduced by the machine learning researcher Ian Goodfellow in 2014. In its name, "G" is for "generative", which is quoted here to indicate that the model generates image-like information, rather than the predicted values related to the input data. And "AN" is for "adversarial network", as model uses two groups of neural networks that contest with each other like in a cat-and-mouse game, or like cashiers fighting banknote counterfeiters: the counterfeiter tries to deceive the cashier to believe that he is holding the real money, and the cashier tries to identify the authenticity.

1.5.4   Will Everyone Be Unemployed?

Throughout the course of human development, people are always seeking ways to enhance efficiency, namely, to harvest more with fewer resources. We used sharp stones to hunt and gathered food more efficiently, and invented steam engine to reduce the reliance on horses. In the era of AI , AI will replace the jobs of high repetitiveness, low creativity and seldom social interactions, while the jobs of high creativity will not be easily replaced.

1.6   The Development Trends for AI

1. Easier Development Framework
   All the AI development frameworks are evolving to be simpler in operation while omnipotent in functions. The threshold for AI development has been continuously lowered.
2. Algorithms and Models with Better Performance
   In computer vision, GAN is able to generate high-quality images that cannot be distinguished by the human eyes. And the GAN-related algorithms have begun to be applied to other vision-related tasks, such as semantic segmentation, facial recognition, video synthesis and unsupervised clustering. In natural language processing, major breakthroughs have been made in the Transformer-based pre-training models. The relevant models such as BERT, GPT and XLNet have begun to be widely applied to industrial scenarios. In reinforcement learning, AlphaStar of DeepMind defeated the top human players at the game *StarCraft II*.
3. Smaller Deep Models
   Models with better performance are often accompanied by larger parameters, and larger models will have to face the problem of operational efficiency during industrial implementation. Therefore, an increasing number of model compression techniques have been proposed to further reduce the size and parameters of the models, accelerate the inference speed, and meet the requirements of industrial applications while ensuring the performance.
4. All-round development of the computing power at device, edge and cloud
   The application of artificial intelligence chips to the cloud, edge devices and mobile terminals is expanding, further solving the problem of computing power for AI.
5. More Sophisticated AI Basic Data Services
   As the AI basic data service is becoming more mature, we will see more and more related data labeling platforms and tools being introduced to the market.
6. Safer Data Sharing
   On the premise of ensuring data privacy and security, federated learning makes use of different data sources to collaboratively train the models, so as to overcome the bottleneck of data as shown in Fig. 1.24.

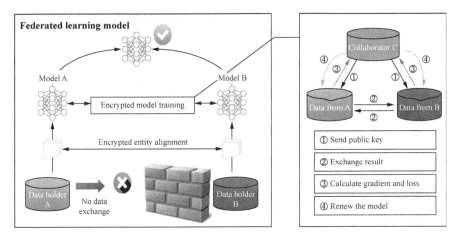

Fig. 1.24 Federated learning

Huawei's global industry outlook report GIV 2020 (GIV 2025 for short) lists the 10 major development trends of intelligent technologies in the future.

1. Popularization of intelligent robots

   Huawei predicts that by 2025, 14% of the families across the globe will own a smart robot, which will play an important role in people's daily life.

2. Popularization of AR/VR

   The report predicts that the percentage of the companies using VR/AR technology will reach 10% in the future. The application of technologies including virtual reality will bring vigor and opportunities to the industries such as commercial presentation and audio-visual entertainment.

3. Application of AI in a wide range of fields

   It is predicted that 97% of the large enterprises will adopt AI technology, mainly exemplified by the employment of speech intelligence, image recognition, facial recognition, human-computer interaction and so on.

4. Popularization of big data applications

   The enterprises will be making efficient use of 86% of the data they produce. The Big data analysis and processing will save time and enhance efficiency for the enterprises.

5. Weakening of search engine

   In the future, 90% of the people will have a smart personal assistant, which means that the chance for you to search something from a search portal will be greatly reduced.

6. Popularization of the Internet of Vehicles

   The cellular vehicle-to-everything (C-V2X) technology will be installed in 15% of the vehicles in the world. Smart vehicles and cars on the Internet will be substantially popularized, providing a safer and more reliable driving experience.

7. Popularization of industrial robots

   Industrial robots will work side by side with people in manufacturing, with 103 robots for every 10,000 employees. The hazardous, high-precision and high-intensity tasks will be assisted or completed by industrial robots independently.

8. Popularization of cloud technology and applications

The usage rate of cloud-based applications will reach 85%. A majority of applications and program collaboration will be performed on the cloud.

9. Popularization of 5G

Fifty-eight percent of the world's population will enjoy 5G services. We may anticipate a revolution of communications industry in the future, when the technology and speed of communications will be greatly advanced.

10. Popularization of digital economy and big data

The amount of global storage data produced annually will reach as high as 180 ZB. Digital economy and blockchain technology will be widely combined with the Internet.

1.7 Chapter Summary

This chapter introduces the basic concepts, development history and application background of AI. By reading this chapter, the readers can find that, as an interdisciplinary science, the application and development of artificial intelligence will not be achieved without the support of other disciplines. Its physical implementation is reliant on the large-scale hardware, and its upper-layer application is reliant upon software design and methods of implementation. As learners, the readers are expected to understand the boundaries of the application of artificial intelligence so as to ameliorate and improve themselves on this basis.

1.8 Exercises

1. There are different interpretations of artificial intelligence in different contexts. Please elaborate on the artificial intelligence in your eyes.
2. Artificial intelligence, machine learning and deep learning are three concepts often mentioned together. What is the relationship between them? What are the similarities and differences between the three terms?
3. After reading the artificial intelligence application scenarios in this chapter, please describe in detail a field of AI application and its scenarios in real life based on your own life experience.
4. CANN is a chip enablement layer that Huawei introduced for deep neural networks and Ascend AI processors. Please brief the four major modules of CANN.
5. Based on your current knowledge and understanding, please elaborate on the development trends of artificial intelligence in the future in your view.

Chapter 2
Machine Learning

Machine learning is currently a mainstream research hotspot in the AI industry, entailing multiple disciplines such as probability theory, statistics, and convex optimization. This chapter first introduces the definition of "learning" in learning algorithms and the process of machine learning. On this basis, it offers some commonly used machine learning algorithms. Our readers will learn about some key concepts such as hyperparameters, gradient descent, and cross-validation.

2.1 Introduction to Machine Learning

Machine learning (including its branch deep learning) is the study of "learning algorithms". The so-called "learning" here refers to the situation that the performance of a computer program measured by performance metric P on a certain task T improves itself with experience E, then we call this computer program learning from experience E. For instance, identifying junk email is a task T. We can complete such tasks easily, because we have lots of experiences in doing so in daily life. These experiences may come from daily emails, spam messages or even advertisements on TV. We can summarize and conclude from these experiences that emails from unknown users that contain the words like "discount" and "zero risk" are more likely to be spam. Referring to the learnt knowledge, we can distinguish whether an email that has never been read before is spam, as shown in Fig. 2.1a. So, can we write a computer program to simulate the above process? As shown in Fig. 2.1b, we can prepare a number of e-mails, and pick out the junk emails by hands, as the experience E for this program. However, the program cannot automatically summarize these experiences. At this time, it is necessary to train the program through machine learning algorithms. The computer program that has been trained is called a model, and in general the larger the number of emails is used for training, the better the model may be trained, and the larger the value of the performance metric P will be.

© The Author(s) 2023
Huawei Technologies Co., Ltd., *Artificial Intelligence Technology*,
https://doi.org/10.1007/978-981-19-2879-6_2

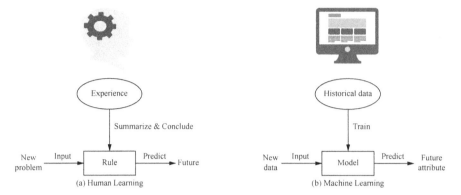

Fig. 2.1 Learning mode

Spam identification is very difficult to achieve through traditional programming methods. Theoretically, we should be able to find a set of rules in line with the features of all junk emails, rather than that of the regular emails. This method of using explicit programming to solve problems is known as a rule-based approach. However, in practice, it is almost impossible to find such a set of rules. Therefore, to solve this problem, machine learning adopts the statistical-based method. We can basically claim that machine learning is a method to let machines to learn rules automatically through samples. Compared with using the rule-based method, machine learning can learn more complex rules and the rules that are difficult to describe, so as to handle more complicated tasks.

Machine learning is highly adaptable and can solve many problems in the AI field, but this does not mean that machine learning will always be used preliminary in all cases. As shown in Fig. 2.2, machine learning is suitable for problems which require a complex solution or involve a large amount of data, but the probability distribution of the data is unknown. Machine learning can certainly solve the problem in other cases, but the cost is often higher than traditional methods. Take the second quadrant shown in Fig. 2.2 as an example. If the size of the problem is small enough to be solved by artificial rules, then there is no need to use machine learning algorithms. There are two main application scenarios in general for machine learning.

1. The rules are quite complicated or unable to be described, such as face recognition and voice recognition.
2. The data distribution itself changes over time, and the program needs to be constantly re-adapted, such as predicting the trend of commodity sales.

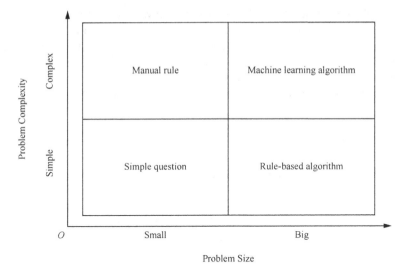

Fig. 2.2 Application scenarios of machine learning

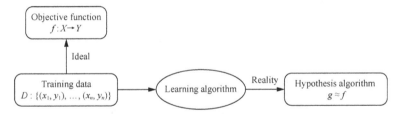

Fig. 2.3 The relationship between the hypothesis function and the objective function

2.1.1 Rational Understanding of Machine Learning Algorithms

The nature of machine learning algorithms is function fitting. Let f be the objective function, the purpose of the machine learning algorithm is to give a hypothetical function g that makes $g(x)$ and $f(x)$ as close as possible to the input x in any defined domain. A simple example is the probability density estimation in statistics. By the law of large numbers, the height of all Chinese population should follow a normal distribution. Although the probability density function f of this normal distribution is unknown, we can estimate the mean and variance of the distribution by sampling, and then estimate f.

The relationship between the hypothesis function and the objective function is shown in Fig. 2.3. For a given task, we can collect a large amount of training data. These data must fit a given objective function f, otherwise, it is meaningless to learn such a task. Next, the learning algorithm can analyze these training data and give a hypothetical function g that is similar to the objective function f as much as possible.

Therefore, the output of the learning algorithm is always not perfect and cannot be completely consistent with the objective function. However, with the expansion of the training data, the degree of approximation of the hypothesis function g to the objective function f is gradually improved, and finally a satisfactory level of accuracy can be achieved in machine learning.

It is worth mentioning that the objective function f is sometimes very abstract in existence. For the classic image classification task, the objective function means the mapping from the image set to the category set. In order to let a program to process logical information such as images and classes, it is necessary to use certain encoding methods to map images or categories one by one into scalars, vectors or matrices. For example, you can number each category from 0, thereby mapping the class to a scalar. You can also use different one-hot vectors to represent different classes, which is called one-hot encoding. The encoding of image is a little more complicated, and is generally represented by a three-dimensional matrix. With this encoding method, we can see the domain of definition the objective function f as a collection of three-dimensional matrices and its range as a collection of a series of serial numbers for classes. Although the encoding process is not part of the learning algorithm, in some cases, the choice of encoding method will also affect the efficiency of the learning algorithm.

2.1.2   Major Problems Solved by Machine Learning

Machine learning can deal with various types of problems, including the most typical ones such as classification, regression, and clustering. Classification and regression are the two major types of prediction problems, taking up of 80–90% of all the problems. The main difference is that the output of classification is discrete serial numbers of classes (generally called as "labels" in machine learning), while the output of regression is continuous value.

The classification problem requires the program to indicate which of the k classes does the input belong to. To solve this problem, machine learning algorithms usually output mapping from domain D to category labels $\{1, 2, \ldots, k\}$. Image classification task is a typical classification problem.

In regression problems, the program needs to predict the output value for a given input. The output of a machine learning algorithm is usually a mapping from the domain D to the real number domain R. For instance, predicting the claim amount of the insured (used to set insurance premium), or predicting the price of securities in the future are all relevant cases. In fact, classification problems can also be reduced to regression problems. By predicting the probability of the image belonging to each class, the machine learning can obtain the result of the classification.

The clustering problem needs to divide the data into multiple categories according to the inherent similarity of the data. Unlike the classification problem, the dataset of the clustering problem does not contain manually labeled labels. The clustering algorithm makes the data similar to each other within the class as much as possible, while the data similarity between the classes is relatively small, so as to implement classification. Clustering algorithms can be used in scenarios like image retrieval, user portrait generation and etc.

2.2 Types of Machine Learning

According to whether the training dataset contains manually tagged labels, machine learning can be generally divided into two types—supervised learning and unsupervised learning. Sometimes, in order to distinguish it from unsupervised learning, supervised learning is also called learning under supervision. If some data in the dataset contains labels and the majority of the data does not, then this learning algorithm is called semi-supervised learning. Reinforcement learning mainly focuses on multi-step decision-making problems, and automatically collects data for learning in the interaction with the environment.

2.2.1 Supervised Learning

Generally speaking, supervised learning is allowing the computer to compare standard answers when it is trained to answer the multiple-choice questions. The computer tries its best to adjust its model parameters, expecting that the inferred answer is as consistent as possible with the standard answer, and finally learn how to solve the question. Using samples of known labels, supervised learning can train an optimal model meeting the required performance. Using this model, any input can be mapped to the corresponding output, so as to predict the unknown data.

Figure 2.4 shows a supervised learning algorithm that is highly simplified. The features in the graph can be understood as data items. Although this interpretation is not sufficient to some extent, it will not affect our description on this supervised learning algorithm. The supervised learning algorithm takes features as input and the predicted value of the targets as output. Figure 2.5 shows a practical example. In this example, we hope to make an overall prediction that whether a user enjoys exercises

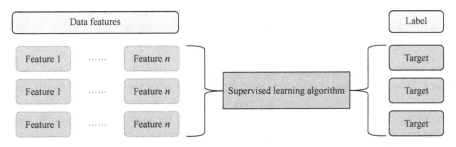

Fig. 2.4 Supervised learning algorithm

Fig. 2.5 Sample data

	Feature		Target
Weather	Temperature	Wind speed	Enjoyment of exercise
Sunny	Warm	Strong	Yes
Rainy	Cold	Medium	No
Sunny	Cold	Weak	Yes

by taking weather conditions into account. Each row in the table is a set of training examples that records the weather characteristics of a specific day and the user's enjoyment of exercises. Similar algorithms can be applied to other scenarios such as product recommendations.

The input (feature) and output (target) of a supervised learning algorithm can be either continuous or discrete. When the value of the target variable is continuous, the output of the supervised learning algorithm is called a regression model. The regression model reflects the features of the attribute values in the sample dataset, and expresses the relationship of the sample mapping through functions to show the dependency between the attribute values. The attribute value mentioned here includes feature and target. Regression model is widely used in time series forecasting. For instance, how much money can you earn form stocks next week? What will the temperature be tomorrow? So on and so forth. Correspondingly, when the target variable takes discrete values, the output of the supervised learning algorithm is called a classification model. Through the classification model, the samples in the sample dataset can be mapped to the given classes. Such as whether there will be traffic jams on a highway during the morning rush hour tomorrow? Which one is more attractive to customers, a five-yuan voucher or a 25%-off discount? Etc.

Although the range of the regression model can be an infinite set, the output of the classification model is often finite. This is because the size of the dataset cannot grow indefinitely, and the number of classes in the dataset should to the most be the same with the number of training examples. Therefore, the number of classes is not infinite. When training a classification model, an artificially designated class set L is often needed for the model to select category output. The size of the set L is generally recorded as K, which is the number of possible classes.

2.2.2 Unsupervised Learning

Compared with supervised learning, unsupervised learning is like letting the computer do multiple-choice questions without telling it what the correct answer is. In this case, it is difficult for the computer to secure the correct answer. But by analyzing the relationship between these questions, the computer can classify the questions so that the multiple-choice questions in each class have the same answer.

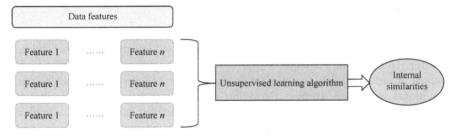

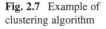

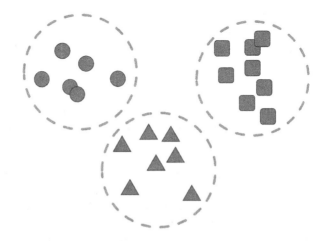

Fig. 2.6 Unsupervised learning algorithm

Fig. 2.7 Example of
clustering algorithm

The unsupervised learning algorithm does not require labeling samples, but directly modeling the input dataset, as shown in Fig. 2.6.

Clustering algorithm is a typical unsupervised learning algorithm that can be summarized by the proverb: "birds of a feather flock together". The algorithm only puts the samples of high similarity together. For newly input samples, it only needs to calculate their similarity with the existing samples, and then classify them according to the degree of similarity. Biologists have used the concept of clustering to study the interspecies relationship for a long time. As shown in Fig. 2.7, after classifying the iris flowers based on the size of sepal and petal, the iris has been divided into three categories. Through the clustering model, the samples in the sample dataset can be divided into several categories, making the similarity of samples under the same category relatively higher. The scenarios of application for the clustering model include that what kinds of audiences like to watch movies of the same subject, and which components are damaged similarly, etc.

2.2.3 Semi-supervised Learning

Semi-supervised learning is a combination of supervised learning and unsupervised learning. This algorithm attempts to allow the learner to automatically utilize a large amount of unlabeled data to assist the learning of a small amount of labeled data. Traditional supervised learning algorithms need to learn from a large number of labeled training samples to build a model for predicting the labels of new samples. For example, in a classification task, the label suggests the class of the sample. And in a regression task, the label suggests the real-valued output of the sample. With the rapid development of human's ability to collect and store data, in many practical tasks, it is very easy to acquire a large amount of unlabeled data, and labeling them often consumes a lot of efforts and materials. For example, for webpage recommendation, users are required to mark web pages they interest in. But few users are willing to spend a lot of time to mark, so the web pages with marked information are limited. But there are countless web pages that are not marked, or marked, which can be used as unmarked data.

As shown in Fig. 2.8, semi-supervised learning does not require manual labeling on all the samples like supervised learning, nor is it completely independent from the target like unsupervised learning. In the semi-supervised learning datasets, generally speaking, there are only a few samples labeled. Taking the iris classification problem presented in Fig. 2.7 as an example. A small amount of supervised information is added to the dataset, as shown in Fig. 2.9. Let's assume the circle represents the Setosa sample, the triangle represents the Versicolor sample, the square represents the Virginica sample, and the star represents the unknown sample. The clustering algorithm has been introduced in unsupervised learning, suppose its output is shown by the dotted circle in Fig. 2.9. Counting the circles including the highest number of known samples and then this class can be used as the class for this cluster. To be more specific, the upper-left cluster belongs to Setosa, while the upper right cluster obviously belongs to Virginica. By combining unsupervised algorithm and supervised information, semi-supervised algorithm can achieve higher accuracy with lower labor costs.

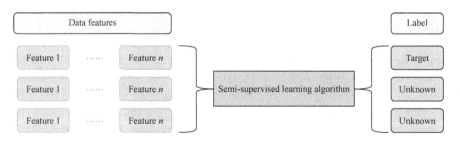

Fig. 2.8 Semi-supervised learning algorithm

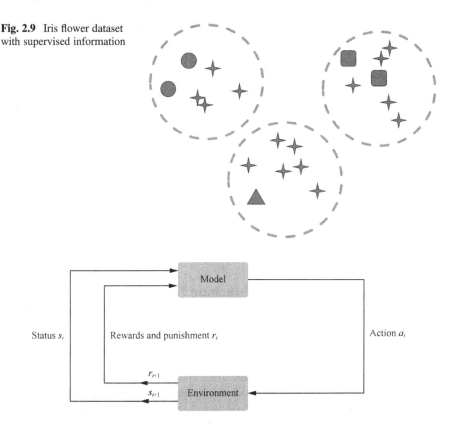

Fig. 2.9 Iris flower dataset with supervised information

Fig. 2.10 Reinforcement learning algorithm

2.2.4 *Reinforcement Learning*

Reinforcement learning is mainly used to solve multi-step decision-making problems, such as Go game, video games, and visual navigation. Unlike the problems studied by supervised learning and unsupervised learning, these problems are often difficult to find accurate answers. Taking Go as an example. It takes about 10,170 operations to exhaust the results of the game (there are only 1080 atoms in the universe). So, for a given and common situation, it is difficult to find the perfect move.

Another characteristic of the multi-step decision problem is that it is easy to define a reward function to evaluate whether the task has been completed. The reward function of Go can be defined as whether to win the game; the reward function of electronic games can be defined as the score. The goal of reinforcement learning is to find an action strategy to maximize the value of the reward function.

As shown in Fig. 2.10, the two most important parts of a reinforcement learning algorithm are the model and the environment. In different environments, the model can determine its own actions, and different actions may have different effects on the environment. Still, in the case of solving test questions, the computer can give the answer randomly, and the teacher will give a score based on the answer given. But if the situation is only limited to this case, it is impossible for the computer to learn how to solve the question, because the teacher's grading does not contribute to the training process. In this case, the importance of status and rewards and punishments are highlighted. A higher test score can make the teacher satisfied and then give the computer a certain reward. On the contrary, a lower test score may incur penalties. As a "motivated" computer, it is bound to hope that by adjusting its own model parameters, it can get more rewards because of its answers. In this process, no one provides training data for the learning algorithm or tells the reinforcement learning system how to make the correct move. All data and reward signals are dynamically generated during the interaction between the model and the environment and are automatically and dynamically learned. No matter it is good behavior or bad behavior, it can help the model to learn.

2.3   The Overall Process of Machine Learning

A complete machine learning project often involves data collection, data cleaning, feature extraction and selection, model training, model evaluation and testing, model deployment and integration, as shown in Fig. 2.11. This section introduces the concepts related to data collection and data cleaning, which are fundamental to understand what is feature selection. After selecting reasonable features, it is necessary to train and evaluate the model based on these features. This is not a one-kick process, but requires constant feedback and iteration to harvest satisfactory results. At last, the model needs to be deployed to the specific application scenarios to put theories into practice.

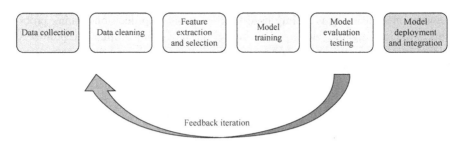

Fig. 2.11   The overall process of machine learning

2.3.1   Data Collection

A dataset is a set of data used in a machine learning project, and each data is called a sample. The items or attributes that reflect the performance or nature of the sample in a certain aspect are called features. The dataset used in the training process is called the training set, and each sample is called a training sample. Learning (training) is the process of learning a model from data. The process of using the model to make predictions is called testing, and the dataset used for testing is known as the test set. Each sample in the test set is called a test sample.

Figure 2.12 shows a typical dataset. In this dataset, each row indicates a sample, and each column refers to a feature or label. When the task is determined, such as predicting housing prices based on floor area, school district, and house orientation, the features and labels are also determined. Therefore, the row and column headers of the dataset should remain unchanged throughout the machine learning project. The training set and the test set are relatively free to split, and the researcher can determine which samples belong to the training set based on experience. A too low proportion of the test set may result in randomness of model testing, not able to properly evaluate the performance of the model. While a high proportion of the training set may result in low sample utilization and the model cannot learn thoroughly. Therefore, the common ratio between training set and dataset is that the training set accounts for 80% of the total number of samples, and the test set accounts for 20%. In this example, there are four samples in the training set and one sample in the test set.

2.3.2   Data Cleaning

Data is vital to the model and determines the limit of the model's capabilities. Without good data, there will be no good models. However, data quality is a

		Feature 1	Feature 2	Feature 3	Label
	Serial number	Floor area	School district	Orientation	Housing price
Training set	1	100	8	South	1000
	2	120	9	Southwest	1300
	3	60	6	North	700
	4	80	9	Southeast	1100
Test set	5	95	3	South	850

Fig. 2.12 Sample dataset

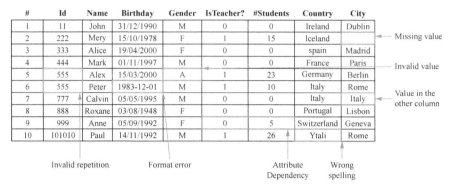

#	Id	Name	Birthday	Gender	IsTeacher?	#Students	Country	City
1	11	John	31/12/1990	M	0	0	Ireland	Dublin
2	222	Mery	15/10/1978	F	1	15	Iceland	
3	333	Alice	19/04/2000	F	0	0	spain	Madrid
4	444	Mark	01/11/1997	M	0	0	France	Paris
5	555	Alex	15/03/2000	A	1	23	Germany	Berlin
6	555	Peter	1983-12-01	M	1	10	Italy	Rome
7	777	Calvin	05/05/1995	M	0	0	Italy	Italy
8	888	Roxane	03/08/1948	F	0	0	Portugal	Lisbon
9	999	Anne	05/09/1992	F	0	5	Switzerland	Geneva
10	101010	Paul	14/11/1992	M	1	26	Ytali	Rome

Missing value — row 2

Invalid value — row 4

Value in the other column — row 7

Invalid repetition   Format error   Attribute Dependency   Wrong spelling

Fig. 2.13 "Dirty" data

commonly problem bothering real data, as shown in Fig. 2.13. Following are some typical problems on data quality.

1. Incomplete: Data lacks attributes or containing missing values.
2. Noisy: Data contains erroneous records or outliers.
3. Inconsistent: Data contains conflicting records or discrepancies.

Such data is called "dirty" data. The process of filling in missing values, finding and eliminating data abnormalities is called data cleaning. In addition, data preprocessing often involves data dimensionality reduction and data standardization. The purpose of data dimensionality reduction is to simplify data attributes and avoid dimensional explosion; while the purpose of data standardization is to unify the dimensions of each feature, thereby reducing the difficulty of training. The content of data dimensionality reduction and data standardization will be introduced in detail in the later passages, and this section only talks about data cleaning.

What are handled by the machine learning model are all features. The so-called feature is the numerical representation of the input variable that can be used in the model. In most cases, the collected data can be used by the algorithm after preprocessing. The preprocessing operation mainly includes the following procedures.

1. Data filtering.
2. Handling missing data.
3. Handling possible errors or outliers.
4. Combining data from multiple sources.
5. Data aggregation.

The workload of data cleaning is often quite heavy. Research shows that data scientists spend 60% of their time on cleaning and organizing data in machine learning researches, as shown in Fig. 2.14. On the one hand, this shows how difficult data cleaning is, and that the data collection featuring different methods and contents will require different methods for data cleaning. What is more, it also shows that data cleaning plays a crucial role in subsequent model training and optimization. Another

Fig. 2.14 The importance of data cleaning

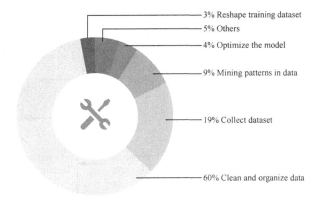

————3% Reshape training dataset

————5% Others

————4% Optimize the model

————9% Mining patterns in data

————19% Collect dataset

————60% Clean and organize data

Fig. 2.15 The machine learning process using the filtering

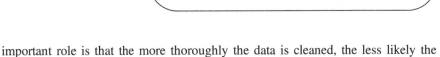

Traverse all the features → Choose the best subset → Learning algorithm → Performance evaluation

important role is that the more thoroughly the data is cleaned, the less likely the model is to be affected by abnormal data, thus ensuring the model's training performance.

2.3.3 Feature Selection

Usually, there are many different features in a dataset, some of which may be redundant or unrelated to the target. For example, when predicting housing prices based on floor area, school district, and daily temperature, the daily temperature is apparently an irrelevant feature. Through feature selection, these redundant or irrelevant features can be eliminated, so that the model is simplified and easier to be interpreted by users. At the same time, feature selection can also effectively reduce the time of model training, avoid dimensional explosion, improve the generalization performance of the model, and avoid overfitting. Common methods for feature selection include filter methods, wrapper methods, and embedded methods, which will be introduced successively in the following passages.

The filter method is independent when selecting features and has nothing to do with the model itself. By measuring the correlation between each feature and the target attribute, filter method applies a statistical measurement to score each feature. By sorting these features on the basis of the scores, you can decide to keep or eliminate specific features. Figure 2.15 shows the machine learning process using filter methods. Statistical measures commonly used in filtering include Pearson's correlation coefficient, Chi-Square coefficient, and mutual information. Since filter

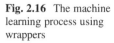

Fig. 2.16 The machine learning process using wrappers

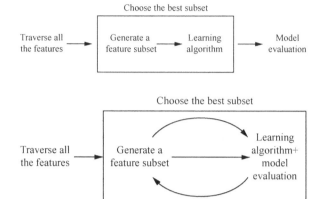

Fig. 2.17 The machine learning process using embedded method

does not consider the relationship between features, it is only prone to select redundant variables.

The wrapper method uses a predictive model to score a subset of features, and considers the feature selection problem as a search problem, where the wrapper will evaluate and compare different feature combinations, and the predictive model will be used as a tool for evaluating feature combinations. The higher the accuracy of the prediction model, the more the feature combination should be retained. Figure 2.16 displays the machine learning using the wrapper method. One of the popular wrapper methods is recursive feature elimination (RFE). Wrapper methods usually provide the best-performing feature set for a specific class of model, but it needs to train a new model for each feature subset, so the amount of operations is extensive.

The embedded method uses feature selection as part of model building, as shown in Fig. 2.17. Unlike the filter and wrapper method, the model using the embedded method actively learns how to perform feature selection during training. The most common embedded feature selection method is regularization. Regularization is also called the penalty method. By introducing additional constraints when optimizing the prediction algorithm, the complexity of the model is reduced, namely, the number of features is reduced. Common regularization methods include ridge regression and Lasso regression.

2.3.4   The Construction of Machine Learning Models

After finishing data cleaning and feature extraction, it is time to build the model. Taking supervised learning as an example, model construction generally follows the steps shown in Fig. 2.18. The core of model construction is model training, verification and testing. This section briefly explains the training and prediction process using one simple example. More details will be introduced in the following chapters.

Overall process of model construction

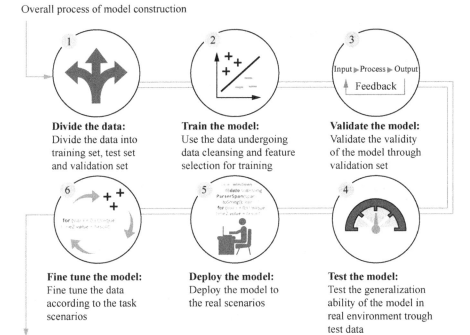

Divide the data:
Divide the data into
training set, test set
and validation set

Train the model:
Use the data undergoing
data cleansing and feature
selection for training

Validate the model:
Validate the validity
of the model through
validation set

Fine tune the model:
Fine tune the data
according to the task
scenarios

Deploy the model:
Deploy the model to
the real scenarios

Test the model:
Test the generalization
ability of the model in
real environment trough
test data

Fig. 2.18   Overall process of model construction

	Feature (attribute)		Target (label)	
Name	City	Age	Change	
Mike	Miami	42	yes	**Training set**
Jerry	New York	32	no	Model finding the relationship between feature and target
Bryan	Orlando	18	no	
Patricia	Miami	45	yes	
Elodie	Phoenix	35	no	**Test set**
Remy	Chicago	72	yes	Using new data to test the validity of the model
John	New York	48	yes	

Divide ✂

Fig. 2.19   Training set and test set

In the example of this section, we need to use a classification model to determine whether someone needs to change suppliers under certain features. Assuming that Fig. 2.19 shows the cleaned dataset, the task of the model is to predict the target as accurately as possible on the basis of the known features. During the training process, the model can learn the mapping relationship between features and targets based on the samples in the training set. After training, we can get the following model:

```
def model(city, age):
 if city == "Miami": return 0.7
 if city == "Orlando": return 0.2
 if age > 42: return 0.05 * age + 0.06
 else: return 0.01 * age + 0.02
```

The output of the model is the probability of truth value of the target. We know that as the training data increases, the accuracy of the model will also increase accordingly. So why not use all the data for training, instead of only taking a part of it as the test set? This is because that the performance of the model in the face of unknown data, not the known data, is what we should look at. The training set is like an exam bank that students read through while preparing for an examination. It is not a surprising thing no matter how high the accuracy rate will be for the students, because the exam bank always has a limitation. As long as they have a good memory, the students can even memorize all the answers after all. Only the formal examination can really test the students' acquisition of knowledge, because the questions in the official examinations may be something they have never seen before. The test set is equivalent to an examination prepared by the researchers for the model. In other words, in the entire dataset (including training set and test set), the model has the right to consult only the features of the training set and test set. The target of the test set can only be used by the researchers when evaluating the performance of the model.

2.3.5   Model Evaluation

What is a good model? The most important evaluation indicator is the model's generalization ability, also known as the prediction accuracy of the model dealing with actual business data. There are also some engineering indicators that can be used to evaluate the model: interpretability, which describes the degree of straight-forwardness of the model's prediction results; prediction rate, which refers to the average time it takes for the model to predict each sample; plasticity, which refers to the acceptability of model prediction rate in actual business process as the business volume expands.

The goal of machine learning is to make the learned model applicable to new samples, not just on training samples. The ability of the learned model to apply to new samples is called generalization ability, also addressed as robustness. The difference between the predicted result of the learned model on the sample and the true result of the sample is called error. The training error refers to the error of the model on the training set, and the generalization error refers to the error of the model on the new sample (test set). Obviously, we want to have a model with smaller generalization error.

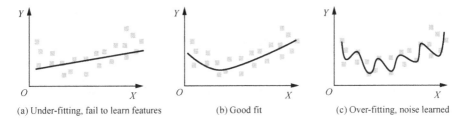

(a) Under-fitting, fail to learn features   (b) Good fit   (c) Over-fitting, noise learned

Fig. 2.20   Underfitting, good fitting and overfitting

Once the model is formed and fixed, all possible functions will construct a space, which is called hypothesis space. The machine learning algorithm can be seen as an algorithm that searches for a suitable fitting function in the hypothesis space. A mathematical model that is too simple, or the training time is too short, will cause an increasing training error for the model. This phenomenon is called underfitting. For the former, it should use a more complex model for retraining; for the latter, it only needs to extend the time to effectively eliminate underfitting. However, to accurately determine the cause of under-fitting often requires certain experience and methods. On the contrary, if the model is too complex, it may lead to a small training error, but a weaker generalization ability, which means a larger generalization error known as overfitting. There are many methods to reduce over-fitting. The common ones include appropriately simplifying the model, ending training before the over-fitting occurs, and using dropout and weight decay. Figure 2.20 shows the results of underfitting, good fitting and overfitting for the same dataset.

The capacity of a model refers to its ability to fit a variety of functions, also known as the complexity of a model. When the capacity is compatible for the complexity of the task and the amount of training data provided, the algorithm will usually have the best performance. A model with insufficient capacity cannot handle the complex tasks, thus underfitting may be provoked. As shown in Fig. 2.20a, the data distribution is in a shape of hook, but the model is linear and cannot describe the data distribution properly. A model with a high capacity can handle complex tasks, but when the capacity surpasses the level that the task needs, overfitting may be provoked. As shown in Fig. 2.20c, the model tries to fit the data with a very complex function. Although the training error is reduced, it can be inferred that such a model cannot predict the target value of a new sample properly. The effective capacity of the model is limited by algorithms, parameters, and regularization methods.

Generally speaking, the generalization error can be interpreted as:

Total error = Bias 2 + Variance + Unresolvable error

Among them, bias and variance are two sub-forms that we need to pay attention to. As shown in Fig. 2.21, the Variance is the degree of deviation of the model's prediction results near the mean, which is an error derived from the sensitivity of the model to small fluctuations on the training set. Bias is the difference between the average value of the model's prediction results and the correct value we are trying to predict. The unresolvable error refers to the error caused by the imperfection of the

Fig. 2.21 Variance and bias

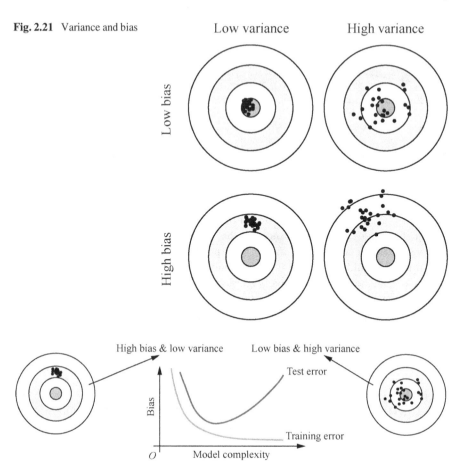

Fig. 2.22 The relationship between model complexity and error

model and the finiteness of the data. In theory, if there is an infinite amount of data and a perfect model, the so-called unresolvable errors can be resolved. But in fact, it is impossible to realize, so the generalization error can never be eliminated.

Ideally, we want to choose a model that can accurately capture the laws in the training data and can also summarize the invisible data (the so-called new data). However, generally speaking, it is impossible for us to accomplish these two things at the same time. As shown in Fig. 2.22, as the complexity of the model increases, the training error gradually decreases. At the same time, the test error will decrease to a certain point as the complexity increases, and then increase in the opposite direction, forming a concave curve. The lowest point of the test error curve suggests the ideal level of model complexity.

When measuring the performance of the regression model, commonly used indicators include mean absolute error (MAE), mean square error (MSE), and correlation coefficient R^2. Assuming that the true target values of the test example

Fig. 2.23 Confusion matrix
for a binary classifier

Predicted / Actual	yes	no	In total
yes	TP	FN	P
no	FP	TN	N
In total	P'	N'	P+N

are y1, y2,. . ., ym, and the corresponding predicted values are $\widehat{y}_1, \widehat{y}_2, \cdots, \widehat{y}_m$, then the definition of the above indicators is as follows:

$$MAE = \frac{1}{m} \sum_{i=1}^{m} |y_i - \widehat{y}_i|$$

$$MSE = \frac{1}{m} \sum_{i=1}^{m} (y_i - \widehat{y}_i)^2$$

$$R^2 = 1 - \frac{RSS}{TSS} = 1 - \frac{\sum_{i=1}^{m}(y_i - \widehat{y}_i)^2}{\sum_{i=1}^{m}(y_i - \overline{y}_i)^2}$$

Where, TSS represents the difference between the sample values, and RSS represents the difference between the predicted value and the sample value. The values of the MAE and MSE indicators are both non-negative, and the closer to 0, the better the performance of the model. The value of R2 is not greater than 1, and the closer to 1, the better the performance of the model.

When evaluating the performance of a classification model, a method called confusion matrix is often used, as shown in Fig. 2.23. The confusion matrix is a k-dimensional square matrix, where k represents the number of all categories. The value in the i-th row and the j-th column in Fig. 2.23 represents the number of samples that are actually the i-th type but are judged to be the j-th type by the model. Ideally, for a classifier with higher accuracy, most of the examples should be represented by the diagonal of the confusion matrix, while other values are 0 or close to 0. For the two-classifier confusion matrix shown in Fig. 2.23, the definition of each symbol is as follows.

1. Positive tuple P: tuple of the major classes of interest.
2. Negative tuple N: other tuples except P.
3. True positive example TP: positive tuples correctly classified by the classifier.
4. True negative example TN: the negative tuple correctly classified by the classifier.

Measurement	Equation
Accuracy rate, recognition rate	$\dfrac{TP+TN}{P+N}$
Error rate, misclassification rate	$\dfrac{FP+FN}{P+N}$
True positive rate and recall rate	$\dfrac{TP}{P}$
True negative rate	$\dfrac{TN}{P}$
Precision rate	$\dfrac{TP}{TP+FP}$
F_1 value (harmonic mean of precision and recall)	$\dfrac{2 \times precision \times recall}{precision+recall}$
F_β value (β is non-negative real number)	$\dfrac{(1+\beta^2) \times precision \times recall}{\beta^2 \times precision+recall}$

Fig. 2.24 The other concepts in confusion matrix for a binary classifier

5. False positive example FP: a negative tuple that is incorrectly marked as a positive tuple.
6. False negative example FN: A positive tuple that is incorrectly marked as a negative tuple.

Figure 2.24 shows the rest concepts in the binary classifier confusion matrix.

Here let us cite the example of document retrieval to clarify the concepts of precision and recall. The precision describes the proportion of documents that are truly related to the subject among all the documents retrieved. The recall describes the retrieved documents related to the search subject, and the proportion of all related documents in the library.

At the end of this section, let's take an example to illustrate the calculation of the confusion matrix of the binary classifiers. Assuming that a classifier can identify whether there is a cat in an image and 200 images are now used to verify the performance of this model. Among them, 170 are labeled as images with cats and 30 are labeled not. The performance of the model is as shown in Fig. 2.25. It can be seen that the recognition result of the model is that 160 images are marked with cats and 40 pictures not. It can be calculated that the precision of the model is 140/160 = 87.5%, the recall is 140/170 = 82.4%, and the accuracy is (140 + 10)/200 = 75%.

Fig. 2.25 Cases of confusion matrix

Predicted / Actual	yes	no	In total
yes	140	30	170
no	20	10	30
In total	160	40	200

2.4 Model Parameters and Hyperparameters

Parameters, as part of what the model has learned from historical training data, are the key to machine learning algorithms. Generally speaking, the model parameters are not manually set by the researchers, but are obtained by data estimation or data learning. Identifying the parameter values of the model is equivalent to defining the function of the model, so the model parameters are usually saved as part of the learning model. When implementing model predictions, parameters are also an indispensable component. Examples of model parameters include weights in artificial neural networks, support vectors in support vector machines, and coefficients in linear regression or logistic regression.

There are not only parameters but also hyperparameters in the model. Different from parameters, hyperparameters are external configurations of the model and are often used in the process of estimating model parameters. The most fundamental difference between the two is that the parameters are automatically learned by the model, while the hyperparameters are manually engineered. When handling different prediction modeling problems, it is usually necessary to adjust the model hyperparameters. In addition to being directly specified by the researcher, model hyperparameters can also be set using heuristic methods. Common model hyperparameters include the penalty coefficient in Lasso or ridge regression, the learning rate, number of iterations, batch size, activation function, and number of neurons in the training neural network, the C and σ of the support vector machine, and the K in *KNN*, the number of decision tree models in the random forest, etc.

Model training generally refers to optimizing model parameters, and this process is completed by a gradient descent algorithm. According to the training effect of the model, a series of hyperparameter search algorithms can be used to optimize the hyperparameters of the model. This section first introduces the gradient descent algorithm, and then the concept of the validation set, and then elaborates on the hyperparameter search algorithm and cross-validation.

2.4.1   Gradient Descent

The optimization idea of the gradient descent algorithm is to use the negative gradient direction of the current position as the search direction, which is the fastest descent direction of the current position, as shown in Fig. 2.26a. The formula for gradient descent is as follows:

$$w_{k+1} = w_k - \eta \nabla f_{wk}(x)$$

Where, η is called the learning rate, and w represents the parameters of the model. As w gets closer to the target value, the amount of change in w gradually decreases. When the value of the objective function barely changes or reaches the maximum number of iterations of gradient descent, then it reaches algorithm convergence. It is worth noting that when using the gradient descent algorithm to find the minimum value of a non-convex function, different initial values may lead to different results, as shown in Fig. 2.26b.

When applying gradient descent to model training, multiple variants can be used. Batch Gradient Descent (BGD) uses the gradient mean of the samples in all datasets at the current point to update the weight parameters. Stochastic Gradient Descent (SGD) randomly selects a sample in a dataset, and updates the weight parameters through the gradient of this sample. Mini-batch Gradient Descent (MBGD) combines the characteristics of BGD and SGD, and selects the gradient mean of n samples in the dataset to update the weight parameters each time. Figure 2.27 shows the different performances of the three variants of gradient descent. Among them, the bottom-up curve corresponds to BGD, the top-down curve corresponds to SGD, and the right-to-left curve corresponds to MBGD. BGD is the most stable at runtime, but because every update needs to traverse all samples, it consumes a lot of computing resources. Each update of SGD randomly selects samples, although it improves the computational efficiency, it also brings instability, which may cause the loss function to produce turbulence or even reverse displacement during the

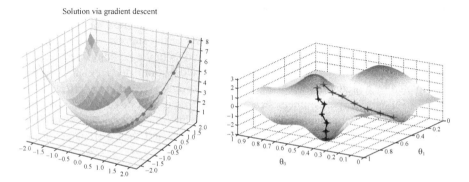

Fig. 2.26 Gradient descent algorithm

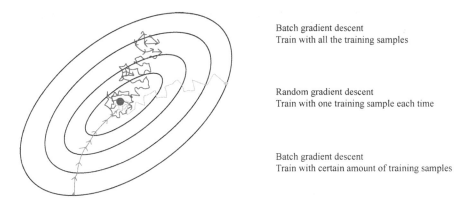

Batch gradient descent
Train with all the training samples

Random gradient descent
Train with one training sample each time

Batch gradient descent
Train with certain amount of training samples

Fig. 2.27 Comparison of the efficiency of gradient descent algorithms

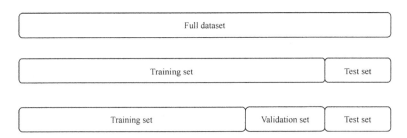

Fig. 2.28 Training set, validation set and test set

process of dropping to the lowest point. MBGD is a method after SGD and BGD are balanced, and it is also the most commonly used gradient descent algorithm in machine learning.

2.4.2 Validation Set and Hyperparameter Search

The training set is a collection of samples used in model training. During the training process, the gradient descent algorithm will try to improve the model's prediction accuracy for the samples in the training set. This causes the model to perform better on the training set than on the unknown dataset. In order to measure the generalization ability of the model, people often randomly select a part of the entire dataset as a test set before training, as shown in Fig. 2.28. The samples in the test set are not involved in training, so they are unknown to the model. It can be approximated that the performance of the model on the test set is the performance of the model under unknown samples.

The optimization goal of hyperparameters is to improve the generalization ability of the model. The most intuitive idea is to try different hyperparameter values, evaluate the performance of these models on the test set, and select the model with

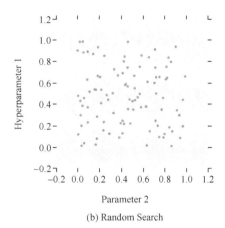

(a) Grid Search   (b) Random Search

Fig. 2.29 Grid search and random search

the strongest generalization ability. The problem is that the test set cannot participate in model training in any form, even for hyperparameter search. Therefore, some samples should be randomly selected from the training set, and the set of these samples is called the validation set. The samples of the validation set also do not participate in training, and are only used to verify the effect of hyperparameters. Generally speaking, the model needs to be optimized repeatedly on the training set and validation set to finally determine the parameters and hyperparameters and be evaluated on the test set. Methods commonly used to search model hyperparameters include grid search, random search, heuristic intelligent search, and Bayesian search.

Grid search attempts to exhaustively search for all possible hyperparameter combinations to form a grid of hyperparameter values, as shown in Fig. 2.29a. In practice, the range and step length of the grid often need to be manually designated. In the case of a relatively small number of hyperparameters, grid search is applicable, so grid search is feasible in general machine learning algorithms. However, in the case of neural networks, grid search is too expensive and time-consuming, so it is not adopted in most cases.

In the case of a large hyperparameter search space, the result of using random search will be better than grid search, as shown in Fig. 2.29b. Random search implements random sampling of parameters, where each setting is to sample from the distribution of possible parameter values, trying to find the best subset of parameters. To use random search, you need to "coarse adjustment" first and then "fine adjustment". Namely, searching in a coarse range first, and then narrowing the search range according to the position where the best result appears. It is worth noticing that some hyperparameters may be more important than others in actual operation. In this case, the most important hyperparameters will directly affect the search bias, while the secondary hyperparameters may not be well optimized.

2.4.3 Cross-validation

The above-mentioned method of dividing the verification set has two main problems: the chance of sample division is great, and the verification result is not convincing; and the number of samples that can be used for model training is further reduced. In order to solve this problem, the training set can be divided into k groups for k-fold cross-validation. K-fold cross-validation will perform k rounds of training and verification, where one set of data is used as the verification set in turn, and the remaining $k - 1$ sets of data are used as the training set. This will get k models and their classification accuracy on the validation set. The average of these k classification accuracy rates can be used as a performance indicator for the generalization ability of the model.

K-fold cross-validation can avoid contingency in the process of dividing the validation set, and the validation results are more convincing. However, using k-fold cross-validation requires training k models. If the dataset is large, the training will be time-consuming. Therefore, k-fold cross-validation is generally applicable to smaller datasets.

The k value in k-fold cross-validation is also a hyperparameter, which needs to be determined through experiments. In an extreme case, the value of k is the same as the number of samples in the training set. This approach is called leave-one-out cross-validation, because one training sample is left as a validation set during each training. The training result of leaving-one-out cross-validation is better, because almost all training samples are involved in the training. But leaving-one-out cross-validation takes a longer time, so it is only suitable for small dataset.

2.5 Common Algorithms of Machine Learning

As shown in Fig. 2.30, there are many common algorithms for machine learning, and a detailed introduction of these algorithms may take a long as a whole book. Therefore, this section only briefly introduces the principles and basic ideas of these algorithms. Readers who are interested in this topic can refer to other books for in-depth understanding.

2.5.1 Linear Regression

Linear regression is a statistical analysis method that uses regression analysis in mathematical statistics to determine the quantitative relationship between two or more variables. It belongs to supervised learning. As shown in Fig. 2.31, the model function of linear regression is a hyperplane:

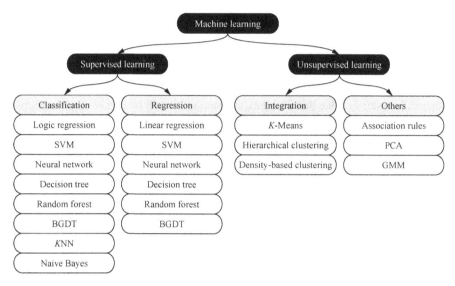

Fig. 2.30 Common algorithms of machine learning

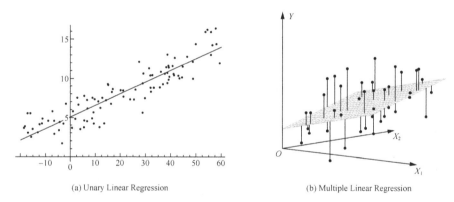

(a) Unary Linear Regression   (b) Multiple Linear Regression

Fig. 2.31 Linear regression

$$h(x) = w^{\mathrm{T}}x + b$$

Where, w is the weight parameter, b is the bias, and x is the sample.

The relationship between the predicted value of the model and the true value is as follows:

$$y = h(x) + \varepsilon$$

Where, y represents the true value and represents the error. The error is affected by many factors. According to the central limit theorem, the error obeys the normal distribution.

$$\varepsilon \sim N\left(0, \sigma^2\right)$$

Where, the probability distribution of the true value can be obtained.

$$y \sim N\left(h(x), \sigma^2\right)$$

According to the maximum likelihood estimation, the goal of model optimization is

$$\arg\max_{h} \prod_{i=1}^{m} P(Y = y_i | X = x_i) = \arg\max_{h} \prod_{i=1}^{m} \frac{1}{\sqrt{2\pi}\sigma} \exp\left(-\frac{(h(x_i) - y_i)^2}{2\sigma^2}\right)$$

Where, argmax represents the maximum point, which is h that maximizes the value of the objective function. In the objective function, $\left(\sqrt{2\pi}\sigma\right)^{-1}$ is a constant that has nothing to do with h, and multiplying or dividing the objective function by a constant will not change the position of the maximum point, so the optimization objective of the model can be transformed into

$$\arg\max_{h} \prod_{i=1}^{m} \exp\left(-\frac{(h(x_i) - y_i)^2}{2\sigma^2}\right)$$

Because the logarithmic function is monotonic, taking ln for the objective function will not affect the maximum point.

$$\arg\max_{h} \ln\left(\prod_{i=1}^{m} \exp\left(-\frac{(h(x_i) - y_i)^2}{2\sigma^2}\right)\right) = \arg\max_{h} \sum_{i=1}^{m} -\frac{(h(x_i) - y_i)^2}{2\sigma^2}$$

By taking the negative of the objective function, the original maximum point will become the minimum point. At the same time, we can also multiply the objective function by a constant to convert the optimization goal of the model into

$$\arg\min_{h} \frac{1}{2m} \sum_{i=1}^{m} (h(x_i) - y_i)^2$$

Obviously, the loss function is

$$J(w) = \frac{1}{2m} \sum_{i=1}^{m} (h(x_i) - y_i)^2$$

We hope that the predicted value is as close as possible to the true value, that is, to minimize the loss value. The method of gradient descent can be used to find the

Fig. 2.32 Comparison of
linear regression and
polynomial regression

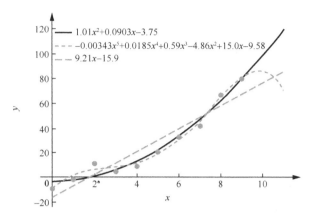

weight parameter w when the loss function is minimized, and then the model construction is completed.

Polynomial regression is a branch of linear regression. Generally, the complexity of the dataset would exceed the possibility of fitting with a straight line, that is, using the original linear regression model will obviously underfit. The solution is to use polynomial regression, as shown in Fig. 2.32, the formula is

$$h(x) = w_1 x + w_2 x^2 + \cdots + w_n x^n + b$$

Where, n represents the polynomial regression dimension.

The polynomial regression dimension is a hyperparameter. If you choose it carelessly, it may cause overfitting. Applying regularization helps reduce overfitting. The most common regularization method is to add a square sum loss on top of the objective function

$$h(x) = w_1 x + w_2 x^2 + \cdots + w_n x^n + b$$

Where $\|\bullet\|_2$ represents the L2 regular term. The linear regression model using this loss function is also called the ridge regression model. Similarly, the linear regression model with the added absolute value loss is called the Lasso regression model, and its formula is

$$J(w) = \frac{1}{2m} \sum_{i=1}^{m} (h(x_i) - y_i)^2 + \lambda \sum \|w\|_1$$

Where $\|\bullet\|_1$ represents the L1 regular term.

2.5.2 *Logistic Regression*

Logistic regression model is a classification model used to solve classification problems. The definition of the model is as follows:

$$h(x) = P(Y = 1|X) = g(w^{\mathrm{T}}x + b)$$

Where g represents the sigmoid function, w represents the weight, and b, the bias. In the formula, is a linear function of x, so logistic regression, like linear regression, belongs to the generalized linear model.

The definition of the sigmoid function is as follows:

$$g(x) = \frac{1}{1 + \exp\{-x\}}$$

The image of the sigmoid function is shown in Fig. 2.33.

By comparing the magnitude relationship between $P(Y = 1|X)$ and the threshold t, the classification result corresponding to x can be obtained. The threshold t here is a hyperparameter of the model, which can be chosen arbitrarily. It can be seen that when the threshold is large, the model tends to judge the sample as a negative example, so the precision rate will be higher; when the threshold is smaller, the model tends to judge the sample as a positive example, so the recall rate will be higher. Generally, 0.5 can be used as the threshold.

According to the idea of maximum likelihood estimation, when the sample is a positive example, we expect $P(Y = 1|X)$ to be larger; when the sample is a negative example, we expect $P(Y = 0|X)$ to be larger. In other words, we expect the following equation to be as large as possible whatever the sample is:

$$P = P(Y = 1|X)^y P(Y = 0|X)^{1-y}$$

Replace $P(Y = 1|X)$ and $P(Y = 0|X)$ with h(x) to get

Fig. 2.33 Sigmoid function

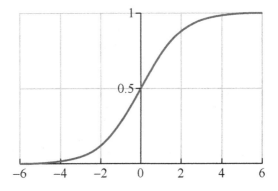

$$P = h(x)^y \cdot (1 - h(x))^{1-y}$$

Therefore, the goal of model optimization is

$$\arg\max_{h} \prod_{i=1}^{m} P_i = \arg\max_{h} \prod_{i=1}^{m} h(x)^y (1 - h(x))^{1-y}$$

The derivation process similar to linear regression can take the logarithm of the objective function without changing the position of the maximum point. Therefore, the optimization goal of the model is equivalent to

$$\arg\max_{h} \sum_{i=1}^{m} (y \ln h(x) + (1 - y) \ln (1 - h(x)))$$

Multiplying the objective function by the constant $-1/m$ will cause the original maximum point to become the minimum value point, which is

$$\arg\min_{h} \frac{-1}{m} \sum_{i=1}^{m} (y \ln h(x) + (1 - y) \ln (1 - h(x)))$$

Therefore, the loss function of logistic regression is

$$J(w) = -\frac{1}{m} \sum (y \ln h(x) + (1 - y) \ln (1 - h(x)))$$

Where, w represents the weight parameter, m is the number of samples, x is the sample, and y is the true value. The value of the weight parameter w can also be obtained through the gradient descent algorithm.

Softmax regression is a generalization of logistic regression, which is applicable for k classification problems. Essentially, the softmax function compresses (maps) a k-dimensional arbitrary real number vector into another k-dimensional real number vector to represent the probability distribution of the category of the sample. The softmax regression probability density function is as follows:

$$P(Y = c|x) = \frac{\exp\left\{w_c^T x + b\right\}}{\sum_{l=1}^{k} \exp\left\{w_c^T x + b\right\}}$$

As shown in Fig. 2.34, the softmax function assigns probability values to each category in the multi-class problem, and these probabilities add up to 1. Among these categories, the probability value of the sample category being apple is the largest, which is 0.68, so the predicted value of the sample should be the apple.

Fig. 2.34 An example of
the softmax function

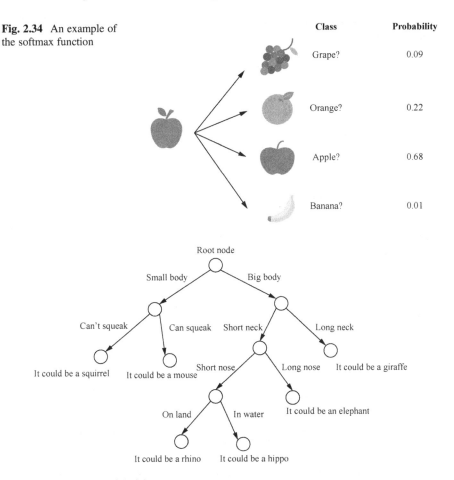

Fig. 2.35 An example of decision tree

2.5.3   Decision Tree

Decision tree is a tree structure (binary or non-binary) classifier, as shown in Fig. 2.35. Each non-leaf node represents a test on a feature attribute, each branch represents the output of this feature attribute in a certain value range, and each leaf node stores a category. The process of using a decision tree to make a decision is to start from the root node, test the corresponding feature attributes in the items to be classified, and select the output branch according to its value until the leaf node is reached, and the category stored in the leaf node is used as the decision result.

The most important thing in the decision tree model is the structure of the tree. The construction of the so-called decision tree is to select attributes to determine the topological structure between each feature attribute. The key step in constructing a decision tree is to perform the division operation according to all the feature

NO.	Tax refund	Marital Status	Taxable income/yuan	Tax fraud
1	Yes	Unmarried	125k	No
2	No	Married	100k	No
3	No	Unmarried	70k	No
4	Yes	Married	120k	No
5	No	Divorced	95k	Yes
6	No	Married	60k	No
7	Yes	Divorced	220k	No
8	No	Unmarried	85k	Yes
9	No	Married	75k	No
10	No	Unmarried	90k	Yes

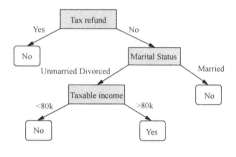

Fig. 2.36 Building a decision tree

attributes, compare the purity of the result set of all the division operations, and select the attribute with the highest purity as the data point of the split dataset. The learning algorithm of the decision tree is the algorithm that constructs the decision tree, and the commonly used algorithms include ID3, C4.5 and CART. The difference between these algorithms is mainly in the quantitative indicators of purity, such as information entropy and Gini coefficient:

$$H(X) = -\sum_{k=1}^{K} p_k \log_2 p_k$$

$$\text{Gini} = 1 - \sum_{k=1}^{K} p^2_k$$

Where, pk represents the probability that the sample belongs to class k, and K represents the total number of categories. The greater the difference in purity before and after segmentation, the more conducive that judging a certain feature is to the improvement of the accuracy of the model, indicating that it should be added to the decision tree model.

In general, the process of building a decision tree consists of the following three stages.

1. Feature selection: select a feature from the features of the training data as the split criterion for the current node (different criteria for feature selection produce different decision tree algorithms).
2. Decision tree generation: According to the selected feature evaluation criteria, child nodes are generated recursively from top to bottom until the dataset is inseparable, then the decision tree growth is stopped.
3. Pruning: By reducing the size of the tree to suppress the overfitting of the model, it can be divided into pre-pruning and post-pruning.

Figure 2.36 shows a case of classification using a decision tree model. The classification result is affected by three attributes: tax refund, marital status and taxable income. From this example, we can see that the decision tree model can not only handle the case where the attribute takes two values, but also the case where the attribute takes multiple values or even continuous values. In addition, the decision tree model is interpretable, and we can intuitively analyze the importance relationship between attributes based on the structure chart shown in Fig. 2.36b.

2.5.4 Support Vector Machine

Support vector machine (SVM) is a linear classifier with the largest interval defined in the feature space. The learning algorithm of SVM is an optimal algorithm for solving convex quadratic linear programming. In summary, the core concepts of SVM include the following two aspects.

1. Search for the optimal hyperplane in the feature space based on the structural risk minimization theory, so that the learner obtains global optimization, and the expectation in the entire sample space satisfies a certain upper bound with a certain probability.
2. For linearly inseparable data, map the linearly inseparable samples of the low-dimensional input space to the high-dimensional feature space to make them linearly separable based on a nonlinear mapping algorithm, so that the high-dimensional feature space adopts the linear algorithm for the nonlinearity of the sample Linear analysis of features becomes possible.

Straight lines are used to divide the data into different categories, but in fact we can find multiple straight lines to separate the data, as shown in Fig. 2.37. The core idea of SVM is to find a straight line that meets the above conditions, and make the points closest to the straight line as distant as possible from this straight line. This will give the model a strong generalization ability. These points closest to the straight line are called support vectors.

Linear SVM can perform properly on linear separable datasets, but we cannot use straight lines to divide non-linear datasets. At this time, a kernel function is needed to construct a nonlinear SVM. The kernel function allows the algorithm to fit the hyperplane in the transformed high-dimensional feature space, as shown in

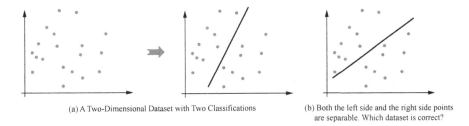

(a) A Two-Dimensional Dataset with Two Classifications   (b) Both the left side and the right side points
                                                                                                          are separable. Which dataset is correct?

Fig. 2.37 Performance of linear classifier

Fig. 2.38 Kernel function

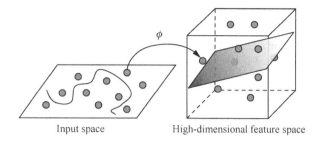

Input space   High-dimensional feature space

Fig. 2.38. Common kernel functions include linear kernel function, polynomial kernel function, Sigmoid kernel function and Gaussian kernel function. The Gaussian kernel function can map samples to infinite dimensional space, so the effect is also better, and it is one of the most commonly used kernel functions.

2.5.5   K-*Nearest Neighbor Algorithm*

The K-nearest neighbor (KNN) algorithm is a theoretically mature method and one of the simplest machine learning algorithms. The KNN algorithm is a non-parametric method, which tends to perform better in datasets with irregular decision boundaries. The idea of this method is: if most of the K nearest samples (i.e., nearest neighbors in the feature space) of a sample in the feature space belong to a certain category, then the sample also belongs to this category.

The core concept of the KNN algorithm is "What's around cinnabar goes red, and what's around ink turns black", featuring a concise logic. But like k-fold cross-validation, K in the KNN algorithm is also a hyperparameter. This means that it is difficult to select the K value appropriately. As shown in Fig. 2.39, when the K value is 3, the prediction result at the question mark will be a triangle; and when the K value is 5, the prediction result at the question mark will become a square. Figure 2.40 shows the decision boundary for different K values. It can be found that as the value of K increases, the decision boundary will become smoother. Generally speaking, a larger K value will reduce the impact of noise on classification but will make the boundaries of classes less obvious. The larger the K value is, the more likely it is to cause under-fitting, because that the decision boundaries are too blur. Correspondingly, the smaller the K value is, the easier it is to cause over-fitting, because that the decision boundaries are too sharp.

The KNN algorithm can not only be used for the classification problems, but also for the regression problems. In the classification prediction problem, it normally adopts the majority voting method. In the regression prediction problem, the average method is widely used. Although these methods are seemingly only about the K samples of the nearest neighbors, the computation volume of the KNN algorithm

Fig. 2.39 An example of
*K*NN algorithm

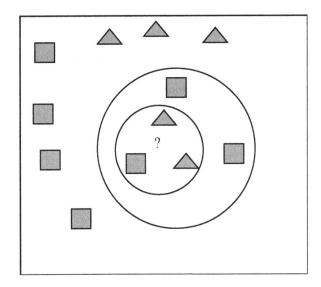

Fig. 2.40 The influence of
K value on decision
boundary

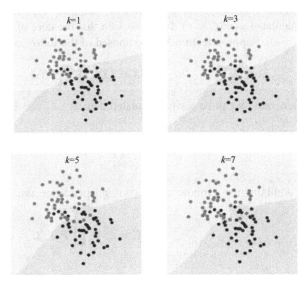

is very large in fact. This is because that the *K*NN algorithm needs to traverse all
samples to determine which *K* samples are the nearest neighbors to the sample to be
tested.

2.5.6 *Naive Bayes*

Naive Bayes is a simple multi-classification algorithm based on Bayes' theorem and assumes that the features are independent. Given the sample feature X, the probability that the sample belongs to class c is

$$P(C = c|X) = \frac{P(X|C = c)P(C = c)}{P(X)}$$

Where, $P(C = c|X)$ is called the posterior probability, $P(C = c)$ represents the prior probability of the target, and $P(X)$ represents the prior probability of the feature. Normally we do not consider $P(X)$, because $P(X)$ can be seen as a fixed value when classifying, that is

$$P(C = c|X) \propto P(X|C = c)P(C = c)$$

$P(C = c)$ has nothing to do with X and needs to be determined before training the model. Generally, the proportion of samples with category c in the dataset is calculated as $P(C = c)$. It can be seen that the core of classification is to find $P(X|C = c)$. Suppose feature X is composed of the following elements:

$$X = (X_1, X_2, \cdots, X_n)$$

Generally, it can be easily calculated that

$$\prod_{i=1}^{n} P(X_i|C = c)$$

Combining the attribute conditional independence assumption, we can prove

$$P(X|C = c) = \prod_{i=1}^{n} P(X_i|C = c)$$

The attribute conditional independence assumption states that given the sample classification as a condition, the distribution of each attribute value is independent of the distribution of other attribute values. The reason why Naive Bayes is naive is precisely because of the attribute independence assumption used in its model. Making this assumption effectively simplifies the calculation and gives the Bayesian classifier a higher accuracy and training speed on large databases.

Here is an example. We want to judge a person's gender C by his height X1 and weight X2. Suppose that the probability of a person with a height of 180 cm and a height of 150 cm is male is 80% and 20%, respectively, and the probability of a person with a weight of 80 kg and 50 kg is male is 70% and 30%, respectively.

According to the Naive Bayes model, the probability that a person with a height of 180 cm and a weight of 50 kg is male is $0.8 \times 0.3 = 0.24$, while the probability that a person with a height of 150 cm and a weight of 80 kg is male is only $0.7 \times 0.2 = 0.14$. It can be considered that the two features of height and weight independently contribute to the probability that this person is male.

The performance of the Naive Bayes model usually depends on the degree to which the feature independence hypothesis is satisfied. As mentioned in the previous example, the two features of height and weight are not completely independent. This correlation will inevitably affect the accuracy of the model, but as long as the correlation is not large, we can continue to use the Naive Bayes model. In practical applications, different features are rarely completely independent.

2.5.7   Ensemble Learning

Integrated learning is a machine learning paradigm. In this paradigm, multiple learners are trained and combined to solve the same problem, as shown in Fig. 2.41. Thanks to the multiple learners involved, the generalization ability of ensemble learning can be much stronger than using a single learner. Let's imagine you randomly ask a complicated question to several thousands of people, and then combine their answers together. In most cases, this integrated answer is even better than an answer provided by an expert. This is the collective intelligence we talk about.

The implementation methods of ensemble learning can be classified into two types—bagging and boosting. Bagging independently builds several basic learners, and then averages their predictions. Typical models of Bagging include random

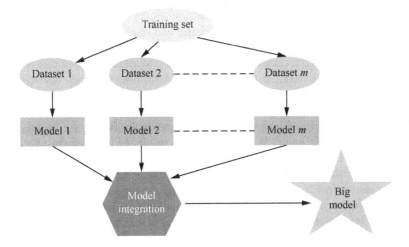

Fig. 2.41 Ensemble learning

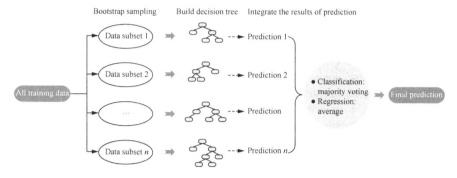

Fig. 2.42 Random forest algorithm

forests and so on. On average, the prediction result of the combined learner is usually better than any single elementary learner because its variance is reduced. Boosting constructs the basic learner in a sequential manner, and gradually reduces the deviation of the comprehensive learner's prediction. Typical models of Boosting include Adaboost, GBDT and XGboost. In general, Bagging can reduce the variance, thereby suppressing over-fitting; while Boosting focuses on reducing the deviation, thereby increasing the capacity of the model, but it may cause over-fitting.

Random forest algorithm is a combination of the bagging method and the CART decision tree. The overall process of the algorithm is shown in Fig. 2.42. Random forest algorithm can be used for classification and regression problems. The basic principle is to build multiple decision trees and merge them to make more accurate and stable predictions. During the training process of the decision tree, sampling is performed at the two levels of sample and feature at the same time. At the sample level, the bootstrap sampling (sampling with replacement) is used to determine the sample subset used for decision tree training. At the feature level, before each node of the decision tree is split, some features are randomly selected to calculate the information gain. By synthesizing the prediction results of multiple decision trees, the random forest model can reduce the variance of a single decision tree model, but the effect of correcting the deviation is not satisfactory. Therefore, the random forest model requires that every decision tree cannot be underfitted, even if this requirement may cause some decision trees to overfit. Also, note that each decision tree model in the random forest is independent, so the training and prediction processes can be performed in parallel.

Gradient boosting decision tree (GBDT) is one of the Boosting methods. The predicted value of the model is the sum of the results of all decision trees. The essence of GBDT is to continuously use new decision trees to learn the residuals of all previous decision trees, that is, the error between the predicted value and the true value. As shown in Fig. 2.43, for a given sample, the prediction result of the first decision tree is 20 years old, while the true age of the sample is 30. The difference between the predicted result and the true value is 10. If we can predict this difference with another decision tree, we can improve the prediction result of 20 and make it closer to 30. Based on this idea, we introduce the second decision tree to learn the

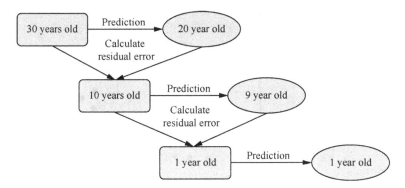

Fig. 2.43 GBDT algorithm

error of the first decision tree, and so on. Finally, the prediction results of the three learners are added together to get the true value of 30. GBDT improves accuracy by continuously correcting the deviation of the decision tree, thus allowing a certain degree of underfitting of the decision tree. However, GBDT cannot correct the variance, so it is generally not allowed to overfit the decision tree. This is also one of the biggest differences between the boosting and bagging methods. In addition, the training data of each decision tree in GBDT depends on the output of the previous decision tree, so the training process cannot be parallelized.

2.5.8   Clustering Algorithm

K-means clustering algorithm (K-Means clustering) is an algorithm that inputs the number of clusters K and a dataset containing n data objects, and outputs K clusters that meet the minimum variance standard, as shown in Fig. 2.44. It shows that the final obtained cluster meets: the similarity of objects in the same cluster is higher; and the similarity of objects in different clusters is lower.

Compared to the K-Means algorithm, the hierarchical clustering algorithm also outputs the tree-like relationship between the samples while outputting the clusters. As shown in Fig. 2.45, the hierarchical clustering algorithm tries to divide the dataset at different levels so as to form a tree-shaped clustering structure. The dataset can be divided either by a "bottom-up" agglomerative strategy, or a "top-down" divisive strategy. The hierarchy of clusters is represented as a tree diagram, where the root of the tree represents the ancestor class of all samples, and the leaves are clusters with only one sample.

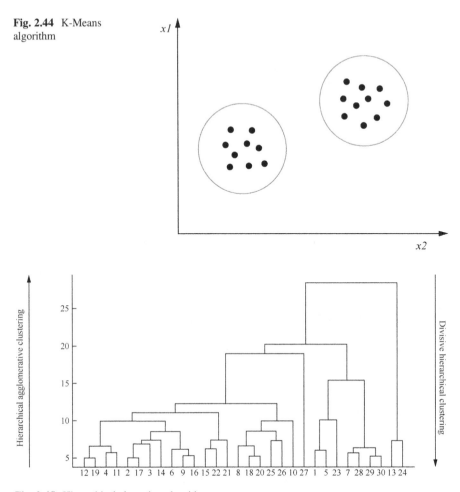

Fig. 2.44 K-Means algorithm

Fig. 2.45 Hierarchical clustering algorithm

2.6   Case Study

By the end of this chapter, we are about to review the overall process of a machine learning project with one case. Suppose there is a dataset that gives the living area (1 square foot $\approx$ 0.09 square meter) and price of 21,613 houses sold in a certain city, as shown in Fig. 2.46. Based on such data, we hope to train a model to predict the prices of other houses in the city.

It can be inferred from the data in the house price dataset that the input (house area) and output (price) in the data are continuous values, so the regression model in supervised learning can be used. The goal of the project is to build a model function h(x) to make the model infinitely approximate the function that expresses the true

Fig. 2.46 Housing price dataset

Floor area/square foot	Price/USD
1180	221,900
2570	538,000
770	180,000
1960	604,000
1680	510,000
5420	1,225,000
1715	257,500
1060	291,850
1160	468,000
1430	310,000
1370	400,000
1810	530,000
...	...

x — Floor area/square foot, y — Price/USD

Dataset

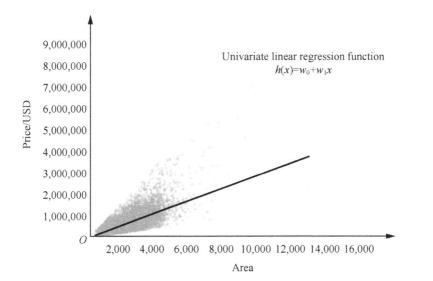

Univariate linear regression function
$h(x)=w_0+w_1x$

Fig. 2.47 Model assumptions/square foot

distribution of the dataset. Figure 2.47 shows a scatter plot of the data and a possible model function.

The goal of linear regression is to find a straight line that best fits the dataset, that is, to determine the parameters in the model. In order to find the best parameters, we need to construct a loss function and find the parameter value when the loss function reaches the minimum value. The equation of the loss function is as follows:

Fig. 2.48 Geometric
meaning of error

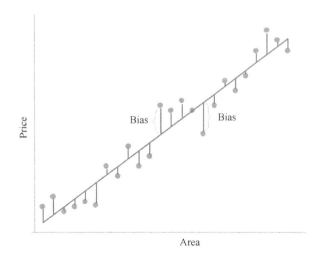

Fig. 2.49 Loss surface

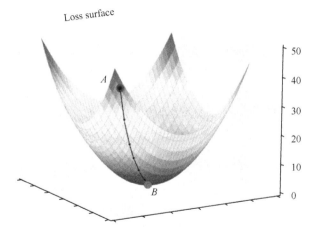

$$J(w) = \frac{1}{2m} \sum (h(x) - y)^2$$

Where m represents the number of samples, $h(x)$ is the predicted value, and y is the true value. Intuitively, the loss function represents the sum of squared errors from all samples to the model function, as shown in Fig. 2.48. When this loss function is reduced to the minimum, all samples should be evenly distributed on both sides of the fitted straight line. At this time, the fitted straight line is the model function we require.

As mentioned earlier, the gradient descent algorithm uses an iterative method to find the minimum value of a function. The gradient descent algorithm first randomly selects an initial point on the loss function, and then finds the global minimum value of the loss function according to the negative gradient direction. The parameter value at this time is the best parameter value we require, as shown in Fig. 2.49. Point

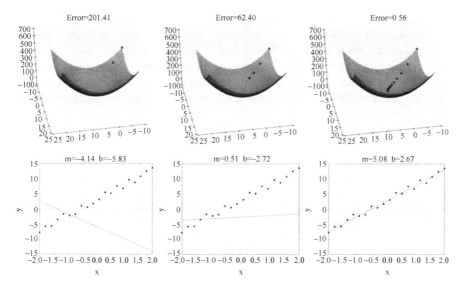

Fig. 2.50   Visualization of the gradient descent process

A represents the position where the parameter *w* is randomly initialized; point *B* represents the global minimum of the loss function, which is the final parameter value; the connected line between *A* and *B* represents the trajectory formed by the negative gradient direction. For every iteration, the value of parameter *w* will change, resulting in the constant change of the regression line.

Figure 2.50 shows an example of an iterative process using gradient descent. It can be observed that as the points on the loss surface gradually approach the lowest point, the linear regression fitting line fits the data better and better. Finally, we can get the best model function $h(x) = 280.62x - 43,581$.

After the model training is completed, we need to use the test set for testing to ensure that the model has sufficient generalization capabilities. If there is overfitting in the test, we can add a regular term to the loss function and adjust the hyperparameters. If it is under-fitting, we can use more complex regression models, such as GBDT. After that, the model needs to be retrained, and the test set is reused for testing until the generalization ability of the model meets expectations. It should be noted that since real data is used in the project, the role of data cleaning and feature selection cannot be ignored either.

2.7   Chapter Summary

This chapter mainly introduces the definition, classification and major challenges of machine learning. Meanwhile, the overall process of machine learning (data collection, data cleaning, feature extraction and selection, model training, model evaluation and testing, model deployment and integration, etc.), common machine learning algorithms (linear regression, logistic regression, decision trees, support vector machines, naive Bayes, *K*NN, ensemble learning, *K*-Means, etc.), gradient descent algorithms, hyperparameters and other important machine learning knowledge are sorted out and explained; finally, through the use of linear regression, the housing price prediction case is completed, showcasing the overall process of machine learning.

2.8 Exercises

1. Machine learning is the core technology of artificial intelligence. Please tell us the definition of machine learning.
2. The generalization error of the model can be classified into variance, bias, and irresolvable errors. What is the difference between variance and bias? What are the characteristics of the variance and bias of an overfitting model?
3. In accordance with the confusion matrix shown in Fig. 2.25, please find the F1 value.
4. In machine learning, the entire dataset is generally divided into three parts: training set, validation set, and test set. What is the difference between the verification set and the test set? Why introduce a validation set?
5. Linear regression models use linear functions to fit the data. For nonlinear data, how to deal with the linear regression model?
6. Many classification models can only handle two classification problems. Taking SVM as an example, try to find a solution for multi-classification problems.
7. Please refer to the relevant information and answer how does the Gaussian kernel function in SVM map features to infinite dimensional space?
8. Is gradient descent the only way to train the model? What are the limitations of this method?

Chapter 3
Overview of Deep Learning

As a machine learning model based on neural networks, deep learning is particularly advantageous in fields like computer vision, speech recognition and natural language processing. This chapter mainly introduces the basic knowledge related to deep learning, including the history, the components of neural networks, the types of deep learning neural networks, and the common problems researchers may encounter in the deep learning projects.

3.1 Introduction to Deep Learning

In traditional machine learning, the features are selected by hands. The more features are included, the more information can the model transmit to the outside world, and thus the model is deemed as more expressive. However, as the number of features increases, the complexity of the algorithm also enhances, and the searching space of the model will also expand accordingly. The training data will look sparse in the feature space and affect the judgment of similarity. This is the so-called explosion of dimensionality. What is more important, if the features are not conducive to the task, they may interfere with the learning efficiency. Limited by the amount of features, the traditional machine learning algorithms are more suitable for the training of small data. When the scale of data accumulates to a certain degree, it will be difficult to ameliorate the performance simply by adding more data. Therefore, traditional machine learning has low requirements for computer hardware and limited needs of calculation, thus generally does not need GPUs and graphics cards to support the parallel operations.

Figure 3.1 shows the general process of traditional machine learning, where the features are highly interpretable as they are selected manually. However, as it is not necessarily the more features the better, high-quality features will decide if the model can perform successful recognition. How many features are required should be determined by what the problem of the model is designed to solve. In order to

Huawei Technologies Co., Ltd., *Artificial Intelligence Technology*, https://doi.org/10.1007/978-981-19-2879-6_3

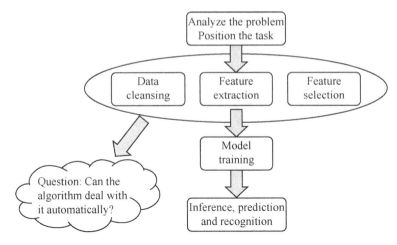

Fig. 3.1 The general process of traditional machine learning

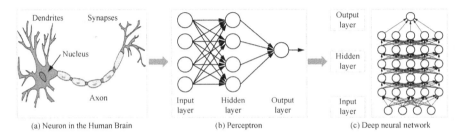

Fig. 3.2 Neurons in the human brain and artificial neural network

avoid the bias that are internet to people's selection of features, deep learning pursues algorithm that can automatically extract features. Although this reduces the interpretability of features, it improves the adaptability of the model to different problems. In addition, deep learning adopts an "end-to-end" learning mode and is combined with high-dimensional weight parameters, which makes it capable of achieving higher performance by handling large training data than the traditional ways. The massive data also put more requirements on the hardware: the large number of matrix operations are processed slowly on the CPU, thus the GPU needs to be included to provide parallel acceleration.

3.1.1 Deep Neural Network

Generally speaking, deep learning is based on deep neural networks, namely the multi-layer neural networks. This is a model built to simulate the human neural network. As shown in Fig. 3.2, a deep neural network is made of a group of stacked perceptrons, and a perceptron simulates the neurons in human brain. In Fig. 3.2b, c, each circle represents a neuron. In the following passages, we will see the similarities between this design and the neurons. The design and application research of artificial neural networks will normally need to take three things into consideration, namely neuron as a function, the connection between neurons, and learning (training) of network.

What exactly is a neural network? At present, people haven't reached a consensus on the definition of neural network. According to the American neural network scientist Robert Hecht-Nielsen, a neural network is a computing system made up of a number of very simple, highly interconnected processing elements which are formed in a certain way, which process information by their dynamic state response to external inputs. Combining the origin, characteristics and various interpretations of the neural network, it can be simply put as: artificial neural network is an information processing system that is designed to imitate the structure and functions of the human brain. The artificial neural networks feature the basic characteristics of human brain, such as parallel information processing, learning, association, classi-fication, and memorizing. Or we can just say that the artificial neural network is a network interconnected by a number of artificial neurons, an abstract and simplified version of human brain in terms of the microstructure and function and is an important approach to imitate human intelligence.

3.1.2 The Development of Deep Learning

In fact, the history of deep learning is the history of neural networks. Since the last 1950s, with the ongoing development of computer hardware, neural networks developed from an initial single layer to multiple layers, and eventually became the deep neural network well-known today. Generally speaking, the development of neural networks can be divided into three stages, as shown in Fig. 3.3.

In 1958, Frank Rosenblatt invented the Perceptron algorithm, which marked the beginning of the initial development stage of neural networks. However, as machine learning had not been an independent subject of artificial intelligence research, the development of perceptron algorithm was restrained. In 1969, Marvin Lee Minsky, a

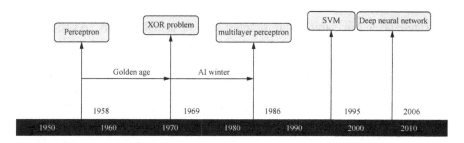

Fig. 3.3 The history of neural network

pioneer of artificial intelligence from the US, questioned that perceptrons could only handle linear classification problems but not even the simplest XOR problem. His questioning and the doubts followed were like a death penalty of the perceptron algorithm, and also heralded the coming winter of deep learning that lasted for two decades.

In 1986, Geoffrey Hinton invented the Multi-Layer Perceptron (MLP) and improved the situation. Hinton proposed to use a sigmoid function to perform nonlinear mapping on the output of perceptron, which effectively solved the problem of nonlinear classification and learning. In addition, Hinton also invented the Back Propagation (BP) algorithm to train MLP. The algorithm and its derivative algorithms are still used for deep neural network training even today. In 1989, Robert Hecht-Nielsen proved the universal approximation theorem (UAT). The theorem states that any continuous function f in a specific closed range can be approximated by a BP network with one hidden layer. In short, a neural network can fit any continuous function. In 1995, Vladimir Vapnik and Corinna Cortes proposed support vector machine (SVM), one of the most decisive breakthroughs in machine learning. The algorithm not only solid in theoretical foundation, but also has outstanding performance in experiments. In 1998, a number of neural networks were invented, including the well-recognized convolutional neural network (CNN) and recurrent neural network (RNN). However, due to the vanishing gradient and gradient explosion problems that occasionally occurred during the over-deep training of neural network, the neural network was once gain gradually forgotten by the public.

The year 2006 marks the advent of the era of deep learning. In this year, Hinton proposed the combination of unsupervised pre-training and supervised fine-tuning as a solution to the gradient vanishing problem of deep neural network training. In 2012, the AlexNet designed by Hinton's team won the world's top image recognition competition ImageNet by defeating all the other methods, which triggered a heat of deep learning. In 2016, AlphaGo, a deep learning artificial intelligence program of Google, defeated the world Go champion and nine-dan Go player Lee sedol. The victory brought the world's attention to deep learning to a new level.

3.1.3 Perceptron Algorithm

The single-layer perceptron is the simplest type of neural network. As shown in Fig. 3.4, the input vector $X = [x_0, x_1, \cdots, x_n]^T$ firstly calculates the dot product with the weight $W = [w_0, w_1, \cdots, w_n]^T$, denoted as *net*. Among them, x_0 equals to 1, and w_0 is called bias. For regression, *net* can be directly used as the perceptron output. And for classification problems, it needs to let *net* to be activated by an activation function called Sgn(*net*) so as to be taken an output. The Sign function equals 1 in the range of x > 0, and equals −1 if it is the other way around.

The perceptron shown in Fig. 3.4 is actually like a classifier which adopts a high-dimensional input vector x to classify the input samples in dichotomies in the

Fig. 3.4 Single-layer
perceptron

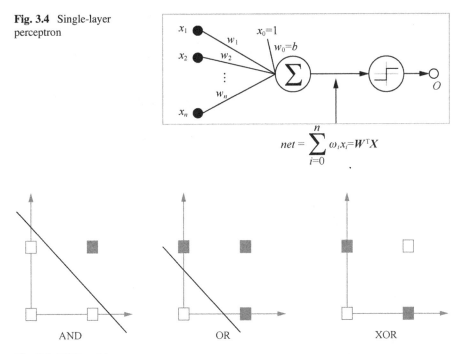

$$net = \sum_{i=0}^{n} \omega_i x_i = W^{\mathrm{T}} X$$

AND   OR   XOR

Fig. 3.5 XOR problem

high-dimensional spaces. To put it more specifically, when Sgn(net) is 1, it means that the sample is classified as positive, and if Sgn(net) is −1, then the sample is classified as negative. The boundary of the two situations is $W^{\mathrm{T}} X = 0$, a hyperplane in high-dimensional space.

In nature, the perceptron is nothing but a linear model, which means that it can only implement linear classification but cannot handle nonlinear data. As shown in Fig. 3.5, for AND and OR logical operators, the perceptron can easily find a line to classify them correctly. But it can do nothing about the exclusive OR (XOR) logical operations, which is the example that Minsky quoted to prove the limitations of perceptron in a straight-forward manner.

In order to let the perceptron to process non-linear data, people produced multilayer perceptron, also known as feedforward neural network, as shown in Fig. 3.6. Feedforward neural network is a version neural network with the simplest architecture, featuring hierarchically arranged neurons (perceptrons), and currently one of the most widely applied and fastest-growing artificial neural networks. In Fig. 3.6, the leftmost three neurons in the multilayer perceptron constitute the input layer of the entire network. The neurons in the input layer do not apply any operations. They simply represent the value of each input vector. Except for the input layer, the neuron in each layer of nodes that possesses a computing function is called a computing unit. The neurons in each layer receive the output values of the neurons in the previous layer as input and transmit them to the next. The neurons in the same layer

Fig. 3.6 Multilayer perceptron

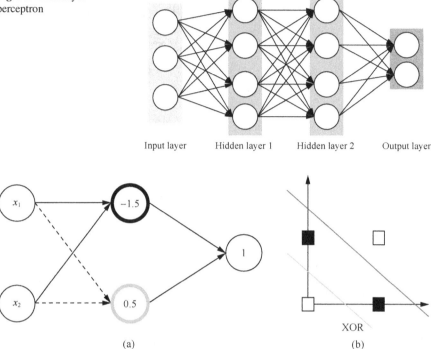

Input layer   Hidden layer 1   Hidden layer 2   Output layer

(a)   (b)

Fig. 3.7 Multilayer perceptron solving the XOR problem

are not connected, and information can only be transmitted one-way between the different layers.

The XOR problem can be solved by merely a very simple multilayer perceptron. In Fig. 3.7a, we can find the structure of multilayer perceptron. The solid line designates that the weight is 1, and the dashed line indicates the weight is -1. The number in circle is the offset. For example, for the point $(0,1)$

$$x_1 = 0, x_2 = 1$$

The output of the neuron -1.5 is

$$\text{sgn}(x_1 + x_2 - 1.5) = \text{sgn}(-0.5) = -1$$

As the two lines on the left side of the -1.5 neuron are both solid, we can conclude the coefficients of x_1 and x_2 are both 1. So the output of this neuron 0.5 is

$$\text{sgn}(-x_1 - x_2 + 0.5) = \text{sgn}(-0.5) = -1$$

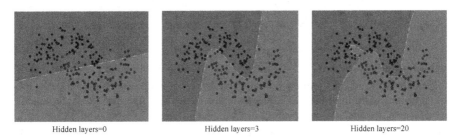

Hidden layers=0   Hidden layers=3   Hidden layers=20

Fig. 3.8 Multi-hidden layer neural network

The coefficients of x_1 and x_2 are both -1, as the two lines on the left side of the 0.5 neuron are both dashed lines. The output of the rightmost neuron is

$$\text{sgn}\,(-1-1+1) = \text{sgn}\,(-1) = -1$$

The two -1 on the left side of the equation are the outputs of the neuron -1.5 and the neuron 0.5, and $+1$ is the offset of the neuron output. Our readers can try to verify, on your own, that for the points (0, 0), (1, 0) and (1, 1), the output of the multilayer perceptron is $1, -1$, and 1 respectively, consistent with the results of the XOR operation. In fact, the two neurons -1.5 and 0.5 are respectively represented by the upper right and lower left lines shown in Fig. 3.7b, adopting the linear classifier to implement the classification of nonlinear samples.

With the increase of hidden layers, the nonlinear classification of neural networks is gradually enhanced, as shown in Fig. 3.8.

3.2 Training Rules

The core of training a machine learning model is loss function, and for deep learning, it is also the same. This section will introduce the rules of model training in deep learning by elaborating on the loss function, including the gradient descent and backpropagation algorithms.

3.2.1 Loss Function

While training a deep neural network, it firstly needs to create a function to detect the error of the target classification. And we call it a loss function (or error function). The loss function reflects the error between the target output value and the actual output value of the perceptron. The most commonly adopted loss function is the mean square error (MSE), with the formula as follows:

$$J(w) = \frac{1}{2n} \sum_{x \in X,\, d \in D} (t_d - o_d)^2$$

In this formula, w = the model parameter, X = training examples set, n = the size of X, D = the gathering of neurons in the output layer, t = the target output, and o = the actual output. Although the parameter w is not directly included in the right side of the equation, the actual output o will need to be calculated in the model, therefore it is decided by the value of the parameter w. Once the training example is settled, both t and o are constants. The actual output of the loss function changes with the value of w, so w is the independent variable of the error function. The feature of the loss function MSE is that its major body is the sum of squares of error, while the error is the difference between the target output t and the actual output o. In the formular, another more complicated component is the 1/2 coefficient. In the following passages, we will learn that this coefficient can bring a more concise form for loss function derivation, by offsetting the exponent 2 into one.

Cross-entropy error is another common loss function, and its formula is as follows:

$$J(w) = -\frac{1}{n} \sum_{x \in X,\, d \in D} (t_d \ln o_d + (1 - t_d) \ln (1 - o_d))$$

The symbols in the formula suggest the same with those in the MSE formula. Cross-entropy error depicts the distance between the two probability distributions. Generally speaking, the MSE function mainly deals with regression, while the cross-entropy error function is more used on classification. The target of model training is to search for the weight vector that minimizes the loss function. However, the neural network model is very complicated, and there is no effective mathematical method to find analytical solutions. Therefore, we need to use the gradient descent to find a numerical solution to minimize loss function.

3.2.2 Gradient Descent

The gradient of the multivariate function $f(x_1, x_2, \ldots, x_n)$ at x is

$$\nabla f(x_1, x_2, \cdots, x_n) = \left[\frac{\partial f}{\partial x_1}, \frac{\partial f}{\partial x_2}, \cdots, \frac{\partial f}{\partial x_n} \right]^{\mathrm{T}} \Big|x$$

The gradient vector indicates the direction of most rapid increase of the function. The negative gradient vector, correspondingly, indicates the direction of the steepest decrease of the function. The gradient descent algorithm is used to let the loss function search along the direction of the negative gradient, iteratively update the parameters, and minimize the loss function.

Fig. 3.9 Batch gradient
descent algorithm

Algorithm 1: Batch gradient descent algorithm
Input: Training examples set D={<x, t>}, learning rate η
Output: optimal parameter value w
1 $w \leftarrow$ Random vector with a relatively small absolute value;
2 repeat
3      $\Delta w \leftarrow \bar{0}$;
4   foreach x, t in D do
5          $\Delta w \leftarrow \Delta w + \dfrac{\partial J}{\partial w}\big|x, t$;
6   end
7      $w = w - \eta \Delta w$;
8 until the model converged or maximum number of iterations is reached;
9 return w;

Each sample in the training examples set X is $<x, t>$, where x is the input vector, t is the target output, o is the actual output, and η is the learning rate. Figure 3.9 shows the pseudo-code for the batch gradient descent (BGD) algorithm.

As a derivative of the direct application of gradient descent to deep learning, the BGD algorithm is actually not used that frequently. The major deficiency of this algorithm is that every time the weight is updated, it needs to compute all training examples, slowing down the convergence. To deal with this problem, a common variant of the gradient descent, the stochastic gradient descent (SGD) algorithm is invented, which is also known as the incremental gradient descent algorithm. Figure 3.10 shows the pseudo-code for SGD algorithm.

SGD algorithm selects one sample at a time to update the gradient. One of the advantages of this method is that the dataset can be expanded during the model training. And this mode of training model during data collection is known as online learning. Compared with the batch gradient descent algorithm, the stochastic gradient descent algorithm enhances the frequency of weight updating but goes from one extreme to the other. Normally, noise exists in training samples. Batch gradient descent can reduce the influence of noise by taking the average of the gradients of the samples. However, as stochastic gradient descent analyzes one sample at a time during weight updating, when it comes to the phase of accurately approximating the extreme value, the gradient may bounce around it, and unable to converge to the extreme value.

The gradient descent algorithm most commonly used in practical tasks is the mini-batch gradient descent (MBGD) algorithm, as shown in Fig. 3.11. To tackle deficiencies of the above two gradient descent algorithms, the mini-batch gradient descent algorithm uses a small batch of samples at a time when updating the weight, giving consideration to both the efficiency and the gradient's stability. The size of a

Fig. 3.10 Stochastic
gradient descent algorithm

Algorithm 2: Stochastic gradient descent algorithm
Input: Training examples set D={<x, t>}, learning rate η
Output: Optimal parameter value w
1 $w \leftarrow$ Random vector with a relatively small absolute value;
2 repeat
3 $\quad$ Any sample in $x, t \leftarrow D$;
4 $\quad \Delta w \leftarrow \frac{\partial J}{\partial w}\vert x, t$;
5 $\quad w = w - \eta \Delta w$;
6 until the model converged or maximum number of iterations is reached;
7 return w;

Fig. 3.11 Mini-batch
gradient descent algorithm

Algorithm 3: Mini-batch gradient descent algorithm
Input: Training examples set D={<x, t>}, learning rate
Output: Optimal parameter value w
1 $w \leftarrow$ Random vector with a relatively small absolute value;
2 repeat
3 $\quad$ foreach batch in D do // batch means a batch of samples in D
4 $\quad\quad \Delta w \leftarrow \overline{0}$;
5 $\quad\quad$ foreach x, t in batch do
6 $\quad\quad\quad \Delta w \leftarrow \Delta w + \frac{\partial J}{\partial w}\vert x, t$;
7 $\quad\quad$ end
8 $\quad\quad w = w - \eta \Delta w$;
9 $\quad$ end
10 until the model converged or maximum number of iterations is reached;
11 return w;

minibatch is generally of 128 elements, but also varies depending on the different situations.

3.2.3   Backpropagation Algorithm

Applying the gradient descent will need to calculate the gradient of the loss function. For the traditional machine learning algorithms, such as linear regression and support vector machines, computing the gradient manually is achievable. However, the model function of the neural network is much more complicated, and it is impossible to find gradients of the loss function with respect to all the parameters by just one formula. Against this backdrop, Geoffrey Hinton invented the backpropagation algorithm, which can update the weights by layers separately through the backpropagation, and effectively speed up the neural network training.

The back propagation of errors works in the opposite direction of the forward propagation, as shown in Fig. 3.12.

$$J(w) = \frac{1}{2n} \sum_{x \in X,\, d \in D} (t_d - o_d)^2$$

For each training example $<x, t>$ in the training examples set X, the output of the model is denoted as o. Assuming that the loss function takes the mean squared error:

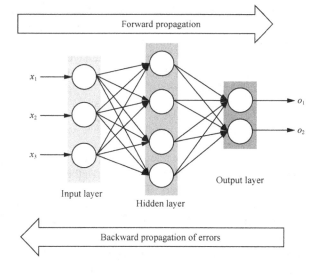

Fig. 3.12 Backward propagation of errors

Fig. 3.13 Backpropagation
algorithm

Algorithm 4: Backpropagation algorithm
Input: parameters of each layer $w_{[1\ to\ L]}$ and output of each layer $o_{[0\ to\ L]}$
Output: parameters of each layer after an iteration $w_{[1\ to\ L]}$
1 $\delta_L \leftarrow \frac{\partial J}{\partial o[L]} \odot f'(w[L]o[L-1])$;
2 for $l \leftarrow L-1$ to 1 do
3 $\quad\quad \delta_l \leftarrow w[l+1]^T \delta_{l+1} \odot f'(w[l]o[l-1])$;
4 end
5 for $l \leftarrow 1$ to L do
6 $\quad\quad w[l] \leftarrow w[l] - \eta\delta_l o[l-1]^T$;
7 end
8 return w;

$$J(w) = \frac{1}{2n} \sum_{x\in X,\ d\in D} (t_d - o_d)^2$$

Suppose that there are L layers in the model (not including the input layer), and the parameters of the first layer are noted as w_1. We can observe that the value of $J(w)$ is not the minimum during iterations because of the deviation between w and optimal parameter values, and this observation works for every layer. In other words, the value of a loss function value is caused by the error of parameters. During the forward propagation process, each layer will cause a certain error. As these errors accumulating layer by layer, they are eventually manifested in the form of a loss function in the output layer. When there is no given model function, we cannot be sure about the relationship between a loss function and the parameters. However, the relationship between the loss function and the model output $\partial J/\partial o$ is evident. This is the key to understand the backpropagation algorithm.

Suppose the output of the penultimate layer as o', and the activation function of the output layer as f, then the loss function can be extended to:

$$J(w) = \frac{1}{2m} \sum_{x\in X,\ d\in D} \left(t_d - f\left(w_L o'_d\right)\right)^2$$

In this formula, o'_d is only relevant to $w_1, w_2, \cdots, w_{L-1}$. It can be observed that the loss function can be divided into two parts, the section caused by w_L and the section caused by other parameters. The latter acts on the loss function as output in the penultimate layer through accumulating errors. Based on the $\partial J/\partial o$ obtained above, we can relatively easily calculate $\partial J/\partial o'$ and $\partial J/\partial w_L$. In this way, we will get the gradient of the loss function with respect to the output layer parameters. Obviously, the derivative of activation function $f'\left(w_L o'_d\right)$ is involved in the computing of $\partial J/\partial o'$ and $\partial J/\partial w_L$ as weight. When the derivative of the activation function is eternally less than 1 (as how Sigmoid function works), the value of $\partial J/\partial o$ will keep decreasing during the backpropagation. This phenomenon is known as the vanishing gradient problem, which will be introduced more specifically in the following passages.

As for the parameters in other layers, we can infer similarly from the relationship between $\partial J/\partial o'$ and $\partial J/\partial o''$. Briefly speaking, the backpropagation is the process of distributing errors layer by layer and is essentially an algorithm that applies the chain rule to calculate the loss function in respect to the parameters of each layer.

In general, the backpropagation algorithm works as shown by Fig. 3.13.

In the code above, $\odot$ represents multiplying by element, and f is the activation function. It is worth noticing that the output of the no. i layer is also the input of the no. $i + 1$ layer. The output of layer no. 0 is deemed as the input of the entire network. Additionally, when the activation function is Sigmoid function, it can be proved that:

$$f'(x) = f(x)(1 - f(x))$$

Therefore, $f'(o[l - 1])$ in the algorithm can also be written as $o[l](1 - o[l])$.

3.3   Activation Function

Activation function plays a very important role in learning neural network models and interpreting complex nonlinear functions. The activation function adds nonlinear characteristics to the neural network. Without the activation function, a neural network can only represent one linear function, no matter how many layers it has. However, the complexity of linear function is limited, and it is even less capable to learn mapping of complex function from data. This section introduces the activation functions commonly used in deep learning and elaborates on their advantages and disadvantages. Our readers can choose from the list based on their demands while doing projects.

As shown in Fig. 3.14a, Sigmoid function is the activation function most frequently adopted in the early stage of the study of feedforward neural network. Similar to the logistic regression model, the sigmoid function can be used in the output layer for binary classification. In general, a sigmoid function is monotonic and continuous, with the derivative easy to compute and output bounded. These features facilitate the convergence of network. However, we can see the derivative of sigmoid function approaches 0 when far away from the origin. When the network is very deep, the backpropagation will drive an increasing number of neurons into the saturation regions, reducing the scope of gradients. Generally speaking, a sigmoid network will degenerate to 0 within 5 layers, which disabling the neural network from further training. This phenomenon is the so-called vanishing gradient problem. Another disadvantage of sigmoid function is that its output is not zero-centered.

As shown in Fig. 3.14b, tanh function is a main alternative to Sigmoid. The tanh activation function rectifies the disadvantage of being not zero-centered in outputs and the gradient is more like the natural gradient in gradient descent, thus reducing the number of iterations required. However, the tanh function is still prone to saturation just like the sigmoid function.

As shown in Fig. 3.14c, Softsign function reduces the saturability of the tanh function and sigmoid function. But be it Softsign, tanh or Sigmoid, an activation function is more likely to cause vanishing gradient problem. At a position far away enough from the central point (the origin) of the function, the derivative of activation function will always approach 0, stopping the update of weights.

As shown in Fig. 3.14d, the rectified linear function or ReLU is currently the most widely applied activation function. Unlike the activation functions such as Sigmoid, ReLU is not bounded by upper limit, so neurons will never reach saturation, which effectively alleviates the vanishing gradient and can converge much faster in gradient descent. Experiments show that the neural network using the ReLU activation function can also generate good performance even without unsupervised pre-training. In addition, the functions like Sigmoid all require exponential equations, which is quite computing-intensive. However, the ReLU activation function spares much efforts in calculation and computation. Although ReLU has lots of advantages, it also has disadvantages. Since the ReLU function has no upper limit, it may diverge during training. Secondly, the ReLU function is not directable at zero, thus it will not be smooth enough in some regression problems. What is mor, the value of ReLU function will remain constantly zero when inputs are negative, which may cause the "death" of neurons.

As shown in Fig. 3.14e, Softplus function is modified on the basis of ReLU. Although the softplus function require more computation than ReLU, it has a continuous derivative, and the curve is relatively smoother.

Softmax function is an extension of the sigmoid function in multiple-dimensional cases. Its function expression is as follows:

$$\sigma(z)_j = \frac{e_j^z}{\sum_k e_k^z}$$

The softmax function is designed to map an arbitrary vector of real numbers of one K dimension to the probability distribution of another K dimension. Therefore, the softmax function is often used as the output layer for multi-classification.

$$f(x) = \frac{1}{1+e^{-x}} \qquad \tanh x = \frac{e^x - e^{-x}}{e^x + e^{-x}} \qquad f(x) = \frac{x}{|x|+1}$$

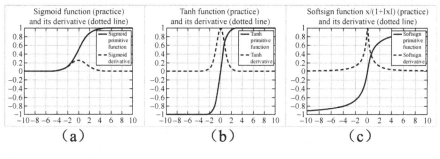

(a)   (b)   (c)

$$y = \begin{cases} x, x \geqslant 0 \\ 0, x < 0 \end{cases} \qquad f(x) = \ln(e^x + 1)$$

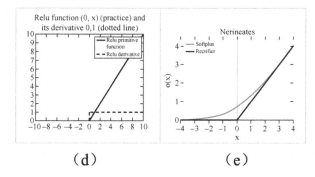

(d)   (e)

Fig. 3.14 Activation functions

3.4 Regularization

Regularization is a rather important and highly effective measure to reduce generalization error in machine learning. Compared to the traditional machine learning model, the capacity of deep learning model is larger, so it is more likely to lead to overfitting. To this end, the researchers have worked out several useful techniques to prevent overfitting, including:

1. Parameter norm penalty, which adds norm constraints such as L1 and L2.
2. Dataset expansion, such as adding noise and changing data.
3. Dropout.
4. Early stopping.

This section will introduce these techniques successively.

3.4.1   Parameter Norm Penalty

For many regularization methods, they constrain the learning capability of the model by adding a parameter norm penalty Z(w) to the objective function J:

$$\widetilde{J} = J + aZ(\boldsymbol{w})$$

Where a is a non-negative penalty term coefficient whose value weights the relative contribution of the norm penalty term Z and the standard objective function J to the general objective function. Setting a to zero results in no regularization; and the larger values of a, the greater regularization will be correspondingly. So a is a hyperparameter. It is worth noticing that in deep learning we normally only penalize the model parameter w, rather than the biases. This is because that, generally speaking, the biases require less data to accurately fit, while adding penalties to the bias parameters will often cause underfitting.

Different Z will generate different methods of regularization. This section will mainly introduce two of them: L1 regularization and L2 regularization. Among the linear regression models, L1 regularization can lead to Lasso regression, and L2 regularization can lead to the ridge regression. In fact, the so-called L1 and L2 denote norms. The L1 norm of a vector is defined as

$$\|\boldsymbol{w}\|_1 = \sum_i |\boldsymbol{w}_i|$$

That is, the sum of the absolute values of all components of the vector. It can be proved that the gradient of L1 norm is Sgn(w). Consequently, the gradient descent algorithm can be used to calculate the L1 regularization model.

The L2 norm is the commonly known Euclidean distance:

$$\|\boldsymbol{w}\|_2 = \sqrt{\sum_i \boldsymbol{w}_i^2}$$

Since the L2 norm has a quite wide application, thus it is often abbreviated as ‖w‖ with the subscript being omitted. However, since the gradient of the L2 norm is relatively complicated, the L2 regularization is generally noted as:

$$Z(\boldsymbol{w}) = \frac{1}{2}\|\boldsymbol{w}\|^2$$

We can see that the penalty term of L2 regularization is proved to be w after the derivative. Therefore, when performing gradient descent on the L2 regularization model, the equation to update weights should be rectified as

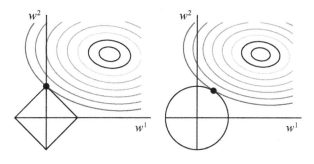

Fig. 3.15 The geometric significance of parameter penalty

$$w = (1 - \eta a)w - \eta \nabla J$$

Compared to the common gradient update equation, it is equivalent to the parameter multiplying a reduction factor, so as to restrain the growth of parameter.

Figure 3.15 displays the difference between L1 regularization and L2 regularization. The contour lines represent the standard objective function J, and the diamond or circle centered at the origin represents the regularizer. The geometric significance of the parameter norm penalty is that for any point in the feature space, what should be considered is not only the standard objective function value corresponding to that point, but also the size of the geometric shapes corresponding to the regularizer of the point. It is not difficult to infer that the larger the penalty coefficient a is, the more likely the diamond or circle will turn smaller, and the closer the parameter will incline to the origin.

As can be seen from Fig. 3.15 that the parameter that can stabilize the L1 regularization model is highly probable to appear at the corners of the diamond shape, which suggests that the parameters of the L1 regularization model are likely to be sparse matrices. The example in the figure reveals that the optimal parameter in correspondence to $w1$ is denoted as zero. Therefore, the L1 regularization can work as a method of feature selection.

To analyze it from the perspective of probability distribution, for many norm constraints, it is simply adding prior distributions to the parameters. The L2 norm is equivalent to parameters obeying the Gaussian prior distribution, and the L1 norm is parameters obeying the Laplace prior distribution.

3.4.2 Dataset Expansion

The most effective method to prevent overfitting is increasing the size of training set, as the probability of overfitting will decrease with the increase of training set. But collecting data (especially the labeling data) is a time-consuming and costly task. To this end, dataset expansion is an alternative that is less time-consuming but as efficient, although there is hardly a universal method of expansion for the different datasets in different tasks.

In target recognition, the popular methods of dataset expansion include image rotation, image scaling and so on. The premise of transforming the forms of images is that the category of the image is changed. For instance, while recognizing handwritten numbers, 6 and 9 are two categories that can be easily confused after rotation thus need special attention. In speech recognition, it often adds random noise into the input data. And in natural language recognition, a common method is replacing the synonyms.

Noise injection is a popular approach of dataset expansion. The noise can be injected to either the input layer, the hidden layer or the output layer. For Softmax classification, the noise I added to the output layer through Label Smoothing. Suppose that there are K candidate classes for a classification task, the standard output provided by the dataset is generally represented as a one-hot encoded K-dimensional vector. The element that represents the correct class is "1", and "0" for the rest. By injecting noise, the element corresponding to the correct category will turn to $1 - (k - 1)e/k$, and the rest will be e/k, where e represents a constant that is sufficiently small. Intuitively, label smoothing reduces the difference between the correct sample and the wrong sample in terms of label value, which increases the difficulty of model training. For an overfitting model, it will effectively reduce the overfitting problem, thereby facilitating the model performance.

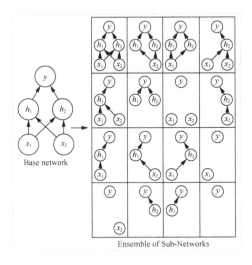
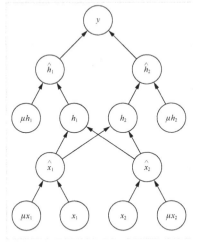

Fig. 3.16 Dropout

3.4.3 Dropout

Dropout is a regularization method that is very popular and simple in computation, widely applied since it was proposed in 2014. To put it simply, Dropout is to randomly discard a part of the output of neurons during the training phase. The parameters of these discarded neurons will not be updated. By randomly dropping the output, Dropout builds a series of subnets featuring different structures, as shown in Fig. 3.16. These subnets will converge in a certain way in the same deep neural network, which equals to taking the method of integrated learning. While running the model, we will leverage the collective intelligence of all the trained subnets, so that the neuron outputs will no longer be discarded.

Dropout is less complex in computation and easier in implementation compared to parameter norm penalty. The random process of Dropout during the training is neither a sufficient condition nor a necessary condition, thus it can absolutely make constant shields parameters, and generate competitive models.

3.4.4 Early Stopping

Early stopping of training should be allowed. As shown in Fig. 3.17, examining the validation dataset regularly, and when the loss function of the validation dataset starts to rise, the training can be stopped in advance to avoid overfitting. However, it may also bring the risk of underfitting. This is because that the samples in validation dataset are not sufficient enough, which makes it difficult to stop training at the exact moment when the generalization error of the model is the minimum. In some extreme cases, the generalization error of the model on the validation dataset may rapidly drop soon after a slight uplift while an early stopping of the training will cause the model underfitting.

Fig. 3.17 Early stopping of training

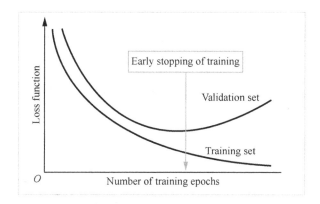

3.5   Optimizer

There are various optimized versions of the gradient descent algorithm. In the implementation of object-oriented language, it often encapsulates different gradient descent algorithms into one object, which is called an optimizer. The optimizers we commonly use include SGD, Momentum, Nesterov, Adagrad, Adadelta, RMSprop, Adam, Adamax and Nadam, etc. These optimizers mainly improve algorithm in terms of the convergence speed, the stability after converging to a local extremum, and the efficiency of adjusting hyperparameters. This section will introduce the most commonly used optimizers and their design.

3.5.1   Momentum

The Momentum optimizer is a fundamental improvement of the gradient descent algorithm, which supplements momentum term to the weight update equation, as shown in Fig. 3.18. Suppose the value of weight change in the n-th iteration is $d(n)$, then the weight update equation shall turn into:

$$d(n) = -\eta \nabla_w J + ad(n-1)$$

Where a is a constant number between 0 and 1, known as momentum, and $ad(n-1)$ is called the momentum term. Let's imagine a small ball rolling down along the error surface from a random point. The ordinary gradient descent algorithm will drive the ball moving along the force curve, but it is actually against the laws of physics. The real situation is that the momentum of the small ball will accumulate as it is rolling down, and its speed will increase faster along the downhill direction.

In places where the gradient is relatively stable, the small ball will roll much faster so as to quickly pass the flat region. In consequence, the model convergence will

Fig. 3.18 The role of momentum term

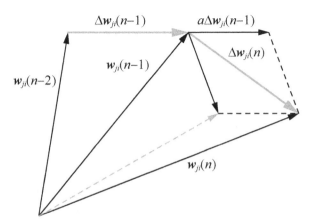

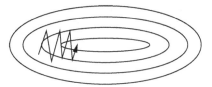 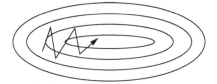

Fig. 3.19 The momentum term accelerates model convergence

accelerate. On the other hand, as shown in Fig. 3.19, the momentum term rectifies the direction of the gradient and reduces the occurrence of abrupt changes. In addition, a small ball carried with inertia is more likely to overcome the narrow local extrema, thus the model will be less likely to get stuck in the local extreme points.

The disadvantage of the momentum optimizer is that the momentum may carry the small ball so far away that it may miss the optimal solution, thus additional iterations will be needed for convergence. Secondly, the learning rate and momentum a of the momentum optimizer are set manually. It means that a lot of experiments should be carried out to find the values that are appropriate to use.

3.5.2 Adagrad Optimizer

A shared characteristic of stochastic gradient descent, mini-batch gradient descent and momentum optimizer is that each parameter is updated with one same learning rate. However, for Adagrad optimizer, different parameters should adopt different learning rates. The gradient update equation of the Adagrad optimizer is generally written as

$$\Delta w = -\frac{\eta}{e + \sqrt{\sum_{i=1}^{n} g^2(i)}} g(n)$$

In the equation, $g(n)$ represents the gradient dJ/dw of the cost function in the n-th iteration, and e is a small constant. With the increase of n, the denominator of the equation will increase, and the degree of the weight update will gradually decrease, which is equivalent to learning rate having been reduced dynamically. In the initial stage of model training, the initial value is not even close to the optimal solution of the loss function, so it requires a much higher learning rate. But as the frequency of updates increases, the weight parameters will approximate closer to the optimal solution, and the learning rate will keep decreasing accordingly. The advantage of the Adagrad optimizer is that it can automatically update the learning rate, but this feature also brings some disadvantages. Since the update of the learning rate is decided by the gradient of the past iterations, it is likely that the learning rate could already have been reduced to zero when the weight parameters are still far from the optimal solution. If so, the optimization process will become meaningless.

3.5.3 RMSprop Optimizer

The Root Mean Square Propagation (RMSprop) optimizer is an ameliorated version of the Adagrad optimizer by introducing an attenuation coefficient, to the algorithm, which attenuates the historical records gradient by a certain percentage for every iteration. The gradient update equations of the RMSprop optimizer is as follows:

$$r(n) = br(n-1) + (1-b)g^2(n)$$

$$\Delta w = -\frac{\eta}{e + \sqrt{r(n)}}g(n)$$

In the equations, b refers to the attenuation factor and e is a small constant. Because of the effect of attenuation factor, r does not have to increase monotonically along with the increase of n. This can effectively prevent the Adagrad optimizer from stopping learning too early, and is very suitable for handling non-stationary targets, especially conducive to the recurrent neural networks.

3.5.4 Adam Optimizer

The Adaptive Moment Estimation (Adam) optimizer is currently the most widely used optimizer that evolved from Adagrad and Adadelta. Adam aims at identifying an adaptive learning rate for each parameter, which is useful in a complex network structure, as the sensitivity different parts of the network to weight adjustment is different, and the learning rate for the sensitive parts should generally be lower. It is difficult and complicated for people to identify the sensitive parts and calculate the specific learning rate manually. The gradient update equation of the Adam optimizer is similar to that of the RMSprop optimizer, as shown below:

$$\Delta w = -\frac{\eta}{e + \sqrt{v(n)}}m(n)$$

Where m and v represent the estimates of the first moment (mean) and second moment (uncentered variance) of the past gradients respectively. Resembling the attenuation-based formula proposed by the RMSprop optimizer, m and v can be defined as:

$$m(n) = am(n-1) + (1-a)g(n)$$

$$v(n) = bv(n-1) + (1-b)g^2(n)$$

In form, m and v are the moving averages of gradient and squares of the gradient respectively. But defining as such will make the algorithm quit unstable in the first several iterations. Let's assume that both $m(0)$ and $v(0)$ are valued zero, so when a and b approximate one, m and v will be very close to zero in the initial iteration. In order to counteract this problem, the final equations put in use will be as:

$$\widetilde{m}(n) = \frac{m(n)}{1-a^n}$$

$$\widetilde{v}(n) = \frac{v(n)}{1-b^n}$$

Although the learning rate, a, and b in the Adam optimizer need to be set up manually, the difficulty has been largely reduced in terms of implementation. The experiments have proved that the default value of a and b is 0.9 and 0.999 respectively, and that of the learning rate is 0.0001. In the practice, the Adam optimizer will facilitate rapid convergence. When the algorithm converges to the point of saturation, the learning rate can be lowered accordingly, and other parameters can stay unadjusted. With several times of the reduction of learning rate, the model will converge to a proper and satisfactory extreme value.

3.6 Types of Neural Network

Since the earliest BP neural network, people have designed a wide range of neural networks to handle different problems. In the domain of computer vision, convolutional neural network is the most widely used deep model currently. In the domain of natural language processing, recurrent neural network once outshined the other models. This section will also introduce a generative model based on game theory—generative adversarial network.

3.6.1 Convolutional Neural Network

Convolutional neural networks (CNNs) are a kind of feedforward neural network. Unlike the fully connected neural networks (FCNNs), the artificial neurons of the convolutional neural networks can respond to a part of the units within the range of coverage, and have good performance in image processing. Generally speaking, a convolutional neural network consists of convolutional layers, pooling layers, and fully connected layers.

In the 1960s, in their study of the neurons of cat's cortex that are sensitive to locality and used to select direction, David Hubel and Torsten Wiesel discovered that the unique network structure of cat's neurons can effectively reduce the complexity of the feedback neural network. Inspired by their discovery, convolutional neural networks were proposed. Today, convolutional neural networks have become one of the heatedly discussed subjects in many scientific fields, particularly in pattern recognition. As the structure of CNNs can avoid the complicated image preprocessing and can directly input the original image, it has been extensively applied in many fields.

The name "convolutional neural network" derives from a mathematical operation called convolution. Convolution is the operation of performing inner product to image (or feature map) and filter matrix (also called filter and convolution kernel). The image is the input of the neural network, and the feature map is the output of convolutional layer or pooling layer of the neural network. Their difference is that the value in feature map is the output of the neuron thus it does not have limitation theoretically, but the value of the image is in line with the brightness of the three channels RGB, valued from 0 to 255. Each convolutional layer in the neural network corresponds to one or more filter matrices, and it works differently from a fully connected neural network. Every neuron in the convolutional layer can only take the output of neurons in a certain local window of the previous layer as input instead of being able to receive the output of all of neurons of the previous layer simultaneously. This feature of convolution is known as local perception.

Generally speaking, people's perceptions on the outside world evolves from the local features to the global features. For the spatial relationship of an image, it is also the same that the local pixels are more closely related, while the distant pixels are less related. Therefore, actually, there is no need for each neuron to perceive the global image. It only needs to perform local perception, and synthesizes the data perceived locally at an upper level to get the global information. The idea of partially connected network is inspired by the structure of the biological visual system where the neurons in the visual cortex also only respond to the stimuli in a certain region and receive information locally.

Another feature of convolution is the parameter-sharing. For the input image, it can be scanned by one or more convolution kernels. The parameters in the convolution kernel equal to the model's weights. In a convolutional layer, all neurons share the same convolution kernel and therefore also share the same weights. Weight-sharing means that every time when a convolution kernel is traversing the image, its parameters will not change. For example, a convolutional layer has three feature convolution kernels, and every convolution kernel will scan the entire image. During the scanning, the parameter values of the convolution kernel are fixed, and namely the pixels of the entire image share the same weights. It means that the features learned in a certain part of the image can also be applied to other parts or other images. This feature is known as position invariance.

1. Convolutional Layer

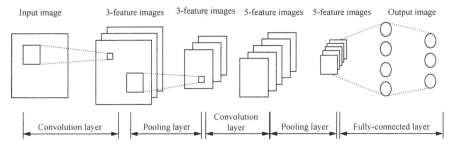

Fig. 3.20   The architecture of the convolutional neural network

Fig. 3.21   An example of convolution operation

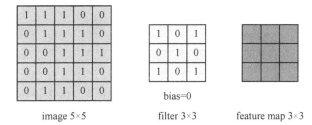

image 5×5   filter 3×3   feature map 3×3

Figure 3.20 displays a typical architecture of convolutional neural network. The leftmost image is the input. The input image first passes through a convolutional layer consisting of three convolution kernels to acquire three feature maps. The parameters of these three convolution kernels are independent from each other, and can be calculated and optimized by the back-propagation algorithm. While performing the convolution operations, a window of the input image is projected to a neuron on the feature map. The convolution operation is performed to detect different features of the input. The first convolutional layer may only present some low-level features, such as the edges, lines and corners of the image. And the following layers can learn more complex features from the low-level features through iterations.

Looking at the convolution operation shown in Fig. 3.21. You can divide up to 3 × 3 different regions in a 5 × 5 square matrix, and the shape of these regions is identical to the convolution kernel. Therefore, the dimension of the feature map is 3 × 3.

As shown in Fig. 3.22, each element in the feature map is calculated by multiplying one section of the original image and the convolution kernel. In the matrix on the left of Fig. 3.22, the 3 × 3 region in the upper left corner is the part relevant to the upper left element in the feature map. Multiplying each element of this part and the corresponding element of the convolution kernel, and summing the result, we will get the first element 4 of the feature map. The example shown here does not include the bias term, namely, the bias equals to zero. In the more common convolution operations, it is often required to sum the result and the bias

Fig. 3.22 An example of convolution operation

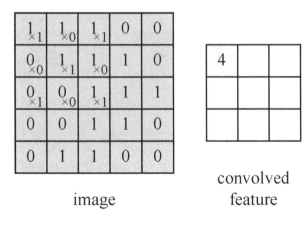

image

convolved feature

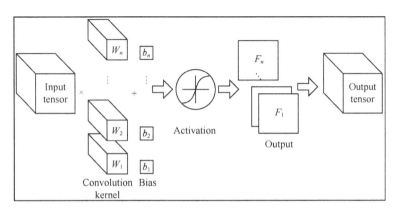

Fig. 3.23 The structure of convolutional layer

term after the multiplications (dot product), so as to output as a feature map. The role of bias term here is similar to that in linear regression.

A convolutional layer is majorly structured by multi-channel convolution. As shown in Fig. 3.23, a convolutional layer can house multiple convolution kernels and biases. A combination of convolution kernel and bias is able to project the input tensor onto a feature map. The role of multi-channel convolution is to collage all the feature maps generated by the convolution kernels and the bias terms to form a three-dimensional matrix as the output. Generally speaking, the input and output tensor and the convolution kernel are three-dimensional matrices, featuring three dimensions referring to width, height and depth respectively. In order to extend the above-mentioned convolution to the three-dimensional sphere, it need to make the rule that the depth of each convolution kernel should be the same with the input tensor. This ensures that the depth of the feature map corresponding to each single convolution kernel is one. The convolution

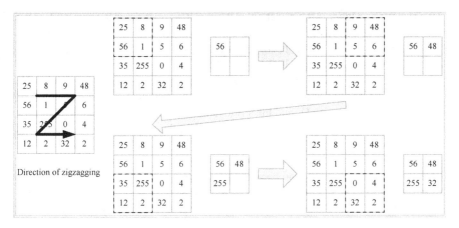

Fig. 3.24 An example of pooling operation

operation does not have specific requirement on the width and height of the convolution kernel, but they are generally valued the same in the operation for the sake of convenience. In addition, in order to stack the feature maps generated by different convolution kernels together, the feature maps need to have the same width and height. In other words, all the convolution kernels in a same convolution layer need to be of the same size.

As the output of the convolutional layer, the feature maps need to be activated. Sometimes, the activation function can be taken as a consisting part of the convolutional layer. But as the activation function and the convolution operation are not so relevant, we can also take activation function as an independent layer. The most commonly used activation layer is the rectified linear layer, which uses the ReLU activation function.

2. Pooling Layer

Pooling layer functions as a tool of dimensionality reduction by grouping the units nearby and reducing the size of the feature maps. The most commonly used pooling layers include max pooling layer and average pooling layer. As shown in Fig. 3.24, the max pooling layer divides the feature map into several rectangular patches and takes the maximum value of each patch as the characteristic value of the entire region. While average pooling is similar to max pooling, except that it replaces the maximum characteristic value with an average value to represent the region. In the feature map, the size of each patch is called a pooling window size.

In the real convolutional neural networks, the convolutional layers and the pooling layers are basically interconnected. Alike the convolution, pooling can also scale up features, thus extracting the features from the previous layer. But unlike the convolution operation, the pooling layer does not have any parameters and has nothing to do with the arrangement of elements in the small patches. It is only relevant to the statistical characteristics of these elements.

The pooling layer is mainly about reducing the size of the input data of the next layer so as to effectively streamline the parameters and lower the intensity of computation, which prevents the occurrence of over-fitting at the same time. Another function of the pooling layer is that it can map the input of any random size to the output of a specified fixed length by giving a reasonable size and stride length to the pooling window. Suppose that the input size is $a \times a$, the size of the pooling window is $a/4$, and the stride length is $a/4$. If a is a multiple of 4, then the pooling window size is equal to the stride length, and it is easy to find that the output size of the pooling layer is 4×4. When a is an integer that is large enough but not divisible by 4, then the pooling window size is always larger than the stride length by one unit, and it can be proved that the output size of the pooling layer remains to be 4×4. The distinguishing feature of pooling layer enables the convolutional neural network to deal with the input images of any sizes.

3. Fully Connected Layer

The fully connected layer is normally used for the output of the convolutional neural network. In pattern recognition, classification or regression are two commonly performed tasks. To be more specific, classification means determining the categories that he objects belong to, or rating the objects in the image. To tackle these problems, taking the feature map as the output is apparently inappropriate. The feature map should be projected to a vector meeting certain requirements, and this will entail embedding the feature maps, which means arranging the neurons in the feature map into a vector in a fixed order.

3.6.2 Recurrent Neural Network

A Recurrent Neural Network (RNN) is a type of neural network that captures dynamic information in serialized data by periodically connecting nodes in the hidden layer, so as to classify serialized data. Unlike the rest feedforward neural networks, recurrent neural networks can maintain the state of context of the serialized data. The recurrent neural network is no longer restricted by the spatial boundary like the traditional neural networks but can be expanded in the time dimension. To put it more simply, the nodes of the memory cells at this moment and the next can be connected. The recurrent neural network is widely used in scenarios featuring sequential data, such as video, audio and sentences.

What is shown in Fig. 3.25 is the typical structure of a recurrent neural network, where $x(t)$ represents the value of the input sequence at a time-step t, and s-(t) represents the state of the memory cell at a time-step t, $o(t)$ represents the output of the hidden layer at a time-step t, and U, V and W represents the model weights. It can be inferred that the update of hidden layer does not only depend on the current input $x(t)$, but also depends on the state of memory cell at the previous time-step $s(t - 1)$. The equation should be $s(t) = f(Ux(t) + Ws(t - 1))$, where f represents the activation function. The output layer of the recurrent neural network is the same with multilayer perceptron, and this chapter will not go into details about it.

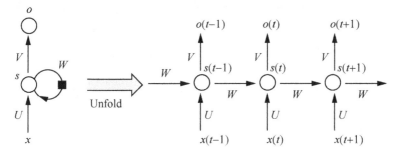

Fig. 3.25 A structure of recurrent neural network

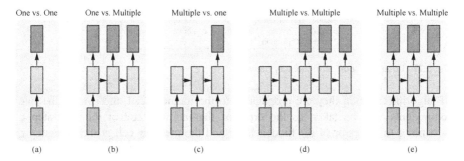

Fig. 3.26 Different structures of recurrent neural network

As shown in Fig. 3.26, there are a variety of structures for different recurrent neural networks. Figure 3.26a depicts a common BP neural network unrelated to time series. Figure 3.26b is a generative model that can generate sequences in line with the specific requirements according to every single input. Figure 3.26c shows a model that can be used for overall classification or regression of the sequence, and it is the most classic structure of recurrent neural network. Figure 3.26d, e shows a model that can be used for the translation of sequences. The structure in Fig. 3.26d is also known as an encoder-decoder architecture.

The calculation of recurrent neural network is operated through the Backpropagation Trough Time (BPTT) algorithm, which is an extension of the traditional backpropagation algorithm in the domain of time. The traditional BP algorithm only considers the propagation of uncertainty (or propagation of error) between different hidden layers, while the BPTT algorithm needs to take into consideration the propagation of uncertainty in the same hidden layer at different time-steps. Specifically, the memory cell error at the time-step t consists of two parts: the component propagated by the hidden layer at the time-step t, and the component propagated by the memory unit at the time step $t + 1$. When these two components are propagated separately, their computational method is the same as the traditional

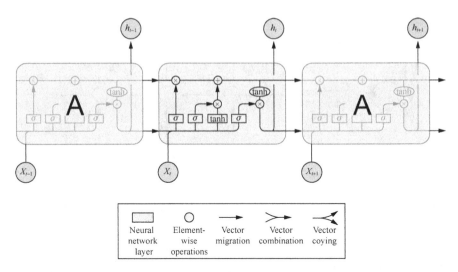

Fig. 3.27 Long and short-term memory network

BP algorithm. When they are propagated to the memory cell, the sum of the two components will be taken as the error of the memory cell at the time-step t. According to the error of the hidden layer and the memory cell at the time-step t, it is easy to infer the gradient of the parameters U, V, and W at the time-step t. After traversing all the time-steps in backpropagation, each parameter including U, V and W will get T gradients, where T is the total length of time. The T gradients summed up is the gradient of the parameters U, V, and W. When we get the gradient of each parameter, the equations of the gradient descent algorithm can be easily solved.

There are still many problems to overcome with recurrent neural networks. Since the memory cell will receive the output from the previous time each time, the problems of gradient vanishing and gradient explosion that characterize deep fully connected neural network are also bothering the recurrent neural network. On the other hand, the state of the memory cell at a certain time-step t cannot be kept for a long time, and the state of the memory cell needs to be mapped by the activation function for every time-step it traverses. For a relatively long sequence, when it loops to the end, the input at the beginning of the sequence may have already vanished alongside the activation function mapping. In other words, the long-term memory of the recurrent neural network will eventually decay.

But for many tasks, we hope that the model can keep the information for a longer time, just like the foreshadowing in a detective fiction can only be revealed until the end of the story. But if memory cell has a limited capacity, the recurrent neural network will certainly unable to memorize all the information in the entire sequence. Therefore, we want the memory cell to selectively remember key information, which can be achieved through Long Short-Term Memory (LSTM). As shown in Fig. 3.27 (*Understanding LSTMs Networks*), the essence of the long and short-term memory network is LSTM block, which an alternative to the hidden layer of the recurrent

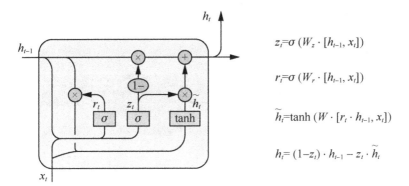

$$z_t = \sigma \left(W_z \cdot [h_{t-1}, x_t] \right)$$

$$r_t = \sigma \left(W_r \cdot [h_{t-1}, x_t] \right)$$

$$\tilde{h}_t = \tanh \left(W \cdot [r_t \cdot h_{t-1}, x_t] \right)$$

$$h_t = (1 - z_t) \cdot h_{t-1} - z_t \cdot \tilde{h}_t$$

Fig. 3.28 Gated recurrent unit (GRU)

neural network. A common LSTM block contains three units for computation: input gate, forget gate and output gate, which allow a LSTM network to selectively remember, forget and output, and therefore realizes the selective memory. We can see that the adjacent LSTM blocks are connected by two lines, representing the cell state and hidden state of the LSTM network.

As shown in Fig. 3.28, the Gated Recurrent Unit (GRU) is a variant of the LSTM network, which combines the forget gate and the input gate into an update gate, and combines the cell state and hidden state into a single hidden state. As a very popular model, the structure of GRU model is more concise than that of a standard LSTM model.

3.6.3 Generative Adversarial Network

Generative Adversarial Networks (GAN) are a type of framework used in scenarios such as image generation, semantic segmentation, text generation, data augmentation, chat bots, information retrieval and ranking. Before the introduction of generative adversarial networks, deep generative models always required Markov chains or approximate maximum likelihood estimation, which may cause many unpredictable problems of uncertainty. Through an adversarial process, GAN trains the generator G and the discriminator D simultaneously and let the two play a zero-sum game. Namely, the discriminator D is designed to determine whether a sample is real, or it is generated by the generator G. While the generator G aims at generating a sample that can fool the discriminator D. The method adopted to train GAN is the mature BP algorithm.

As shown in Fig. 3.29, the input of the generator is taken as noise z. Noise z follows an artificially selected prior probability distribution, such as uniform distribution and Gaussian distribution. The input space can be mapped to the sample space relying on a certain network architecture. The input of the discriminator is the real sample x or the fake sample $G(z)$, and the output is the authenticity of the

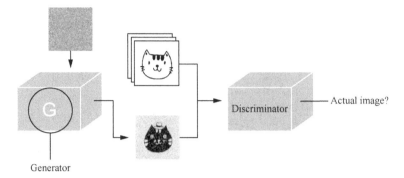

Generator

Fig. 3.29   A structure of generative adversarial network

sample. The discriminator can be designed on the basis of any classification model, such as the convolutional neural networks and fully connected neural networks that are commonly used as discriminators. For instance, we may want to generate a cat-themed image, and the image should be as real as possible. The target of the discriminator is to discriminate whether the image is real or not.

The objective function of the generative adversarial network is:

$$G = \min_G \max_D E_{x \sim P_{datat}}[\log D(x)] + E_{z \sim P_z}[\log (1 - D(G(z)))]$$

The objective function is constituted by two parts. The first part is only related to the discriminator D. When a real sample is the input, the closer the output of the discriminator D is to 1, the greater the value of the first part will be. The second part is related to both the generator G and the discriminator D. If random noise is the input, the generator G can generate a sample. The discriminator D receives this sample as an input, and the closer the output is to 0, the greater the value of the second part will be. Since the discriminator D aims at maximizing the objective function, it needs to output a value 1 in the first part and a value 0 in the second part, so as to classify the sample correctly. Although the generator aims at minimizing the objective function, the first part of the objective function is unrelated to the generator, so the generator can only minimize the second part as much as possible. To achieve that, the generator needs to output a sample that secures that the output value of the discriminator is 1, which equates to making the discriminator unable to distinguish between true and false as much as possible.

Ever since the introduction of GAN in 2014, it has derived more than 200 variants, and has been widely applied to tackle numerous generation problems. But the original GAN also suffers from many problems, such as the instability of the training procedure. The fully connected neural networks, convolutional neural networks, and recurrent neural networks introduced above are all made to minimize the cost function by optimizing parameters through the training procedure. The training of GAN is slightly different, mainly because of the adversarial relationship between the generator G and the discriminator D that makes it hard to strike a balance. The general training procedure is to perform an alternate training of D and G, until $D(G(z))$ stabilizes at a value around 0.5. At this point, the D and G reach a status of the Nash Equilibrium, signifying that the training is over. However, in some cases, it is hard for a model to attain the Nash equilibrium, and it may lead to problems such as mode collapsing. Therefore, how to improve the stability of the GAN model has always been a key topic in the field of study. Generally speaking, GAN does have some issues, but they do no harm to the crucial role of GAN among the generative models.

3.7   Common Problems

The models of deep learning are very complicated, so there could be various problems during the training procedure. This section summarizes the problems that are the most common seen during the training, so that our readers could spend less time to locate and tackle them when they encounter these situations.

3.7.1   Imbalanced Data

Imbalanced data refers to a problem in the dataset of classification tasks where the number of samples in each category is not necessarily equal. The problem of imbalanced data imbalance mainly occurs when the samples of one or more categories for prediction are particularly sparse. For instance, if there are 4251 training images for classification, there could be over 2000 classes having one image, and a few containing two to five images. Under the circumstances, the model cannot examine each class evenly, which may affect the model performance. The common methods fix the imbalanced data include random under-sampling, random over-sampling, and synthetic sampling.

Random under-sampling refers to randomly deleting samples from the classes with sufficient number of observations. This method can save the time of operation and meet the storage requirement when the training set is too big. However, while deleting the samples, some important information contained within could also be discarded randomly. And the samples left might be too biased to accurately represent the majority of the class. Therefore, using random under-sampling may not get accurate results on the actual test set as expected.

Random over-sampling refers to duplicating existing samples in unbalanced classes to increase the number of observations. Unlike random under-sampling, this method will not cause the loss of data, so it often outperforms the random under-sampling on the actual test set. However, as the newly duplicated samples are actually the same as the original one, it is more likely to result in overfitting.

Synthetic Minority Over-sampling Technique (SMOTE) is to use a synthetic method to realize the observation of unbalanced classes, quite similar to the method of nearest neighbor classification. SMOTE first selects a data subset from the minority class, and then generates new samples based on the selected subset, and these synthesized examples will be supplemented to the original dataset. The advantage of this method is that it will do no harm to the valuable data and can effectively ease overfitting by generating synthetic samples through random sampling. But generally speaking, its performance in dealing with the high-dimensional data is not so promising. In addition, when generating synthetic samples, SMOTE will not take into consideration the examples of other classes, which may intensify the class overlap and bring additional noise.

3.7.2 Vanishing Gradient and Exploding Gradient

When there are sufficient network layers, the gradient of model parameters during the process of backpropagation can get very small or very large, and the two situations are called vanishing gradient and exploding gradient respectively. Essentially speaking, the two problems both derive from the backpropagation equations. Let's assume that the model has three layers, and each layer contains only one neuron, then the backpropagation equation can be written as:

$$\delta_1 = \delta_3 f'_2(o_1) w_3 f'_1(o_0) w_2$$

Where f is the activation function. In this example, we use the Sigmoid function. As the number of network layers rises, the frequency that $f(o)w$ appears in the equation will also increase. According to inequality of arithmetic and geometric means, we can get that the maximum value of $f'(x) = f(x)(1 - f(x))$ is 1/4. Therefore, it can be concluded that when w is smaller than 4, $f(o)w$ must be smaller than 1. By multiplying the multiple terms valued less than 1 together, the value of δ_1 will inevitably approximate 0, which causes the vanishing gradient. The exploding gradient is caused by similar reason, mainly occurs when the value of w is very large. It means that we multiply the multiple terms valued larger than 1 together, leading to a very large value of δ_1.

The vanishing gradient and exploding gradient problems arise mainly because that the network is too deep, and the weight update of the network is unstable, which are in essence caused by the multiplicative effect during the gradient backpropagation. The popular approaches to address the vanishing and exploding gradients include pre-training, adopting the ReLU activation function, the LSTM neural network and the residual module and so on. (ResNet, the winner of the 2015 ImageNet Large Scale Visual Recognition Challenge (ILSVRC), elevates the model depth up to 152 layers by introducing a residual module into the model. In comparison, the model depth of the depth of the 2014 ILSVRC winner GoogLeNet is only 27 layers.) The major solution to deal with the exploding gradient is gradient clipping, which is designed to set a gradient threshold, and scale down the gradients that exceed the threshold to a certain limit to prevent the gradients from exploding.

3.7.3 Overfitting

Overfitting refers to the problem that the model performs well on the training set but performs poorly on the test set. There could be many reasons causing overfitting, such as high feature dimensions, complex model assumptions, excessive parameters, limited training data, and excessive noise. But essentially, the overfitting problem is mainly cause by the model overfitting the training set without considering the generalization ability of the network. Consequently, the model can predict the training set well but always fail in new data prediction.

To tackle the overfitting caused by insufficient training data, we can try to obtain more data. One option is to obtain more data from the data source, but it will take much time and strength. Another common option is data augmentation.

If the model is too complex to cause overfitting, there are many ways to suppress it. The simplest method is to adjust the hyperparameters of the model, reduce the number of layers and the number of neurons in the network, etc., thereby limiting the fitting ability of the network. You can also consider adding regularization technology to the model. The related content has been introduced before, so I won't repeat it here.

3.8 Chapter Summary

This chapter mainly elaborates on the definition and evolvement of neural networks, training rules of perceptrons, and the knowledge related to the poplar neural networks such as CNN, RNN and GAN. In addition, this chapter also introduces the problems of neural networks commonly encountered in artificial intelligence engineering and the solutions.

3.9 Exercises

1. Deep learning is a new division deriving from machine learning. In your point of view, how is deep learning different form the traditional machine learning?
2. In 1986, the introduction of multilayer perceptron ended the first winter of AI in the history of machine learning. Why do you think that the multilayer perceptron can solve the XOR problem? What is the role of the activation function in this procedure?

3. The Sigmoid function is a type of activation function widely adopted in the early stage of neural network research. What disadvantages does it have? How does the tanh activation function solve these problems?

4. Regularization techniques are widely applied in deep learning models. What does it aim at? How does Dropout lead to regularization?

5. It is said that the optimizer is an encapsulation of model-training algorithms. The popular optimizers include SGD, Adam and etc. Try to compare their differences in performance.

6. Please refer to the example and complete the convolution operation in Fig. 3.22.

7. The recurrent neural network can maintain the state of contexts in the serialized data. How is this function of memory realized? What problems might be encountered when dealing with long sequences?

8. The generative adversarial network is a type of deep generative network architecture. Please briefly describe its working principles.

9. The vanishing gradient and exploding gradient are two common problems in deep learning. What causes the vanishing and exploding gradient? How to avoid?

Chapter 4
Deep Learning Frameworks

This chapter firstly introduces the development frameworks that are widely used in deep learning and their characteristics, and illustrates one of the representative frameworks, TensorFlow, in detail. This chapter aims at helping readers to deepen their understanding of through practices after learning the concept at the theoretical level, and to tackle the practical problems. In the latter part of this chapter, the MindSpore framework developed by Huawei is introduced. The framework features some advantages that many of today's frameworks cannot outperform. After reading this chapter, our readers can decide whether to read this section based on their own needs.

4.1 Introduction to Deep Learning Frameworks

4.1.1 Introduction to PyTorch

PyTorch is a deep learning development framework launched by Facebook. It is a scientific computing package of machine learning that grew out of Torch. Torch is a scientific computing framework supported by a large amount of machine learning algorithms and a tensor operation library similar to NumPy. Although Torch is characterized by its exceptional flexibility, it adopts Lua, an unpopular programming language, prohibiting it from being widely used. Therefore, the Python-based PyTorch is introduced.

PyTorch has the following characteristics.

1. Put Python First

    PyTorch does not simply construct a Python binding to an entire C++ framework. It supports the Python access at a fine-grained level. You can just use PyTorch as swiftly as using NumPy or SciPy, which not only helps users to

Huawei Technologies Co., Ltd., *Artificial Intelligence Technology*,
https://doi.org/10.1007/978-981-19-2879-6_4

understand Python much more easily, but also guarantees that the code is basically in consistency with the native Python code.

2. Dynamic Neural Network

Many mainstream frameworks today do not support dynamic neural networks, such as TensorFlow 1.x. The running of TensorFlow 1.x requires constructing static computational graphs in advance, and then repeatedly running the graphs through the feed and the run () method. But running PyTorch is much less complicated. The PyTorch programs can dynamically construct and adjust computational graphs at runtime.

3. Easy to Debug

PyTorch can generate dynamic graphs while it is running. Therefore, developers can terminate the interpreter in the debugger session and check the output at a certain node.

Meanwhile, tensors that PyTorch provides to support CPU and GPU can also substantially accelerate the computation.

4.1.2   Introduction to MindSpore

Huawei developed the essential architecture of the MindSpore framework on the basis of user-friendliness, efficiency and flexibility, which consists of four layers: the top layer is MindSpore's expression of native computational graphs; the second layer is the parallel Pipeline execution layer, mainly designed to optimize the depth image computation and the operator fusion; the third layer includes an on-demand collaborative distribution architecture, a communication library, and a basic framework of scheduling and distributed deployment of tasks; and what at the bottom is the execution efficiency layer. The core architecture of MindSpore enables auto-differentiation, automatic parallelization and automatic tuning, offering solid support for the all-scenario API that is in line with Huawei's design pursuits of development-friendliness, efficient operation and flexible deployment.

What lies at the core and plays a decisive role in the programming paradigm of an AI framework is the automatic differentiation technology of the framework. A deep learning model is trained through forward and backward computation. Let's look at the mathematical expression shown in Fig. 4.1. The process of forward computation of this equation suggested by the dark arrow in Fig. 4.1 which finds the output f through the forward computation, and gets the differential values of x and y through backward computation based on the chain rule. When the algorithm engineers design the model, they only cover the forward computation, and the backward computation is implemented by the automatic differentiation technology that the framework features.

What is more, with the expansion of the NPL models, the memory overhead of training large models such as Bert (340M) and GPT-2 (1542M) has exceeded the single-card capacity, thus the model will need to be distributed into multiple GPUs

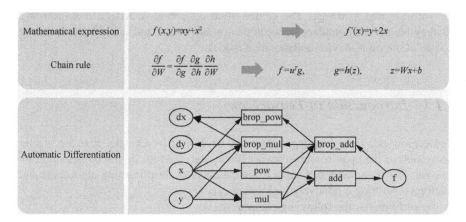

Fig. 4.1 Mathematical expression

for execution. At present, the commonly adopted method is hand-engineered model parallelism, which entails designing model partitioning and being aware cluster topology. Developing such a model is very difficult, not mentioning to ensure high performance and tuning.

MindSpore adopts the automatic graph partitioning, which partitions the graphs based on operator's input/output dimensions, and combines data parallelism with model parallelism. It uses cluster topology-aware scheduling and minimizes the communication overhead through awareness of cluster topology and automatically scheduling subgraph execution. It can keep the logic of the standalone code and put in place the model parallelism, enhancing the development efficiency of the model parallelism by ten times compared to the hand-engineered parallelism.

Currently, the model execution in the context of super computing power chips faces huge challenges, such as memory wall problem, mounting interaction overhead and troublesome data supply. As part of the operation is executed on the host and part is executed on the terminal device, the host-device interaction overhead has even surmounted the execution overhead, reducing the accelerator occupancy.

MindSpore offers the chip-oriented depth graph optimization featuring the wait-reduced synchronization and maximized parallelism of "data-computation-communication", which makes the data and computation graph sink to the Ascend AI processor.

MindSpore also uses the on-device execution method for decentralization. By implementing the gradient data-driven self-adaptive graph partitioning optimization, MindSpore realizes the decentralization of the independent AllReduce, synthesizes the speed of gradient aggregation and sufficiently pipelines computation and communication.

An on-demand collaborative distributed architecture that synergizing the device edge and cloud is also adopted by the MindSpore. The intermediate representation (IR) of the collective model guarantees a consistent deployment experience, and blocks scene differences through the graph optimization technology that collaborate the software and hardware. The device-cloud collaborative federal meta learning strategy breaks the boundary between device and cloud, and realizes the real-time update of the multi-device collaborative model.

4.1.3 Introduction to TensorFlow

TensorFlow is a deep learning framework developed by Google. It is the second generation of the open-source software library designed for digital computation by Google. The framework can support a wide range of deep learning algorithms and platforms featuring a relatively high system stability.

TensorFlow has the following characteristics.

1. Support Multiple Platforms

   All the platforms of Python environments can support TensorFlow. But TensorFlow has to access the supported GPU through another software to such as the NVIDIA CUDA Toolkit and cuDNN.

2. Support GPU

   TensorFlow supports specific NVIDIA GPUs compatible with the related version of the CUDA toolkit that meets specific performance criteria.

3. Support Distributed Computation

   TensorFlow supports distributed computation. It allows portions of the graph to be computed on different processes, which may be on completely different servers.

4. Support Multiple Languages

   The major programming language of TensorFlow is Python. Developers can also use C++, Java, and Go but these languages have no stability promises, as are many third-party bindings for C#, Haskell, Julia, Rust, Ruby, Scala, R and even PHP. Google recently released TensorFlow-Lite library optimized for mobile devices so as to run TensorFlow applications on the Android system.

5. Flexible and Expandable

   One of the major advantages of using TensorFlow is that it has a modular, extensible, and flexible design. Developers can easily move models across CPU, GPU, or TPU processors by making a few modification of the code. Python developers can use the TensorFlow raw, low-level API (or core API) to develop their own models, and use the high-level APIs for built-in models. TensorFlow has many built-in libraries and distributed libraries, and it can overlay an advanced deep learning framework of higher-level such as Keras to serve as a high-level API.

6. Strong Computing Performance

   Although TensorFlow performs best on Google's Tensor Processing Units (TPUs), it also manages to attain higher performance on other platforms, not just servers and desktop systems, but also embedded systems and mobile devices.

TensorFlow's distributed deployment allows it to run on different computer systems. Training models can be generated in real-time on a system either as small as a smart phone or as big as a cluster of computers. The Windows environment is built on the single-GPU mode, and most of the deep learning frameworks rely on cuDNN. So as long as there is no obvious discrepancy in the hardware computing power or memory allocation, the training speed of these frameworks will not differ from each other too much. But for large-scale deep learning, the huge amount of data will make it hard for the single machine to complete training in time. But TensorFlow supports distributed training.

TensorFlow is believed to be one of the most user-friendly libraries for deep learning. With the help of TensorFlow, deep learning development will become a much easier task. Its open-source feature makes it possible for everyone to maintain and update TensorFlow so as to improve its efficiency.

Keras, which receives the third most Stars (namely, being tagged) on GitHub, is encapsulated as a high-level API for Tenser Flow 2.0. Thanks to Keras, TensorFlow 2.0 becomes more flexible and easier to debug.

In TensorFlow 1.0, after a tensor is created, you cannot return to the result directly, but to create session including the graph concept, and you need to execute session.run for operation. This style is more like the hardware programming language VHDL. Compared with the simpler frameworks such as PyTorch, the above unnecessary steps required by TensorFlow 1.0 are pointless except for creating more hurdles for developers in usage. TensorFlow 1.0 is often criticized for its complicated debugging experience, confusing API, and not easy to get started with. And TensorFlow 1.0 is still difficult to use even for the informed developers, thus many developers turned to PyTorch.

4.2 TensorFlow 2.0 Basics

4.2.1 Introduction to TensorFlow 2.0

The core function of TensorFlow 2.0 is eager execution, a dynamic graph mechanism which allows users to write and debug models just as the normal programming does, facilitating the learning and application of TensorFlow. TensorFlow 2.0 bears more platforms and languages, and improves compatibility across components by standardizing exchange formats aligning APIs. The version 2.0 of TensorFlow cleans up deprecated APIs and reduces the duplicated APIs so as to not confuse the users. TensorFlow 2.0 provides modules that are compatible with TensorFlow 1. x, and tf.contrib module will no longer be used, with the maintained modules moved to other places, and the rest deleted.

4.2.2 Introduction to Tensors

The most fundamental data structures in TensorFlow are tensors, which encapsulate all the data.

According to the definition, a tensor is a multi-dimensional array. Among which, a rank 0 tensor is a scalar, a rank 1 tensor is a vector, and a rank 2 tensor is a matrix. In TensorFlow, tensors can be divided into constants and variables.

4.2.3 TensorFlow 2.0 Eager Execution

TensorFlow 1.0 adopts a static graph mechanism which separates the definition of computations from their execution via graph (also known as computational graph). This is a sort of declarative programming model. Under the static graph mechanism, you need first to build a graph, then run a session, and input the data to get the execution result.

The static graph mechanism has many advantages in distributed training, performance optimization and deployment, but it is not easy to use in debugging, just like calling from a compiled C language program where we cannot perform internal debugging. Therefore, the dynamic graph-based (AutoGraph) eager execution is introduced.

Eager execution is an imperative programming environment consistent with native Python. The execution results will be immediately returned after an operation is performed.

4.2.4 TensorFlow 2.0 AutoGraph

In TensorFlow 2.0, eager execution is enabled by default. For users, eager execution is straightforward and flexible, featuring easier and faster operation. But this may be achieved at the cost of performance and deployment.

To obtain the best performance and ensure that the model can be deployed anywhere, we can apply the @tf.function decorator to build the graph in the program, enhancing the efficiency of the Python code.

A very cool feature of tf.function is AutoGraph, which can convert the TensorFlow operation function into a graph, thus executing the function in Graph mode. In this way, the function is encapsulated into a graph of TensorFlow operation.

4.3   Introduction to TensorFlow 2.0 Module

4.3.1   Introduction to Common Modules

Functions under the TensorFlow 2.0 tf.modules are designed to handle common operations.

For instances, most of the operations in tf.abs (computing the absolute value), tf. add (element-by-element addition), tf.concat (concatenation of tensors), etc. can be fulfilled by NumPy.

The tf.modules also include:

1. tf.errors: exception types for TensorFlow errors.
2. tf.data: perform the operation on dataset. For example, use the input pipeline created by tf.data to read training data. The module also supports easy input of data from memory (such as NumPy).
3. tf.gfile: perform the operation on file. The functions under this module can perform file I/O operations, and copy and rename the file.
4. tf.image: perform the operation on image. The functions under this module can process images like OpenCV, featuring a series of functions such as image brightness, saturation, inversion, cropping, resizing, image format conversion (from RGB format to HSV, YUV, YIQ, Gray formats), rotation and Sobel edge detection. It is equal to a small-scale OpenCV image processing toolkit.
5. tf.keras: call a Python API from the Keras tool. This module is a relatively large, which contains all kinds of operations of the network.
6. tf.nn: the functional support module of the neural network. It is the most commonly used module for building classic convolutional networks. It also contains the rnn_cell sub-module, which is applied in recurrent neural network building. The frequently used functions in this module include: average pooling avg_pool (), batch normalization batch_normalization(), adding bias bias_add(), two-dimensional convolution conv2d(), random dropout neural network cell dropout(), ReLu activation layer relu(), sigmoid cross entropy after activation sigmoid_cross_entropy_with_logits(), softmax activation layer softmax().

4.3.2   Keras Interface

Keras is the program recommended in TensorFlow 2.0 for network building. The keras.layer module has included all the popular neural networks.

Keras is a high-level API designed for building and training deep learning models. It can be used for fast prototyping, advanced research and production. Keras has the following three major advantages.

1. User-Friendly
    Keras has a simple and consistent interface optimized for common use case which provides clear and actionable feedback for user errors.

2. Modular and Composable

You can build Keras models by connecting configurable building blocks together, with almost no restrictions.

3. Easy to Extend

You can write custom building blocks to express new research ideas, create new layers, loss functions, and develop advanced models.

Following are the modules commonly used in Keras.

1. tf.keras.layers

The tf.keras.layers namespace provides extensive interfaces for common network layers, such as fully connected layer, activation function layer, pooling layer, convolutional layer, recurrent neural network layer, etc. For these network layer classes, the forward computation can be accomplished by specifying the relevant parameters of the network layers when creating them, and calling the _call_ method. Keras will automatically call the forward propagation logic of each layer while calling the _call_method, which is implemented by the call function of the class.

2. Network Container

In the often-used networks, users need to manually call the class instances of each layer to accomplish the forward propagation. When the number of network layers go deeper, the code of this part will become very redundant. The network container Sequential provided by Keras can encapsulate the multiple network layers into a big network model, where users only need to call instance of the network model once to complete the sequential operation of the data from the first layer to the last.

4.4   Get Started with TensorFlow 2.0

4.4.1   Environment Setup

To set up an TensorFlow 2.0 development environment, you need to do as the follows.

1. Setup in Windows Environment

   (a) Operating system: Windows 10.
   (b) Python development environment: Anaconda3 (a version adapted to Python 3) equipped with pip software.

Install TensorFlow: Open Anaconda Prompt, and install TensorFlow directly executing the pip command.

As shown in Fig. 4.2, type the following command in Anaconda Prompt.

```
pip install tensorflow
```

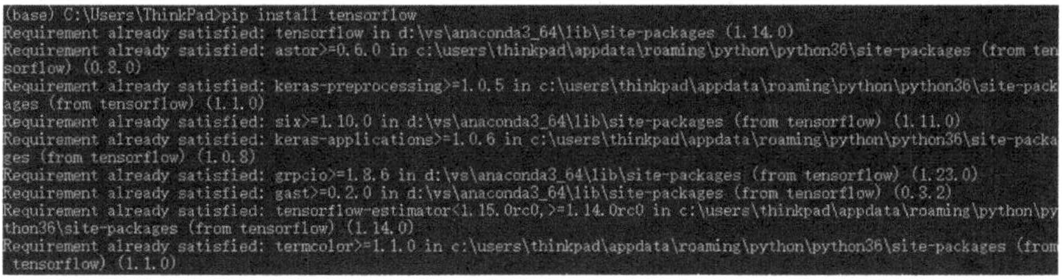

```
(base) C:\Users\ThinkPad>pip install tensorflow
Requirement already satisfied: tensorflow in d:\vs\anaconda3_64\lib\site-packages (1.14.0)
Requirement already satisfied: astor>=0.6.0 in c:\users\thinkpad\appdata\roaming\python\python36\site-packages (from ten
sorflow) (0.8.0)
Requirement already satisfied: keras-preprocessing>=1.0.5 in c:\users\thinkpad\appdata\roaming\python\python36\site-pack
ages (from tensorflow) (1.1.0)
Requirement already satisfied: six>=1.10.0 in d:\vs\anaconda3_64\lib\site-packages (from tensorflow) (1.11.0)
Requirement already satisfied: keras-applications>=1.0.6 in c:\users\thinkpad\appdata\roaming\python\python36\site-packa
ges (from tensorflow) (1.0.8)
Requirement already satisfied: grpcio>=1.8.6 in d:\vs\anaconda3_64\lib\site-packages (from tensorflow) (1.23.0)
Requirement already satisfied: gast>=0.2.0 in d:\vs\anaconda3_64\lib\site-packages (from tensorflow) (0.3.2)
Requirement already satisfied: tensorflow-estimator<1.15.0rc0,>=1.14.0rc0 in c:\users\thinkpad\appdata\roaming\python\py
thon36\site-packages (from tensorflow) (1.14.0)
Requirement already satisfied: termcolor>=1.1.0 in c:\users\thinkpad\appdata\roaming\python\python36\site-packages (from
tensorflow) (1.1.0)
```

Fig. 4.2 Installation command

2. Linux Environment Setup

The simplest way to install TensorFlow in a Linux environment is using pip. If the installation goes on slowly, you can use Tsinghua Open Source Mirror to execute the following command in the terminal.

```
pip install pip-U
pip config set global.index-url https://pypi.tuna.tsinghua.edu.cn/
simple
```

At last, run the pip installation command.

```
pip install tensorflow==2.0.0
```

4.4.2   Development Process

The development process of TensorFlow 2.0 includes five steps.

1. Data preparation, including data exploration and data processing.
2. Building the network, including defining the network structure, defining the loss function, choosing the optimizer, and defining the model evaluation standards.
3. Training and validating the model.
4. Saving the model.
5. Restoring and calling the model.

The above-mentioned process will be further elaborated in the following passage by a real project—MNIST handwritten digit recognition.

The handwritten digit recognition is a common task of image recognition where computers are required to recognize digits from pictures of handwritten digits. Unlike the print, the handwriting of different people has different styles, and the size of handwritten digits varies from one to another, which makes the recognition of handwritten digits by computers much harder. In this project, deep learning and TensorFlow framework are employed to perform a handwritten digit recognition on the MNIST dataset.

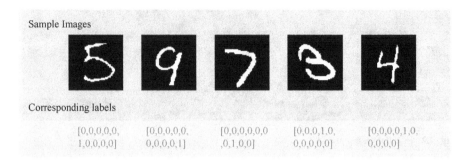

Fig. 4.3 An example from the dataset

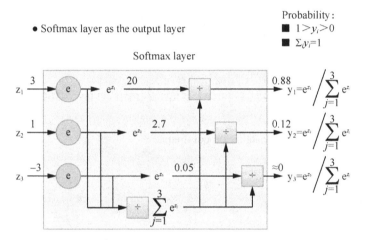

Fig. 4.4 Computation of the softmax function

1. Data Preparation

Download the MNIST dataset.

The MNIST dataset is composed of a training set and a test set.

The training set contains 60,000 images of handwritten digits and the corresponding labels.

The test set contains 10,000 images of handwritten digits and the corresponding labels.

Figure 4.3 shows an example from the dataset.

2. Building the Network

The activation function used in this project is the Softmax regression model. The Softmax function is also known as the normalized exponential function, which is a derivative of binary function Sigmoid in multiclass classification. Figure 4.4 shows how is the Softmax function computed.

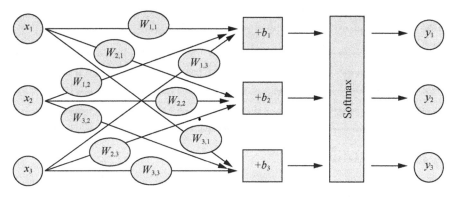

Fig. 4.5 Calculation process of the model

Import TensorFlow
`import tensorflow as tf`
Define the input variables with operator symbol variables
"""

Where *x* is not a particular value, but a placeholder, which will be entered when running TensorFlow. For the
computation, each input image will be flattened into a vector of 784 dimensions, featuring a shape of [None,
784]. None refers to the first dimension of the vector. It can be of any length.
"""

`x = tf.placeholder(tf.float32, [None, 784])`
"""

Weight (w) and bias (b) are expressed by the Variable that is changeable. The initial values of the two are both zero.
"""

`w = tf.Variable(tf.zeros([784, 10]))`
`b = tf.Variable(tf.zeros([10]))`
"""

Use tf.matmul (x.w) to express x multiplying w. The equation of Softmax regression is y=softmax (wx+b)
"""

`y = tf.nn.softmax(tf.matmul(x, w) + b)`

Fig. 4.6   Code implementing softmax

The process of model building is the key of network construction. Figure 4.5
shows a model's calculation process, defining how the model is built, and how the
output is generated based on the input.

The quintessential code for TensorFlow to implement the Softmax regression
model is presented in Fig. 4.6.

Creating a model mainly needs to determine the following two things first.

Loss function: In either machine learning or deep learning, we often need to
define a loss function as an indicator to express whether a model is suitable, and
then to minimize the loss function. The indicator is called the cost or the loss. The
loss function used in this project is cross entropy loss function.

Optimizer: After the loss function is defined, we need to optimize the loss
function by the optimizer, so as to find the optimal parameters and minimize the

```
# Fitting the model on training data through model.fit
model.fit(mnist.train.images, mnist.train.labels, epochs=5)

Epoch 1/5
55000/55000 [==============================] - 4s 74us/sample - loss: 0.3043 - categorical_accuracy: 0.9110
Epoch 2/5
55000/55000 [==============================] - 4s 73us/sample - loss: 0.1460 - categorical_accuracy: 0.9569
Epoch 3/5
55000/55000 [==============================] - 4s 79us/sample - loss: 0.1104 - categorical_accuracy: 0.9669
Epoch 4/5
55000/55000 [==============================] - 4s 74us/sample - loss: 0.0881 - categorical_accuracy: 0.9722
Epoch 5/5
55000/55000 [==============================] - 4s 73us/sample - loss: 0.0767 - categorical_accuracy: 0.9760
```

Fig. 4.7 Training process

Fig. 4.8 Test validation

value of the loss function. The optimizer that is more frequently used in finding the optimal parameters of machine learning is the gradient descent-based optimizer.

3. Training and Validating the Model

Training all the data in batches or in bulk iterations. In this project, we train the data directly with model.fit, and train the data in bulk iterations for five times, as shown in Fig. 4.7. An epoch represents the number of times of training iterations.

As shown in Fig. 4.8, we test and validate the model with the test set and compare the predicted outcome and the actual outcome, so as to find out the correct label, and estimate the accuracy of the model on the test set.

4.5 Chapter Summary

This chapter introduces the development frameworks that are commonly used in the AI industry and their characteristics, with the module composition and basic procedure of the TensorFlow framework developing particularly emphasized. What is more, this chapter offers a project to introduce the application of TensorFlow functions and modules in practical cases. Readers can take this chapter as a guide while setting up the framework environment and operating the sample projects. With these steps, we hope our readers can have a deeper understanding of AI.

4.6 Exercises

1. As the implementation of AI is getting wider and wider, what are the most popular development frameworks for AI today? What characteristics do they have?
2. TensorFlow is a representative development framework for AI that has attracted many users. The most important change during its maintenance is the transformation from TensorFlow 1.0 to TensorFlow 2.0. Please describe the differences between the two versions.
3. TensorFlow has a variety of modules designed for users' demands. Please describe three common Tensor Flow modules.
4. Compared with other frameworks, Keras is quite special as a frontend framework. Please briefly describe the features of Keras' interface.
5. Please try to configure an AI development framework according to the guidelines provided in this chapter.

Chapter 5
Huawei MindSpore AI Development Framework

This chapter focuses on the AI development framework developed by Huawei—MindSpore. Firstly, it introduces the architecture of MindSpore and how it is designed. Next, it analyses the problems and difficulties of AI development frameworks. Lastly, it further presents the framework base on the development and application of MindSpore.

5.1 Introduction to MindSpore Development Framework

MindSpore is a Huawei self-developed AI development framework which can achieve device-edge-cloud all-scenario on-demand collaboration. It provides a unified all-scenario API which enable end-to-end model development, execution and deployment.

MindSpore adopts a device-edge-cloud on-demand collaborative distributed architecture, a new paradigm of native differential programming, and a new AI Native execution mode to achieve higher resource efficiency, security and reliability, while lowering the entrance standards for AI development and giving a full play to the computing power of the Ascend AI processor to realize inclusive AI application.

5.1.1 MindSpore Architecture

The architecture of MindSpore consists of three parts: development, execution and deployment. As shown by Fig. 5.1, the processors that can be deployed include CPU, GPU and Ascend AI processors (Ascend310, Ascend910).

The development is a unified all-scenario API (Python API) which provides users with a unified model training, inference, and export interface, as well as a unified data processing, enhancement, and format conversion interface.

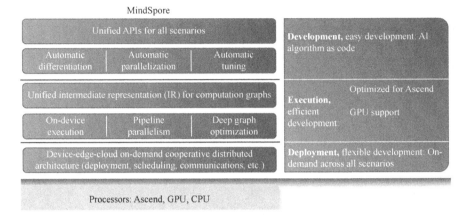

Fig. 5.1 The architecture of MindSpore

The development includes functions such as graph high level optimization (GHLO), hardware-independent optimization (e.g., dead code elimination, etc.), automatic parallelism, and automatic differentiation. These functions also support the design concept of a unified all-scenario API.

MindSpore IR in execution has a native computational graph representation, and a unified intermediate representation (IR), based on which MindSpore performs the optimization on compiler pass.

The execution includes hardware-related optimization, parallel Pipeline execution layer, and deep optimization related to combination of software and hardware, such as operator fusion and buffer fusion. These features enable the automatic differentiation, automatic parallel, and automatic tuning.

The deployment adopts distributed architecture of the on-demand device-edge-cloud collaboration, with deployment, scheduling, and communication acting on the same layer, contributing to the all-scenario on-demand collaboration.

In a nutshell, MindSpore integrates the easy development (AI algorithm as code), efficient operation (supporting optimization of Ascend AI processor and GPU), and flexible deployment (all-scenario on-demand collaboration) together in one framework.

5.1.2   How Is MindSpore Designed

In response to the challenges faced by AI developers in the industry, such as high development entrance standards, high operating costs, and difficulties of deployment, MindSpore proposes three technological innovations correspondingly: new programming paradigm, new execution mode, and new collaboration mode to help the developers realize the development and deployment of AI applications in an easier and more efficient manner.

1. New Programming Paradigm

The design concept of the new programming paradigm is proposed to deal with the challenges for the AI development.

The challenges for the development mainly include:

(a) High skill requirements. Developers are required to have relevant theoretical knowledge and mathematical skills of AI, computer systems, software to get engaged in AI development, raising the bar of entrance.
(b) Difficult black-box optimization. The un-interpretability and the "black-box" feature of AI algorithms make it more difficult to tune parameters.
(c) Difficult parallel planning. Influenced by the technological progress, the volume of data is getting larger and larger, and the models are getting bigger and bigger, making parallel computing inevitable. Parallel planning relies heavily on the technicians' personal experience, requiring technicians to not only be a professional of data and models but also be acquainted with the distributed systems architecture.

The AI algorithm in the new programming paradigm is code itself, which lowers the bar of AI development. The new AI programming paradigm based on the mathematical native expression allows algorithm experts to focus on AI innovation and exploration, as shown in Fig. 5.2.

(a) Automatic Differentiation

Automatic differentiation (AD) is the soul of the deep learning framework. Generally speaking, AD refers to a method of automatically computing the

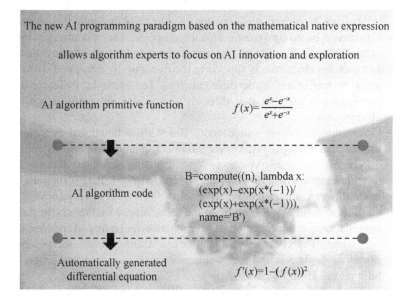

The new AI programming paradigm based on the mathematical native expression

allows algorithm experts to focus on AI innovation and exploration

AI algorithm primitive function $\quad f(x)=\dfrac{e^{x}-e^{-x}}{e^{x}+e^{-x}}$

AI algorithm code $\qquad$ B=compute((n), lambda x: (exp(x)−exp(x*(−1))/ (exp(x)+exp(x*(−1)))), name='B')

Automatically generated differential equation $\qquad f'(x)=1-(f(x))^2$

Fig. 5.2 New programming paradigm of MindSpore

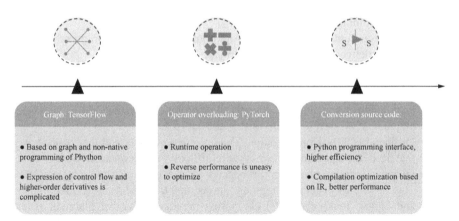

Fig. 5.3 The development of automatic differentiation

derivative of a function. In machine learning, these derivatives can update the weights. In the natural science with a broader connotation, these derivatives can also be used in subsequent computations. The development of automatic differentiation is shown in Fig. 5.3.

During the development of automatic differentiation, there are three types of automatic differentiation techniques as follows.

- Conversion based on static calculation graph: The network is converted into static calculation diagram at compile time, and then the chain rule is applied to the calculation diagram to realize automatic differentiation. For example, Tensorflow can optimize the network performance by static compilation technology. However, it is very complex to build or debug the network.
- Conversion based on dynamic calculation graph: The operation track of the network during forward propagation is recorded by operator overloading, and then the chain rule is applied to the dynamically generated calculation graph to realize automatic differentiation. For example, PyTorch is very convenient to use, but it is difficult to optimize the performance to the ultimate level.
- Conversion based on source code: Based on a functional programming framework, it adopts just-in-time (JIT) compilation to perform automatic differentiation transformation on the intermediate representation (a representation of a program during compilation). It also supports automatic differentiation of automatic control flow. So it is very convenient to build models, just as PyTorch. At the same time, MindSpore can do static compilation and optimization of neural networks, so its performance is also very good. The comparison of automatic differentiation technologies is shown in Table 5.1, and the comparison of performance and programmability is shown in Fig. 5.4.

The MindSpore automatic differentiation technology has the following advantages.

Table 5.1 Comparison of automatic differentiation technologies

Schools of AD	General	Fast	Portable	Differentiable	Typical framework
Graph	No	√	√	Partially	TensorFlow
OO	√	Partially	Partially	√	PyTorch
SCT	√	√	√	√	MindSpore

Fig. 5.4 Comparison of automatic differentiation performance and programmability

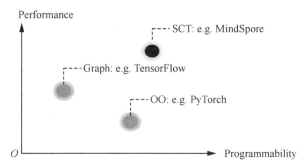

- Programmability: Differentiability can be achieved by Python universal languages based on IR primitives (each primitive operation in MindSpore IR corresponds to the basic function in basic algebra).
- Performance: Compiler optimization, operator reverse auto-tuning.
- Debugging: Diversified visual interfaces and supports dynamic execution.

(b) Automatic Parallel

The deep learning models today often need to be parallelized because of their huge size. Currently, the manual model parallelism is adopted, which requires design model segmentation and awareness of cluster topology, which is difficult to realize. And it is also uneasy to assure high performance by the manual parallelism, not to mention tuning.

MindSpore can automatically parallel the code written in serial, realize distributed parallel training automatically and keep high performance.

Generally speaking, parallel training can be divided into model parallel and data parallel. Data parallel is easier to understand, which means each sample can complete the forward propagation independently, and finally summarize the propagation results. In contrast, model parallel is more complicated, and we need to manually write all the parts that need to be paralleled with logic of "parallel thinking".

MindSpore introduces a key innovation technology—automatic full-graph segmentation. As shown in Fig. 5.5, the full graph is segmented according to the operator input and output data, that is, each operator in the graph is divided into clusters and then complete the parallel operation. This technology combines data parallel and model parallel. Cluster topology is adopted to automatically schedule the execution of sub-graphs to minimize communication overhead.

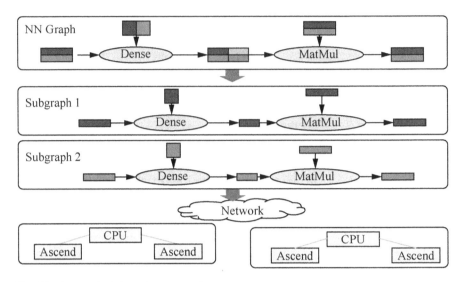

Fig. 5.5 Automatic full-graph segmentation

The goal of MindSpore automatic parallel is to build a training method that combines data parallelism, model parallelism, and hybrid parallelism. It will automatically select a model segmentation method featuring the lowest cost to implement automatic distributed parallel training.

The operator fine-granularity method of MindSpore segmentation is very complicated. But developers do not need to take into account the underlying implementation, as long as they endow the top-level API with high efficiency of calculations.

Generally speaking, the new programming paradigm not only realizes the "AI algorithm as code", lowering the threshold of AI development, but also enables efficient development and debugging. For example, it can efficiently complete automatic differentiation, realize the automatic parallel of one line of code, and complete debugging and running of one line of code.

Transformer, a classic algorithm used by developers to implement natural language processing, is made real by the MindSpore framework. During the development and debugging process, both dynamic and static implementation combined, and the debugging is transparent and simple. From the final structure, the amount of code on the MindSpore framework is 2000, which, compared with 2500 lines of Tensorflow, is about 20% less, but with efficiency improved more than 50%.

2. New Execution Mode

The design concept of the new execution mode is proposed in response to the challenges of the execution.

The challenges posed to the execution are as follows:

Fig. 5.6 On-device execution

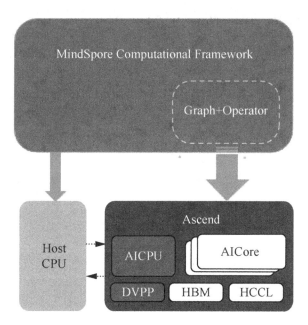

(a) The complexity of AI computation and the diversity of computing power: various types of computing powers, such as CPU core, cube unit, vector unit; computation of scalar quantity, vector quantity, and tensor quantity; mixed precision computation; dense matrix and sparse matrix computation.
(b) In the case of multi-GPU operation, as the number of nodes increases, the performance is difficult to increase linearly, resulting in high parallel control overhead.

The new execution mode adopts Ascend Native execution engine of and proposes on-device execution, as shown in Fig. 5.6. The full graph offload execution and the depth map optimization are utilized, giving full play to the strong computing power of Ascend AI processor.

There are two technical cores of On-Device implementation, as follows.

(a) Full graph sink execution, giving full play to the strong computing power of the Ascend AI processor. This technique addresses the challenges faced by model execution under super chip computing power, such as memory wall, high interaction overhead, difficulty in data supply, etc. Execution is partly done on the host and partly on terminal devices, which leads to much higher overhead of interaction than the overhead of execution, resulting in a low accelerator occupancy rate. MindSpore, adopting chip-oriented depth map optimization technology, minimizes synchronization waiting and maximizes the parallel degree of data-calculation-communication synergy, sinking the entire data+ full graph calculation to the Ascend AI processor, thus offering the best and optimal result. The final result is a 10 times improvement in

Fig. 5.7 Decentralized
autonomous AllReduce
algorithm

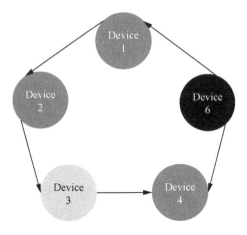

Fig. 5.8 Comparison
between MindSpore and
TensorFlow

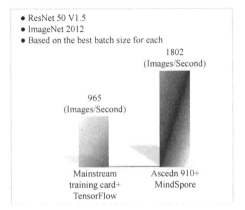

training performance compared to the graph scheduling method on the
host side.

(b) Data-driven large-scale distributed gradient aggregation. This technology
addresses the challenges of distributed gradient aggregation under super
chip computing power, i.e., the synchronization overhead of central control
and the communication overhead of frequent synchronization in a single
iteration of ResNet-50 in 20 ms. The traditional method requires three
synchronization steps to complete AllReduce and the data-driven autonomous AllReduce without control overhead.

MindSpore achieves a decentralized autonomous AllReduce algorithm through
adaptive graph segmentation optimization driven by gradient data, so as to keep
gradient aggregation in the same step and the parallel of computation and
communications, as shown in Fig. 5.7.

Figure 5.8 shows an example in computer vision. Neural network ResNet-50
V1.5 is adopted to carry out training on the ImageNet 2012 dataset based on their
best batch size respectively. It can be seen that the speed of MindSpore

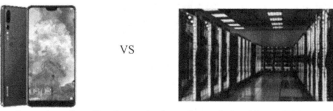

Scenarios of application at device, edge and cloud have different
demands, targets and restrictions

Different hardware has different precision and speed

Fig. 5.9 Challenges of the deployment

framework on Ascend 910 is much higher than that on other frameworks and
other mainstream training cards.

3. New Collaborative Model

   The design concept of the new collaboration model is proposed in response to
the challenges of the deployment.

   The challenges to the deployment are as follows.

(a) Device, edge, and cloud application scenarios have different requirements,
    goals and constraints. For instance, the devide of mobile phone may prefer a
    lighter model, while the cloud may require higher precision.
(b) Different hardware has different accuracy and speed, as shown in Fig. 5.9.
(c) The diversity of hardware architectures leads to deployment differences and
    performance uncertainties in all scenarios, and the separation of training and
    inference leads to model isolation.

In the new collaboration mode, all scenarios can be coordinated on-demand,
resulting in better resource efficiency and privacy protection, security and credibility, and supporting one-time development and multiple deployments. The
models can be big or small and can be deployed flexibly, offering a consistent
development experience.

   MindSpore has the following three key technologies regarding the new collaborative model.

(a) The unified model IR can cope with differences in different language scenar-
    ios, compatible with customized data structure, bringing a consistent deploy-
    ment experience.

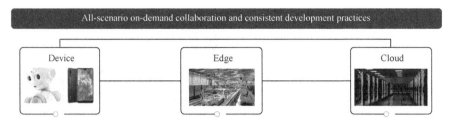

Fig. 5.10 On-demand collaboration and consistent development

(b) The hardware of the framework is also developed by Huawei, and the software-hardware collaborative graph optimization technology can shield the scene differences.

(c) The device-cloud collaborative federated meta learning strategy breaks the boundary between the device and cloud, realizing real-time update of the multi-device collaborative model.

The final effect of these three key technologies is under a unified architecture, the deployment performance of the all-scenario model is consistent, and the accuracy of the personalized model is significantly improved, as shown in Fig. 5.10.

The vision and value of MindSpore is to provide an AI computing platform of efficient development, excellent performance, and flexible deployment, to lower the entrance bar for AI development, release the computing power of the Ascend AI processor, and realize inclusive AI, as shown in Fig. 5.11.

5.1.3   Advantages of MindSpore

MindSpore has the following advantages.

1. User-Friendliness in Development

   (a) Automatic differentiation, unified programming of network and operator, native expression of functional formulas and algorithms, and automatic generation of reverse network operators.

   (b) Automatic parallelism, optimal efficiency model parallelism achieved by automatic model segmentation.

   (c) Automatic tuning, the same set of codes for dynamic graph and static graph.

2. High Efficiency in execution

   (a) On-device execution, giving full play to the strong computing power of Ascend AI processor.

   (b) Pipeline optimization, maximizing parallel performance.

   (c) Depth map optimization, computing power and precision of adaptive AI Core (Da Vinci architecture, check Chap. 6 for details).

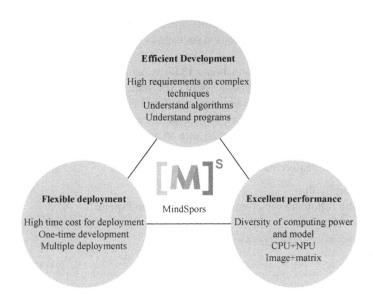

Fig. 5.11 Vision and value of MindSpore

3. Flexibility in Deployment

   (a) On-demand collaborative computing of device, edge and cloud to better protect privacy.
   (b) The unified architecture of device, edge and cloud enables one-time development and deployment on demand.

4. Equivalent to Industrial Open-Source Frameworks

   MindSpore ranks abreast with the industry's open source frameworks, supporting CPU, GPU and other hardware, with the self-developed chips and cloud services prioritized in services.

5. Upward

   MindSpore is enabled to dock with third-party frameworks. It can connect with third-party frameworks through Graph IR (training front-end docking, inference model docking), and developers can extend.

6. Downward

   MindSpore can interface with third-party chips to help developers expand MindSpore's application scenarios and prosper the AI ecosystem.

5.2 MindSpore Development and Application

5.2.1 Environment Setup

Setting up the MindSpore development environment requires the installation of Python version 3.7.5 or above. MindSpore supports hardware platforms such as

CPU, GPU, and Ascend910, and supports operating systems such as Ubuntu. It can be installed directly with the installation package or compiled source code, as shown in Fig. 5.12.

Now take the installation in an Ubuntu 18.04 system with CPU environment as an example to introduce the installation steps. The requirements of MindSpore CPU version on system and software are shown in Table 5.2.

GCC 7.3.0 can be installed directly through the apt command.

If Python is already installed, make sure to add Python to the system variable. You can also use the command "Python-Version" to check whether the version of Python meets the requirements.

1. Installation by Pip

Use the following pip command to install MindSpore.

```
pip install –y MindSpore-cpu
```

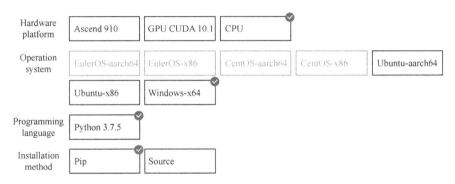

Fig. 5.12 Installation of MindSpore

Table 5.2 Mindspore's requirements on system and software

Item	Requirement
Version number	MindSpore master
Operation system	• Ubuntu 18.04 × 86_64 • Ubuntu 18.04 aarch64
Installation reliance of executable file	• Python 3.7.5 • For other reliance, check requirements.txt (see Fig. 5.13)
Source code compilation and installation reliance	Compilation reliance • Python 3.7.5 • wheel 0.32.0 or above • GCC 7.3.0 • CMake 3.14.1 or above • patch 2.5 or above Installation reliance • Same with installation reliance of executable file

   Please add pip to the system variable to ensure that Python-related toolkits can be installed directly through pip. If pip is not installed in the current system, you can download from the official website and install it. Requirements.txt contents are shown in Fig. 5.13.

   When the Internet is connected, reliance items will be automatically downloaded during whl package installation. In other cases, you need to manually install reliance items.

2. Installation by Source Code Compilation
   The procedures to install MindSpore by source code are as follows.

(a) Source code for downloading source code from code repository are as follows:

(b) Run the following command in the root directory of the source code to compile MindSpore:

   - Before executing the above commands, make sure that the path where the executable file cmake and path store has been added to the environment variable PATH.
   - Confirm that the git tool is installed. Then the command "git clone" will be executed in build.sh to obtain the code of the third-party code repository.
   - If the compiler performance is strong, you can add -j{Number of threads} in to script to increase the number of threads. For example, bash build.sh -e cpu -j12.

Fig. 5.13 Contents of requirements.txt

```
numpy >= 1.17.0, <= 1.17.5
protobuf >= 3.8.0
asttokens >= 1.1.13
pillow >= 6.2.0
scipy >= 1.3.3
easydict >= 1.9
sympy >= 1.4
cffi >= 1.13.2
wheel >= 0.32.0
decorator >= 4.4.0
setuptools >= 40.8.0
matplotlib >= 3.1.3          # for ut test
opencv-python >= 4.1.2.30    # for ut test
sklearn >= 0.0               # for st test
pandas >= 1.0.2              # for ut test
bs4
astunparse
packaging >= 20.0
pycocotools >= 2.0.0         # for st test
tables >= 3.6.1              # for st test
```

Table 5.3 MindSpore components and descriptions

Component	Description
Tensor	Data storage
model_zoo	Definition of common network models
communication	Data loading modules, including the definition of dataloader, dataset and some image, text and other data processing functions
dataset	Dataset processing modules, such as data reading and data preprocessing
common	Definition of tensor, parameter, dtype and initializer
context	The definition of the Context class, set the parameters of model operation, such as switching between graph and pynative modes
akg	Automatic differentiation and custom operator library
nn	Definition of MindSpore neural network unit, loss function, optimizer
ops	Basic operator definition and registration of reverse operator
train	Related to training model and summary function module
utils	Utilities, mainly for parameter verification (used internally by the framework)

(c) Execute the following command to install MindSpore.

```
chmod +x build/package/MindSpore-{version}-cp37-cp37m-linux_
{arch}.whl
  pip install build/package/MindSpore-{version}-cp37-cp37m-
linux_{arch}.whl
```

(d) Execute the following command. If the output is "No module named 'mindspore'", it means that the installation was not successful.

```
python -c 'import MindSpore'
```

5.2.2   Components and Concepts Related to MindSpore

1. Component
   Some commonly used components and descriptions by MindSpore are shown in Table 5.3.
      In MindSpore, the most basic data structure is also the tensor. There are several common tensor operations as follows:

```
asnumpy()
size()
dim()
dtype()
set_dtype()
tensor_add(other: Tensor)
```

```
tensor_mul(ohter: Tensor)
shape()
__str__ # convert into string
```

These tensor operations can basically be understood by reading their names, such as asnumpy() means conversion to NumPy array, tensor_add() means tensor addition.

2. Programming Concept: Operation

There are several common operations in MindSpore as follows.

(a) Array: Array-related operators as follows:

```
-ExpandDims  - Squeeze
-Concat      - OnesLike
-Select      - StridedSlice
-ScatterNd   ...
```

(b) Math: mathematical calculations related operators as follows:

```
-AddN        - Cos
-Sub         - Sin
-Mul         - LogicalAnd
-MatMul      - LogicalNot
-RealDiv     - Less
-ReduceMean  - Greater
...
```

(c) Nn: Network operators as follows:

```
-Conv2D      - MaxPool
-Flatten     - AvgPool
-Softmax     - TopK
-ReLU        - SoftmaxCrossEntropy
-Sigmoid     - SmoothL1Loss
-Pooling     - SGD
-BatchNorm   - SigmoidCrossEntropy
...
```

(d) Control: control operators as follows:

```
ControlDepend
```

3. Programming Concept: Cell

   (a) Cell defines the basic modules for performing calculations. Cell objects can be executed directly.

- __init__, initialize parameters (parameter), sub-module (cell), operator (primitive) and other components, and perform initialization verification.
- Construct, which defines the execution process. In graph mode, it will be compiled into graphs for execution. There are some grammatical restrictions.
- Bprop (optional), the reverse of the custom module. When this function is not defined, automatic differentiation will be used to calculate the reverse of the construct part.

   (b) The predefined cells in MindSpore mainly include: commonly used loss functions (such as SoftmaxCrossEntropyWithLogits, MSELoss), commonly used optimizers (such as Momentum, SGD, Adam), and commonly used network packaging functions (such as TrainOneStepCell, WithGradCell).

4. Programming Concept: MindSporeIR

   (a) MindSporeIR is a concise, efficient, and flexible graph-based functional IR that can express functional semantics such as free variables, higher-order functions and recursion.

   (b) Each graph represents a function definition, and the graph consists of ParameterNode, ValueNode, and ComplexNode (CNode).

5.2.3   Realization of Handwritten Digit Recognition with Mindspore

1. Overview

This tutorial uses a simple image classification example to demonstrate the basic functions of MindSpore. For general users, it takes 20–30 min to complete the entire sample practice. This is a simple and basic application process, and other advanced and complex applications can be extended based on this basic process.

This sample will implement a simple image classification, and the overall process is as follows:

   (a) Process the needed dataset. The MNIST dataset is used in this example.

   (b) Define a network. The LeNet network is used in this example.

   (c) Define the loss function and optimizer.

(d) Load the dataset and perform training. After the training is complete, check the result and save the model file.

(e) Load the saved model for inference.

(f) Validate the model, load the test dataset and trained model, and validate the result accuracy.

2. Preparation

Before the practice, check whether MindSpore has been correctly installed. If not, install MindSpore on your computer by referring to Sect. 5.2.1. In addition, you shall have basic mathematical knowledge such as Python programming basics, probability, and matrix.

Next, let's embark on the journey of MindSpore.

(a) Download the MNIST Dataset.

The MNIST dataset used in this example consists of 10 classes of 28×28 pixels grayscale images. It has a training set of 60,000 examples, and a test set of 10,000 examples.

The download page of the MNIST provides four download links of dataset files. The first two links are required for data training, and the last two links are required for data test.

Download the files, decompress them, and store them in the workspace directory: ./MNIST_Data/train and ./MNIST_Data/test.

The directory structure is as follows:

```
└─MNIST_Data
 ├─test
 │   t10k-images.idx3-ubyte
 │   t10k-labels.idx1-ubyte
 └─train
     train-images.idx3-ubyte
     train-labels.idx1-ubyte
```

To facilitate the operation, we add the function of automatically downloading datasets in the sample script code.

(b) Import Python Libraries and Modules

Before the usage, import Python libraries.

Now the libraries are used. For better understanding, other required libraries will be introduced when we use them in practices.

import os

(c) Configure the Running Information

Before officially compiling the code, we need to know the basic information about the hardware and backend required for MindSpore at run-time.

We can use context.set_context to configure the information required at run-time, such as the running mode, backend information, and hardware information.

Import the context module and configure the required information. The codes are exemplified as follows.

```
import argparse
from MindSpore import context

if __name__ == "__main__":
    parser = argparse.ArgumentParser(description='MindSpore LeNet
Example')
    parser.add_argument('--device_target', type=str,
default="Ascend", choices=['Ascend', 'GPU', 'CPU'], help='device
where the code will be implemented (default: Ascend)')
    args = parser.parse_args()
    context.set_context(mode=context.GRAPH_MODE, device_target=args.
device_target, enable_ mem_reuse=False)
    ...
```

We use graph mode when deploy the above-mentioned example. You can configure hardware information according to the site requirements. For instance, if the code runs on the Ascend AI processor, then device_target chooses Ascend. This rule also applies to the code running on the CPU and GPU. For details about parameters, see context.set_context () interface for more details.

3. Processing Data

Datasets are important for training. A good dataset can effectively improve training accuracy and efficiency. Generally speaking, before loading a dataset, you need to perform some operations on the dataset.

Define the create_dataset() function to create a dataset. In this function, we need to define the data augmentation and processes to be performed.

(a) Define the dataset.
(b) Define parameters required for data augmentation and processing.
(c) Generate corresponding data augmentation according to the parameters.
(d) Use the map() mapping function to apply data processes to the dataset.
(e) Process the generated dataset.

The sample codes for processing the dataset are as follows:

```
import MindSpore.dataset as ds
import MindSpore.dataset.transforms.c_transforms as C
import MindSpore.dataset.transforms.vision.c_transforms as CV
from MindSpore.dataset.transforms.vision import Inter
from MindSpore.common import dtype as mstype

def create_dataset(data_path, batch_size=32, repeat_size=1,
        num_parallel_workers=1):
    """ create dataset for train or test
    Args:
```

```
    data_path: Data path
    batch_size: The number of data records in each group
    repeat_size: The number of replicated data records
    num_parallel_workers: The number of parallel workers
    """
    # define dataset
    mnist_ds = ds.MnistDataset(data_path)

    # define operation parameters
    resize_height, resize_width = 32, 32
    rescale = 1.0 / 255.0
    shift = 0.0
    rescale_nml = 1 / 0.3081
    shift_nml = -1 * 0.1307 / 0.3081

    # define map operations
    resize_op = CV.Resize((resize_height, resize_width),
interpolation=Inter.LINEAR) # resize images to (32, 32)
    rescale_nml_op = CV.Rescale(rescale_nml, shift_nml) # normalize
images
    rescale_op = CV.Rescale(rescale, shift) # rescale images
    hwc2chw_op = CV.HWC2CHW() # change shape from (height, width,
channel) to (channel, height, width) to fit network.
    type_cast_op = C.TypeCast(mstype.int32) # change data type of label
to int32 to fit network

    # apply map operations on images
    mnist_ds = mnist_ds.map(input_columns="label",
operations=type_cast_op, num_parallel_
workers=num_parallel_workers)
    mnist_ds = mnist_ds.map(input_columns="image",
operations=resize_op, num_parallel_ workers=num_parallel_workers)
    mnist_ds = mnist_ds.map(input_columns="image",
operations=rescale_op, num_parallel_ workers=num_parallel_workers)
    mnist_ds = mnist_ds.map(input_columns="image",
operations=rescale_nml_op, num_parallel_
workers=num_parallel_workers)
    mnist_ds = mnist_ds.map(input_columns="image",
operations=hwc2chw_op, num_parallel_ workers=num_parallel_workers)

    # apply DatasetOps
    buffer_size = 10000
    mnist_ds = mnist_ds.shuffle(buffer_size=buffer_size) # 10000 as in
LeNet train script
    mnist_ds = mnist_ds.batch(batch_size, drop_remainder=True)
    mnist_ds = mnist_ds.repeat(repeat_size)

    return mnist_ds
```

The notes for the codes are as follows.

Batch_size: the amount of data in each group. Currently, each group contains 32 data records.

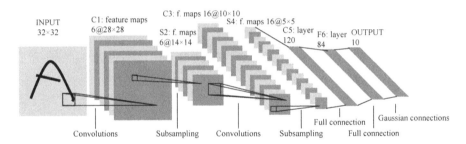

Fig. 5.14 LeNet-5 architecture

Repeat_size: the number of replicated datasets.

Firstly, implement the shuffle and batch operations, and then perform the repeat operation to ensure that data is nonrepetitive during one epoch.

MindSpore supports multiple data processing and augmentation operations, which are usually used in combination.

4. Defining the Network

Here we choose the relatively simple LeNet network. In addition to the input layer, the LeNet network has seven layers, including two convolutional layers, two down-sampling layers (pooling layers), and three full-connected layers. Each layer contains different numbers of training parameters, as shown in Fig. 5.14:

We need to initialize the full-connected layers and convolutional layers.

Mindspore supports multiple parameter initialization methods, such as TruncatedNormal, Normal, and Uniform. For details, see the illustration in the Mindspore.common.initializer module of the MindSpore API. This case uses the parameter initialization method TruncatedNormal.

Following are the sample codes exemplified for initializing the full-connected layers and convolutional layers:

```
import MindSpore.nn as nn
from MindSpore.common.initializer import TruncatedNormal

def weight_variable():
    """
    weight initial
    """
    return TruncatedNormal(0.02)

def conv(in_channels, out_channels, kernel_size, stride=1,
padding=0):
    """
    conv layer weight initial
    """
    weight = weight_variable()
    return nn.Conv2d(in_channels, out_channels, _size=kernel_size,
```

```
stride=stride, padding= padding weight_init=weight, has_bias=False,
pad_mode="valid")
  def fc_with_initialize(input_channels, out_channels):
    """
    fc layer weight initial
    """
    weight = weight_variable()
    bias = weight_variable()
    return nn.Dense(input_channels, out_channels, weight, bias)
```

To use MindSpore to define the neural network, inheriting MindSpore.nn.Cell is required. Cell is the base class of all neural networks (such as Conv2d).

Each layer of a neural network will need to be defined by the __init__ () method in advance, and then define the construct() method to complete the forward construction of the neural network. According to the structure of the LeNet network, define the network layers as follows:

5. Defining the Loss Function and Optimizer

(a) The concept of loss function and optimizer.

Loss function: Also known as objective function, loss function is used to measure the differences between the predicted value and the actual value. Deep learning reduces the value of the loss function by iteration. Defining a good loss function can effectively improve the model performance.

Optimizer: It is used to minimize the loss function so as to optimize the model during training.

After the loss function is defined, the weight-related gradient of the loss function can also be obtained. The gradient is used to indicate the weight optimization direction for the optimizer and improve the model performance.

(b) Defining the Loss Function

The loss functions supported by MindSpore include SoftmaxCrossEntropyWithLogits, L1Loss, MSELoss. The loss function SoftmaxCrossEntropyWithLogits is used in the following sample codes:

```
class LeNet5(nn.Cell):
    """
    Lenet network structure
    """
    #define the operator required
    def __init__(self):
        super(LeNet5, self).__init__()
        self.batch_size = 32
        self.conv1 = conv(1, 6, 5)
        self.conv2 = conv(6, 16, 5)
        self.fc1 = fc_with_initialize(16 * 5 * 5, 120)
        self.fc2 = fc_with_initialize(120, 84)
        self.fc3 = fc_with_initialize(84, 10)
        self.relu = nn.ReLU()
        self.max_pool2d = nn.MaxPool2d(kernel_size=2, stride=2)
        self.flatten = nn.Flatten()
```

```
#use the preceding operators to construct networks
def construct(self, x):
  x = self.conv1(x)
  x = self.relu(x)
  x = self.max_pool2d(x)
  x = self.conv2(x)
  x = self.relu(x)
  x = self.max_pool2d(x)
  x = self.flatten(x)
  x = self.fc1(x)
  x = self.relu(x)
  x = self.fc2(x)
  x = self.relu(x)
  x = self.fc3(x)
  return x
from MindSpore.nn.loss import SoftmaxCrossEntropyWithLogits
```

Call the defined loss funciton in __main__ function. The sample codes are as follows.

```
if __name__ == "__main__":
   ...
   #define the loss function
   net_loss = SoftmaxCrossEntropyWithLogits(is_grad=False,
sparse=True, reduction='mean')
   ...
```

(c) Defining the Optimizer

The optimizers supported by MindSpore include Adam, AdamWeightDecay and Momentum. The following sample codes are based on the Momentum optimizer, which is quite popular:

```
if __name__ == "__main__":
   ...
   #learning rate setting
   lr = 0.01
   momentum = 0.9
   #create the network
   network = LeNet5()
   #define the optimizer
   net_opt = nn.Momentum(network.trainable_params(), lr,
momentum)
   ...
```

6. Training the Network

(a) Save the Configured Model

MindSpore provides the callback mechanism to execute customized logic during training. Here we list ModelCheckpoint and LossMonitor provided by the framework as examples.

```
from MindSpore.train.callback import ModelCheckpoint,
CheckpointConfig

if __name__ == "__main__":
    ...
    # set parameters of check point
    config_ck = CheckpointConfig(save_checkpoint_steps=1875,
keep_checkpoint_max=10)
    # apply parameters of check point
    ckpoint_cb = ModelCheckpoint(prefix="checkpoint_lenet",
config=config_ck)
    ...
```

ModelCheckpoint can save network models and parameters for subsequent fine-tuning. And LossMonitor can monitor the changes of the loss value during training.

(b) Configure the Network Training

Through the model.train() API provided by MindSpore we can easily train the network. Here, we set epoch-size as 1 to train the dataset for 1 iteration.

```
from MindSpore.nn.metrics import Accuracy
from MindSpore.train.callback import LossMonitor
from MindSpore.train import Model
...
def train_net(args, model, epoch_size, mnist_path,
repeat_size, ckpoint_cb):
    """define the training method"""
    print("============== Starting Training ==============")
    #load training dataset
    ds_train = create_dataset(os.path.join(mnist_path, "train"),
32, repeat_size)
    model.train(epoch_size, ds_train, callbacks=[ckpoint_cb,
LossMonitor()], dataset_ sink_mode=False)
    ...

if __name__ == "__main__":
    ...
    epoch_size = 1
    mnist_path = "./MNIST_Data"
    repeat_size = epoch_size
    model = Model(network, net_loss, net_opt, metrics={"Accuracy":
Accuracy()})
    train_net(args, model, epoch_size, mnist_path, repeat_size,
ckpoint_cb)
    ...
```

Here in the train_net() method, we load the training dataset we downloaded before, and mnist_path is the MNIST dataset path.

7. Run and View the Result

Run the script code using the following command:

```
python lenet.py --device_target=CPU
```

Explanation is as follows.

lenet.py: the script file you wrote.

--device_target CPU: Specify the hardware platform. The parameters are 'CPU', 'GPU' or 'Ascend'.

Loss values are printed during training, as shown in the following figure. Although loss values may fluctuate, they would gradually decrease. Loss values for every running may be different because of their randomicity. The following is an example of loss values output during training.

```
epoch: 1 step: 262, loss is 1.9212162
epoch: 1 step: 263, loss is 1.8498616
epoch: 1 step: 264, loss is 1.7990671
epoch: 1 step: 265, loss is 1.9492403
epoch: 1 step: 266, loss is 2.0305142
epoch: 1 step: 267, loss is 2.0657792
epoch: 1 step: 268, loss is 1.9582214
epoch: 1 step: 269, loss is 0.9459006
epoch: 1 step: 270, loss is 0.8167224
epoch: 1 step: 271, loss is 0.7432692
. . .
```

The following is an example of model files saved after training, namely saving the model parameter files:

```
checkpoint_lenet-1_1875.ckpt
```

Explanation is as follows.

checkpoint_lenet-1_1875.ckpt: It refers to the saved model parameter file. The checkpoint_network means the name of network, epoch No. means the serial number of epoch, and .ckpt means the serial number of the step.

8. Validate the Model

After obtaining the model file, we verify the generalization ability of the model.

Use the model.eval() interface to load testing dataset.

Inference by using the saved model after training.

The sample codes are as follows:

```
from MindSpore.train.serialization import load_checkpoint,
load_param_into_net
    . . .
    def test_net(args,network,model,mnist_path):
      """"define the evaluation method"""
```

```
print ("=============== Starting Testing ==============")
#load the saved model for evaluation
param_dict = load_checkpoint ("checkpoint_lenet-1_1875.ckpt")
#load parameter to the network
load_param_into_net (network, param_dict)
#load testing dataset
ds_eval = create_dataset (os.path.join (mnist_path, "test"))
acc = model.eval (ds_eval, dataset_sink_mode=False)
print ("=========== Accuracy:{}=========".format (acc))

if __name__ == "__main__":
  ...
  test_net (args, network, model, mnist_path)
```

Explanation is as follows.

load_checkpoint(): This interface is used to load the CheckPoint model parameter file and return a parameter dictionary.

checkpoint_lenet-1_1875.ckpt: name of the saved CheckPoint model file.

load_param_into_net(): This interface is used to load parameters to the network.

Run the script code with the following command:

```
python lenet.py --device_target=CPU
```

An example of the result of running the verification model sample code is presented as follows:

```
============== Starting Testing ==============
========== Accuracy:{'Accuracy':0.9742588141025641} ==========
```

Here we can find that model accuracy is displayed in the output content. In the example, the accuracy reaches 97.4%, which indicates that the model quality is satisfactory.

5.3 Chapter Summary

This chapter mainly introduces the deep learning framework MindSpore independently developed by Huawei. It firstly presents the three technological innovation of MindSpore in design, namely, the new execution mode, new collaboration mode, and the advantages such as friendly development, efficient execution, and flexible deployment. At last the chapter briefs about the development and application of MindSpore, and uses an example of image classification to illustrate the development procedure of MindSpore.

As MindSpore is still undergoing a rapid version iteration, please refer to the latest official materials to learn the specific operations.

5.4   Exercises

1. MindSpore is an on-demand collaborative AI computing framework for all device-edge-cloud scenarios developed by Huawei. It provides a unified API for all scenarios, and provides device-to-device capability for model development, model operation and model deployment of all-scenario AI. What are the main features of the MindSpore architecture?
2. To tackle the challenges faced by AI developers including high entrance standards, high costs of operation and difficult deployment, MindSpore proposes three technological innovations so as to achieve easier and more efficient development and deployment of AI application. What are them?
3. The challenges of execution mode under super chip computing power: memory wall problem, high interaction overhead, difficult data supply, and the low occupancy rate of accelerator caused by the fact that the interaction overheads even surpasses the execution overhead as part of the operation is executed on host and part on device. What is the countermeasure offered by MindSpore?
4. Use MindSpore to perform MNIST handwritten digit recognition.

Chapter 6
Huawei Atlas AI Computing Solution

This chapter mainly introduces Huawei Ascend AI processor and Huawei Atlas AI computing solution, focusing on the hardware and software architecture of Ascend AI processor and Huawei's full-stack and all-scenario AI solution.

6.1 The Hardware Architecture of Ascend AI Processor

6.1.1 The Logic Architecture of Ascend AI Processor Hardware

The logic architecture of Ascend AI processor hardware is mainly composed of four modules, i.e., Control CPU, AI computing engine (including AI Core and AI CPU), multi-level system-on-chip cache or Buffer, Digital Vision Pre-Processing (DVPP), etc., as shown in Fig. 6.1. The following will focus on the AI Core of AI computing engine, namely, Da Vinci Architecture.

6.1.2 Da Vinci Architecture

Da Vinci Architecture, which is both the AI computing engine and the core of the Ascend AI processor, is specially developed to enhance AI computing power.

Da Vinci Architecture is mainly composed of three parts: computing unit, memory system and control unit.

1. The computing unit includes three basic computing resources: Cube Unit, Vector Unit and Scalar Unit.
2. The memory system includes AI Core's on-chip memory unit and the corresponding data path.

© The Author(s) 2023
Huawei Technologies Co., Ltd., *Artificial Intelligence Technology*,
https://doi.org/10.1007/978-981-19-2879-6_6

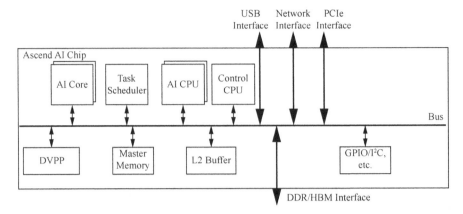

Fig. 6.1 The logic architecture of Ascend AI processor hardware

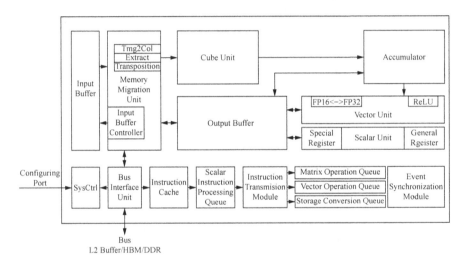

Fig. 6.2 Da Vinci Architecture

3. The control unit provides command control for the whole calculation process, which is equivalent to the headquarters of AI core and is responsible for the operation of the whole AI Core.

Da Vinci Architecture is shown in Fig. 6.2.

1. Computing Unit

There are three basic computing units in Da Vinci Architecture: Cube Unit, Vector Unit and Scalar Unit, which respectively correspond to the three common computing modes, namely, cube, vector and scalar, as shown in Fig. 6.3.

Cube Unit: The main function of Cube Unit and accumulator is to complete matrix correlation operations. One beat completes 16×16 and 16×16 matrix

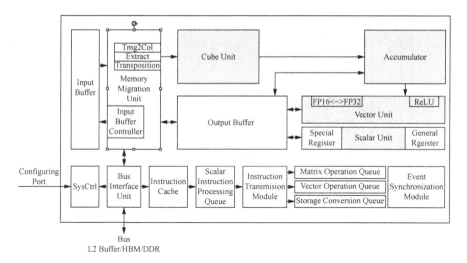

Fig. 6.3 Da Vinci Architecture—computing unit

multiplication (4096) of one FP16; if the input data belongs to Int 8 type, then one beat will complete 16×32 and 32×16 matrix multiplication (8192).

Vector Unit: It implements the calculation between vector and scalar, as well as dual vector. Its functions cover various basic calculation types and many customized calculation types, such as FP16, FP32, Int32, Int8 and other data types.

Scalar Unit: It is equivalent to a micro CPU, which controls the entire AI Core operation, completing the cycle control and branch judgment of the whole program, providing data address and related parameter calculation for matrix and vector, as well as basic arithmetic operation.

2. Memory System

Memory Unit and the corresponding data path constitute Memory System of Da Vinci Architecture, as shown in Fig. 6.4.

(a) Memory Unit is composed of memory control unit, buffer and register.

- Storage Control Unit: A direct access to lower-level caches in addition to AI Core can be achieved via bus interface. It can also directly access the memory through Double Data Rate Synchronous Dynamic Random Access Memory (SDRAM, DDR for short) or High Bandwidth Memory (HBM). The memory migration unit, which is responsible for the read-write management of the internal data of AI Core between different buffers, is also set as the transmission controller of the internal data path of AI Core, completing a series of format conversion operations, such as filling, Img2Col, transposition, extract, etc.
- Input Buffer: It is used to temporarily reserve the data that needs frequent use, which avoids external reading to AI Core via the bus interface every time. The frequency of data access on the bus is reduced as well as the risk

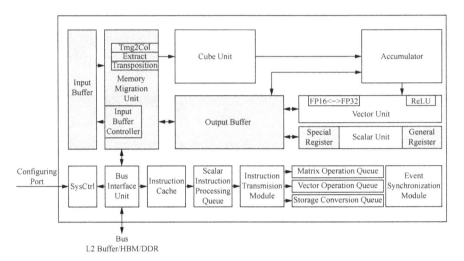

Fig. 6.4 Da Vinci Architecture—memory system

of data congestion on the bus, so as to minimize power dissipation and improve performance.

- Output Buffer: It is used to store the intermediate results of each calculation layer in the neural network, for obtaining data conveniently when entering the next layer. In contrast, the bandwidth of reading data through the bus is low and the delay is large, and the calculation efficiency can be greatly improved through the output buffer.
- Register: All kinds of register resources in AI Core are mainly used by scalar units.

(b) Data path refers to the flow path of data in AI Core when AI Core completes a computing task.

Da Vinci Architecture data path is characterized by multiple-input and single-output, which is mainly due to the various and numerous input data in the computing process of neural network. Parallel input can be used to promote the efficiency of data inflow. On the contrary, only the output characteristic matrix is generated after the procession of multiple input data, and the data type is relatively unitary. Therefore, single-output data path can save chip hardware resources.

3. Control Unit

The control unit is made up of system control module, command cache, scalar command processing queue, command transmission module, matrix execution queue and event synchronization module, as shown in Fig. 6.5.

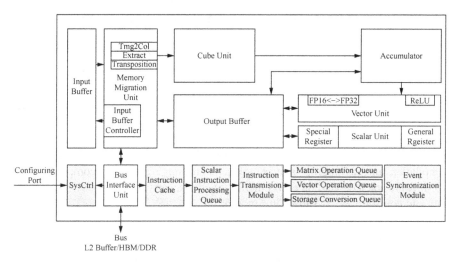

Fig. 6.5 Da Vinci Architecture—control unit

(a) System Control Module: It controls the execution process of task block (the minimum computing task granularity in AI Core). After the execution of task block, the system control module will interrupt processing and declare the state. If an error occurs in the execution process, the error status will be reported to Task Scheduler.

(b) Command Cache: In the process of command execution, subsequent commands can be prefetched in advance, and multiple commands can be read into the cache at one time to improve the efficiency of command execution.

(c) Scalar Command Processing Queue: After the command is decoded, it will be imported into scalar queue to realize address decoding and computing control. The commands include matrix computing command, vector computing command and memory conversion command.

(d) Command Transmission Module: It reads the command address and decoding parameters configured in the scalar command queue, and then send them to the corresponding command execution queue according to their command types, while the scalar command resides in the scalar command processing queue for subsequent execution.

(e) Command Execution Queue: It is composed of matrix queue, vector queue and memory conversion queue. Different commands enter different queues, and the commands in the queue are executed in the order of entry.

(f) Event Synchronization Module: It controls the executing state of each command pipeline at any time, analyzing the dependencies of different pipelines, so as to adjust the data dependence and synchronization between command pipelines.

6.2   The Software Architecture of Ascend AI Processor

6.2.1   The Logic Architecture of Ascend AI Processor Software

The software stack of Ascend AI processor is mainly divided into four levels and one auxiliary tool chain. The four layers are L3 application enabling layer, L2 execution framework layer, L1 chip enabling layer and L0 computing resource layer. The tool chain mainly provides auxiliary capabilities such as engineering management, compilation and debugging, matrix, log and profiling. The main components of the software stack depend on each other in functions, carrying data flow, calculation flow and control flow, as shown in Fig. 6.6.

1. L3 Application Enabling Layer

   L3 application enabling layer is application-level encapsulation, which provides different processing algorithms for specific applications, in addition to offering the engine of computing and processing for various fields. It can also directly use the framework scheduling capability provided by L2 execution framework layer, and generate the corresponding neural network through the general framework to realize specific engine functions.

   L3 application enabling layer includes computer vision engine, language engine, general business execution engine, etc.

   (a) Computer Vision Engine: It provides some video or image processing algorithms encapsulation, which is specialized to deal with algorithms and applications in the field of computer vision.

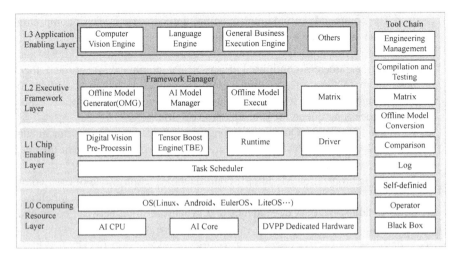

Fig. 6.6 The logic architecture of ascend AI processor software

(b) Language Engine: It provides some basic processing algorithm encapsulation for voice, text and other data, in which language processing can be carried out according to specific application scenarios.

(c) General Business Execution Engine: It provides general neural network reasoning ability.

2. L2 Executive Framework Layer

L2 executive framework layer is the encapsulation of framework calling ability and offline model generation capability. After the L3 application enabling layer develops the application algorithm and encapsulates it into an engine, the calls (such as Caffe or Tensorflow) suitable for deep learning framework will be made according to the characteristics of relevant algorithms, then the neural network with corresponding functions is obtained, and the offline model (OM) is generated by Framework Manager.

L2 executive framework layer contains the framework manager and the process choreographer.

(a) Framework Manager contains Offline Model Generator (OMG), Offline Model Executor (OME) and Offline Model Reasoning Interface, which supports model generation, loading, unloading and reasoning.

The online framework generally uses mainstream deep learning open source frameworks (such as Caffe, Tensorflow, etc.) to accelerate computations on Ascend AI processors through offline model transformation and loading.

While the offline framework refers to for Ascend AI processor, L2 executive framework layer provides offline generation and executive capability of neural network, which can be separated from deep learning open source framework (such as Caffe, TensorFlow, etc.) to enable offline model to have the same capability (mainly reasoning ability).

- Offline Model Generator is responsible for transforming the models trained by Caffe or TensorFlow into offline models supported by Ascend AI processor.
- Offline Model Executor is responsible for loading and unloading the off-line model, converting the successfully loaded model file into an executable instruction sequence on Ascend AI processor, and completing the program compilation before execution.

(b) Matrix: It provides developers with a development platform for deep learning computing, including computing resources, operating framework and related supporting tools, which allows developers to conveniently and efficiently write AI applications running on specific hardware devices, responsible for the generation, loading and scheduling of models.

After L2 executive framework layer transforms the original model of neural network into an offline model that can run on Ascend AI processor, Offline Model Executor transmits the offline model to L1 chip enabling layer for task allocation.

3. L1 Chip Enabling Layer

L1 chip enabling layer is the bridge between offline model and Ascend AI processor. After receiving the offline model generated by L2 execution framework layer, L1 chip enabling layer will provide acceleration function for offline model calculation through Acceleration Library based on different computing tasks.

L1 chip enabling layer is the layer closest to the underlying computing resources, responsible for dispatching operator-level tasks to hardware. It is mainly composed of Digital Vision Pre-Processing (DVPP), Tensor Boost Engine (TBE), Runtime, Driver and Task Scheduler.

In L1 chip enabling layer, TBE of the chip acts as the core, which supports online and offline model acceleration, including standard operator acceleration library and custom operator capabilities. The tensor acceleration engine includes the standard operator acceleration library, and these operators have good performance after optimization. The operator interacts with Runtime on the upper layer of the operator accelerator library in the executive process. At the same time, Runtime communicates with L2 executive framework layer, providing standard operator acceleration library interface to perform the calling, so that the specific network model can find the optimized, executable and accelerated operators for the optimal implementation of functions. If there is no operator needed by L2 executive framework layer in the standard operator acceleration Library of L1 chip enabling layer, new custom operators can be written by TBE to meet the needs of L2 executive framework layer. Therefore, TBE provides fully functional operators for L2 executive framework layer by offering standard operator library and the capability to customize operators.

Under TBE is Task Scheduler. After specific computing kernel function is generated based on the corresponding operator, Task Scheduler processes and distributes the corresponding computing kernel function to the AI CPU or AI Core according to specific task types, activating the hardware through the driver. Task Scheduler itself runs on a dedicated CPU core.

Digital Vision Pre-Processing (DVPP) module is a multi-functional capsule for the field of image and video. In the case of pre-processing common image or video scene, the module provides the upper layer with various data pre-processing capabilities by using the bottom dedicated hardware.

4. L0 Computing Resource Layer

L0 computing resource layer is the hardware computing power foundation for Ascend AI processor, which provides computing resources and performs specific computing tasks.

After L1 chip enabling layer completes the distribution of tasks corresponding to operators, the execution of specific computing tasks is started by L0 computing resource layer.

L0 computing resource layer is composed of operating system, AI CPU, AI Core and DVPP dedicated hardware modules.

AI Core is the computing core of Ascend AI processor, which mainly completes the matrix correlation calculation of neural network, while AI CPU performs the general calculation of control operator, scalar and vector. If the input data needs to be pre-processed, DVPP dedicated hardware modules will be activated to pre-process the image and video data, providing data formats to AI Core to meet the computing requirements in specific scenarios.

AI Core is mainly responsible for large computing tasks while AI CPU is mainly responsible for complex computing and executive control, and DVPP hardware is responsible for data pre-processing. The role of the operating system is to make the three closely assist each other and form a perfect hardware system, which provides executive guarantee for deep neural network computing of Ascend AI processor.

5. Tool Chain

Tool Chain, designed for the convenience of programmers is a set of tool platform supporting Ascend AI processor. It provides support for the development, debugging, network transplantation, optimization and analysis of custom operators. In addition, a set of desktop programming services is provided in the programmer-oriented programming interface, which lowered the barrier of entry for the development of deep neural network related applications.

It is composed of engineering management, compilation and testing, matrix, offline model conversion, comparison, log, profiling, custom operators, etc. Therefore, tool chain provides multi-level and multi-functional convenient services for application development and implementation on this platform.

6.2.2   The Neural Network Software Flow of Ascend AI Processor

The neural network software flow of Ascend AI Processor is a bridge between deep learning framework and Ascend AI processor, which provides a shortcut for neural network to transform from original model to intermediate computing graph representation, and then to independent offline model.

The neural network software flow of Ascend AI processor is mainly used to generate, load and execute an offline model of neural network application. The neural network software flow of Ascend AI processor gathers functional modules such as Matrix, DVPP module, Tensor Boost Engine, Framework, Runtime and Task Scheduler, thus forming a complete functional cluster.

The neural network software flow of Ascend AI processor is shown in Fig. 6.7.

1. Matrix: It is responsible for the landing and implementation of neural network on Ascend AI processor, coordinating the whole effective process of neural network, governing the loading and executive process of offline model.
2. DVPP Module: It conducts a data processing and modification prior to input to meet the needs of computing format.
3. Tensor Boost Engine: As an arsenal of neural network operators, it provides a steady stream of powerful computing operators for neural network models.

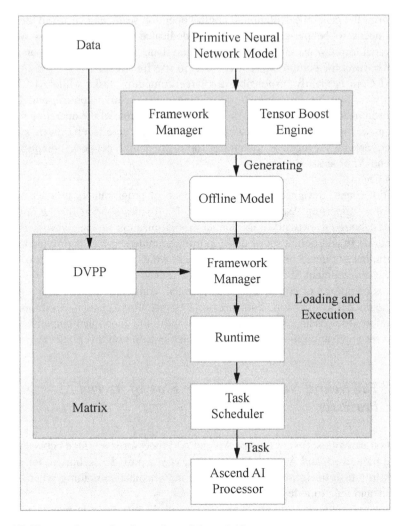

Fig. 6.7 The neural network software flow of Ascend AI processor

4. Framework: It builds the original neural network model into the form supported by Ascend AI processor, and the model is integrated with Ascend AI processor to guide the neural network to run and give full play to its performance.
5. Runtime: It provides various resource management channels for task distribution and allocation of neural network.
6. Task Scheduler: As a task driver of hardware execution, it provides specific target tasks for Ascend AI processor; Runtime and Task Scheduler interact together to form a dam system of neural network task flow system to hardware resources, real-time monitoring and effectively distributing different types of executive tasks.

The whole neural network software provides a fully functional executive process to Ascend AI processor that combines hardware and software, helping the development of related AI applications. The functional modules related to neural network will be introduced separately as follows.

6.2.3   Introduction to the Functional Modules of Ascend AI Processor Software Flow

1. Tensor Boost Engine

    In the construction of neural networks, operators constitute network structures with different application functions. As an arsenal of operators, Tensor Boost Engine (TBE) provides operator development capabilities for neural networks based on Ascend AI processor. The operators written in TBE language are used to construct various neural network models. At the same time, TBE also provides operators with the capabilities to wrap callings. TBE contains an optimized TBE standard operator library of neural network, which can be directly utilized by developers to achieve high-performance of neural network computing. In addition, TBE also provides the fusion capability of TBE operators, opening up a unique path for neural network optimization.

    TBE provides the capability to develop custom operators based on Tensor Virtual Machine (TVM). Users can complete the development of corresponding neural network operators through TBE language and custom operator programming development interface. TBE includes Domain-Specific-language (DSL) Module, Schedule Module, Intermediate Representation (IR) Module, Compiler Transfer Module and CodeGen Module. The structure of TBE is shown in Fig. 6.8.

    TBE operator development is divided into computational logic writing and scheduling development. DSL Module provides the programming interface of operator computational logic, directly based on the calculation process and scheduling process of operators based on domain specific language. The calculation process of operators describes the calculation methods and steps of operators, while the scheduling process describes the plan of data segmentation and data flow. Each operator calculation is processed according to the fixed data shape, which requires data shape segmentation in advance, for the operators executed on different computing units in Ascend AI processor, such as Matrix Unit, Vector Unit and the operators executed on AI CPU, have different requirements for input data shape.

    After the basic implementation process of the operator is defined, it is necessary to start Tiling Sub Module of Scheduling Module, segment the data in the operator according to the scheduling description, and specify the data handling process to ensure the optimal execution on the hardware. In addition to data shape

Fig. 6.8 The structure
of TBE

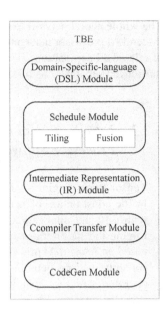

segmentation, the operator fusion and optimization capability of TBE is also provided by Fusion Sub Module of Scheduling Module.

After the operator is written, the intermediate representation needs to be generated for further optimization, and IR Module generates the intermediate representation through IR format similar to TVM. After the intermediate representation is generated, the module needs to be compiled and optimized for various application scenarios, with various optimization methods such as Double Buffer, Pipeline Synchronization, Memory Allocation Management, Command Mapping, Tiling Adapter Cube Unit, etc.

After the operator is processed by Compiler Transfer Module, a temporary file of C-like code is generated by CodeGen Module. The temporary code file can be transferred into an operator implementation file by the compiler, which can be directly loaded and executed via Offline Model Executor.

To sum up, a complete user-defined operator completes the whole development process through sub modules of TBE. After the operator prototype is formed by the operator calculation logic and scheduling description provided by the domain specific language module, the scheduling module performs data segmentation and operator fusion, entering the intermediate representation module to generate the intermediate representation of the operator. The compiler transfer module uses the intermediate representation to optimize the memory allocation. Finally, the code generation module generates C-like code for the compiler to compile directly. In the process of operator definition, TBE not only completes the compilation of operators, but also completes related optimization, which boosts the performance of operators.

The three application scenarios of TBE are shown in Fig. 6.9.

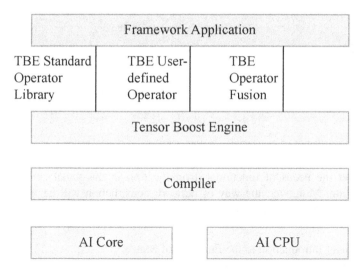

Fig. 6.9 The three application scenarios of TBE

(a) Generally, the neural network model implemented by standard operators in deep learning framework has been trained by GPU or other types of neural network processors. If the neural network model continues to run on Ascend AI processor, it is anticipated to maximize its performance without changing the original code. Therefore, TBE provides a complete set of TBE operator boosting library. The operator functions in the library keep a one-to-one correspondence with the common standard operators in neural network, and the software stack provides a programming interface for calling operators, boosting various frameworks or applications in the upper-level deep learning, refraining from the development of Ascend AI processor underlying adaptation code.

(b) If new operators appear in the neural network model construction, the standard operator library provided by TBE will not meet the development requirements. At this time, it is necessary to develop custom operators through TBE language, which is similar to CUDA C++ on GPU. More versatile operators can be realized and various network models can be flexibly programmed. The completed operators will be transferred to the compiler for compilation, and the final execution takes advantage of the chip acceleration capabilities on AI Core or AI CPU.

(c) In appropriate scenarios, the operator fusion capability provided by TBE can promote the performance of the operator, so that the neural network operator can perform multi-level cache fusion based on buffers of different levels. Ascend AI processor can significantly improve the resource utilization rate when performing the fused operator.

To sum up, because of the capabilities of operator development, standard operator calling and operator fusion optimization provided by TBE, Ascend AI processor

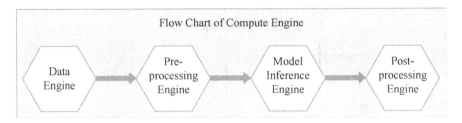

Fig. 6.10 Flow chart of compute engine in deep neural network application

can meet the needs of functional diversification in the actual neural network application. Moreover, the way of network construction will be more flexible and the fusion optimization capability will lead to a better performance.

2. Matrix

(a) A Brief Introduction to the Function of Matrix.

Ascend AI processor divides the execution level of network, regarding the execution of specific functions as a basic execution unit—Compute Engine. Each compute engine completes the basic operation function of the data in process arrangement, such as the image classification and so on. Compute Engine is customized by the developer to complete the required specific functions.

Through the unified call of Matrix, the whole deep neural network application generally includes four engines: Data Engine, Pre-processing Engine, Model Inference Engine and Post-processing Engine, as shown in Fig. 6.10.

- Data Engine mainly prepares the data set required by the neural network (such as MNIST data set) and processes the corresponding data (such as image filtering, etc.) as the data source of the subsequent compute engine.
- Generally, the input media data needs to go through format pre-processing to meet the computing requirements of Ascend AI processor. Pre-processing Engine is mainly used to pre-process the media data, complete the encoding and decoding of images and videos, format conversion and other operations, and each function module of digital vision pre-processing needs to be called through Matrix uniformly.
- Model Inference Engine is used in the neural network inference of data stream. It mainly uses the loaded model and the input data stream to complete the forward algorithm of neural network.
- After Model Reasoning Engine outputs the results, Post-processing Engine performs subsequent processing on the output data, such as framing and labeling of image recognition.

Figure 6.10 shows a typical flow chart of Compute Engine. Each specific data processing node in the flow chart of compute engine is the compute engine. When data flows through each engine according to the arranged path, related processing and calculation are respectively carried out, and the required results are finally output. The final output of the whole flow chart is the corresponding result of the calculation output of the neural network. The connection between two adjacent compute engine nodes is established through the configuration file in the flow chart of compute engine, and the actual data flow between nodes will flow according to the node connection mode of specific network model. After the configurations of node attributes are completed, the whole running process of the compute engine is initiated by pouring data into the starting node of the compute engine flow chart.

Matrix runs above L1 chip enabling layer and below L3 application enabling layer, providing a unified standardized intermediate interface for a variety of operating systems (Linux, Android, etc.), which is responsible for the establishment, destruction and recycling of the whole compute engine flow chart.

In the process of establishing the flow chart of the computing engine, Matrix completes the establishment of the flow chart of the compute engine according to the configuration file of the compute engine. Prior to execution, Matrix provides input data. If the input data such as video, image and other formats that can not meet the requirements of processing, the corresponding programming interface can be used to call the digital vision pre-processing module for data pre-processing. If the data meets the processing requirements, Offline Model Executor is directly called through the interface for reasoning calculation. In the process of execution, Matrix has the functions of multi-node scheduling and multi-process management, which is responsible for the operation of the computing process on the device side, guarding the computing process, and collecting the relevant execution information. After the execution of the model, Matrix will provide the application on the host with the function of obtaining the output results.

(b) Application Scenarios of Matrix.

As Ascend AI processor is targeted at different business needs, different hardware platforms can be built with different specificity. Depending on the collaboration of specific hardware and host side, the application of Matrix is used differently in typical scenarios such as Accelerator and Atlas 200 DK.

- Accelerator Form of Application Scenario

PCIe Accelerator based on Ascend AI processor is mainly oriented to data center and edge server scenarios, as shown in Fig. 6.11.

PCIe Accelerator supports a variety of data accuracy, which has improved its performance compared with other similar accelerators, providing a greater computing power for neural network computing. In the scenario of accelerator, a host is required to be connected with the accelerator. The host can support various servers of PCIe plug-in cards and personal computers, performing the corresponding processing by call the neural network computing power of the accelerator.

Fig. 6.11 PCIe accelerator

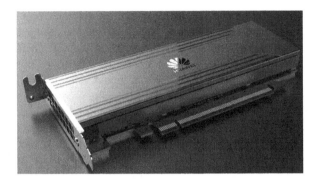

The function of Matrix in accelerator scenario is realized by three sub-processes: Matrix Agent, Matrix Daemon and Matrix service.

Matrix Agent usually runs on the host. It can control and manage Data Engine and Post-processing Engine, complete with the data interaction with the host application, control the application, and communicate with the processing process on the device side.

Matrix Daemon runs on the device side. It can complete the process establishment on the device according to the configuration file. It is responsible for starting and managing the process choreography process on the device, as well as the dissolution of the calculation process and resource recycle after the calculation is completed.

Matrix Service runs on the device side. It controls Pre-processing Engine and Model Reasoning Engine on the device side. It can control Pre-processing Engine to call the programming interface of Digital Vision Pre-Processing Module to realize the pre-processing function of video and image data. It can also call the model manager programming interface in Offline Model Executor to load and reason the offline model.

The offline model of neural network is reasoned through Matrix, and the computing process is shown in Fig. 6.12.

The off-line model of neural network can be divided into the following three steps.

Step 1: The flow chart to create compute engine. Through Matrix, the execution process of neural network is arranged by using different compute engines.

Step 2: The flow chart to perform compute engine. According to the defined compute engine flow chart, the neural network function is calculated and implemented.

After the offline model is loaded, the application notifies Matrix Agents on the host side to input the application data. The application program directly sends the data to the data engine for corresponding processing. If the incoming media data does not meet the computing requirements of Ascend AI processor, the pre-processing engine will start immediately and call the interface of DVPP module to pre-process the media data, such as

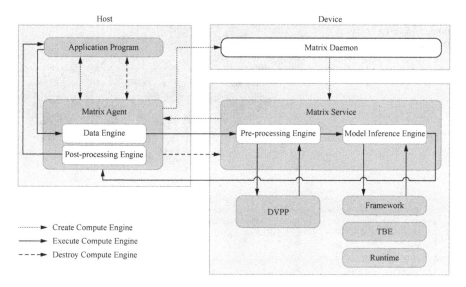

Fig. 6.12 The computing process of the offline model reasoned through matrix

encoding, decoding, scaling, etc. After pre-processing, the data is returned to the pre-processing engine, through which the data is transmitted to the model inference engine. At the same time, the model inference engine calls the processing interface of the model manager to complete the inferential calculation by combining the data with the loaded offline model. After the output results are obtained, the model inference engine calls the sending data interface of the process choreography unit to return the inferential results to the post-processing engine, which completes the post-processing operation of the data, and finally returns the post-processing data to the application program through the process choreographer unit. Thus, the execution calculation engine flow chart is completed.

Step 3: The flow chart to destroy compute engine. After all calculations are completed, the system resources occupied by the compute engine are released.

After all the engine data are processed and returned, the application program notifies Matrix Agent to release the data engine and post-processing engine computing hardware resources, while Matrix Agents notify Matrix Service to release the resources of the pre-processing engine and model inference engine. After all the resources are released, the flow-chart of the compute engine is destroyed, and then Matrix Agents notify the application to implement the next neural network.

- Atlas 200 DK Application Scenario

    Atlas 200 DK Application Scenario refers to Atlas 200 Developer Kit (Atlas 200 DK) scenario based on Ascend AI processor, as shown in Fig. 6.13.

Fig. 6.13 Atlas
200 developer kit (Atlas
200 DK)

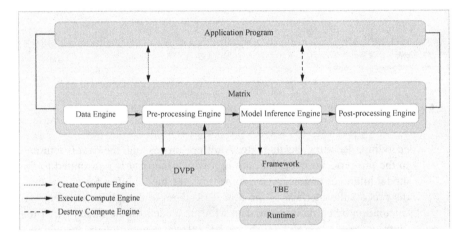

Fig. 6.14 Logical architecture of Atlas 200 Developer Kit

Atlas 200 DK opens up the core functions of Ascend AI processor through the peripheral interface on the developer board, which facilitates the direct external control and development of the chip, enabling the neural network processing ability of Ascend AI processor to be easily and intuitively played. Therefore, Atlas 200 DK, based on Ascend AI processor, can be used in a wide range of different artificial intelligence fields, which will be the backbone of mobile terminal hardware in the future.

For Atlas 200 DK Application Scenario, the host control function is also on the developer board, and its logical architecture is shown in Fig. 6.14.

As the function interface of Ascend AI processor, Matrix can complete the data interaction between the flow chart of the computing engine and the application program. According to the configuration file, Matrix establishes the flow chart of the computing engine, which is responsible for the scheduling, controlling and managing of the process. After the calculation, it also destroys the flow chart of the computing engine and recycles the resources after the calculation. In the process of pre-processing, Matrix calls the interface of pre-processing engine to realize the function of media pre-processing. In the process of inference, Matrix can also call the programming interface of the model manager to realize the offline model loading and inference. In Atlas 200 DK Application Scenario, Matrix coordinates the implementation of the whole computing engine flow chart without interacting with other devices.

3. Task Scheduler

Together with Runtime, Task Scheduler (TS) forms the dam system between hardware and software. During execution, Task Scheduler drives the hardware tasks, providing specific target tasks for Ascend AI processor, completing the task scheduling process with Runtime, and sending the output data back to Runtime which acts as a channel for task delivery and data return.

(a) Introduction to the Function of Task Scheduler

Task Scheduler runs on the task scheduling CPU on the device side and is responsible for further dispatching specific tasks distributed by Runtime to AI CPU. It can also assign tasks to AI Core for execution through hardware Block Scheduler (BS), and return the results of task execution to Runtime after execution. Generally, the main tasks of Task Scheduler includes AI Core task, AI CPU task, Memory Replication, Event Recording, Event Waiting, Maintenance and Profiling.

Memory Replication is mainly carried out asynchronously. Event Recording mainly records the occurrence information of the event. If there are tasks waiting for the event, these tasks can release the waiting and continue to execute after the event recording is completed, so as to eliminate the blocking of the execution flow caused by the event recording. Event Waiting means that if the waiting event has already occurred, the waiting task will be completed directly; if the waiting event has not yet occurred, the waiting task will be filled in the waiting list, and the processing of all subsequent tasks in the execution flow where the waiting event is located will be suspended. When the waiting event occurs, the processing of the waiting event will be executed.

After the task is completed, Maintenance performs the corresponding maintenance according to different task parameters and recover the computing resources. In the process of execution, it is also possible to record and analyze the performance of the calculation, which requires Profiling to control the start and pause of the profiling operation.

The functional framework of Task Scheduler is shown in Fig. 6.15. Task Scheduler is usually located on the device side, with its function completed by task scheduling CPU. Task scheduling CPU is composed of Interface, Engine, Logic Processing, AI CPU Scheduler, Block Scheduler, SysCtrl, Profile and Log.

Task scheduling CPU realizes the communication and interaction between Runtime and Driver through scheduling interface. The task is transmitted to

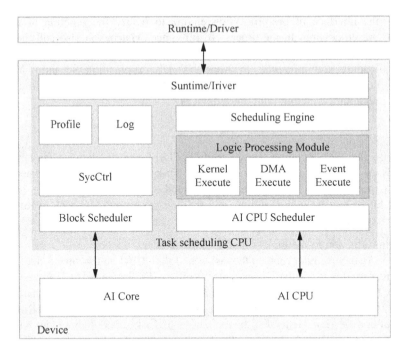

Fig. 6.15 The functional framework of Task Scheduler

the task scheduling engine through the results. As the main body of task scheduling, the task scheduling engine is responsible for the process of task organization, task dependence and task scheduling control, and managing the execution process of the whole task scheduling CPU. According to the specific types of tasks, the task scheduling engine divides the tasks into three types: calculation, storage and control, which are distributed to different scheduling logic processing modules to start the management and scheduling of specific kernel function tasks, memory tasks and event dependencies between execution flows.

The logic processing module is divided into Kernel Execute, DMA Execute and Event Execute. Kernel Execute carries out scheduling processing of computing tasks and realizes the scheduling logic of tasks on AI CPU and AI Core, scheduling specific kernel functions. DMA Execute implements the scheduling logic of storage tasks, and dispatches tasks such as memory replication and other tasks. Event Execute is responsible for the scheduling logic of synchronous control tasks and the logical processing of event dependencies between execution flows. After completing the scheduling logic processing of different types of tasks, it starts to be directly handed over to the corresponding control unit for hardware execution.

For the task execution of AI CPU, AI CPU scheduler in the task scheduling CPU conducts state management and task scheduling of AI CPU by software. For the task execution of AI Core, the task scheduling CPU distributes the processed tasks to AI Core through a separate block scheduler hardware, and the specific calculation is carried out by AI Core. The calculated results are also returned to the task scheduling CPU by the block scheduler.

In the process of task scheduling CPU, SysCtrl configures the system and initializes the chip function. At the same time, Profile and Log monitor the whole execution process and record the key execution parameters and specific execution details. At the end of the whole execution process or when an error is reported, specific performance profiling or error location can be carried out, providing a basis for the subsequent evaluation of implementation accuracy and efficiency.

(b) The Scheduling Process of Task Scheduler.

In the process of neural network's offline model execution, Task Scheduler receives specific tasks from Offline Model Executor. There are dependencies among these tasks, which need to be removed first, followed by task scheduling and other steps, and finally distributed to AI Core or AI CPU according to the specific task type to complete the calculation or execution of specific hardware. In the process of task scheduling, a task is composed of multiple commands (CMD). Task Scheduler and Runtime interact with each other to complete the orderly scheduling of the whole task command. Runtime runs on the CPU of the host, as command queue is located in the memory of the device, and Task Scheduler issues specific commands.

The detailed flow of task scheduler's scheduling process is shown in Fig. 6.16.

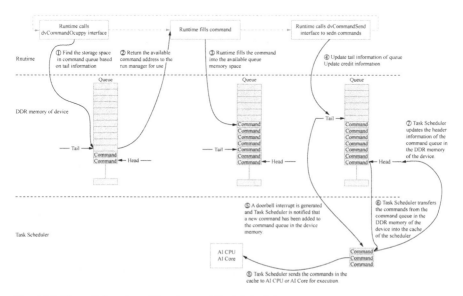

Fig. 6.16 The collaboration of Runtime and Task Scheduler

First, Runtime calls the driver's dvCommandOcuppy interface to enter the command queue, querying the available memory space in the command queue according to the tail information of the command, and returning the address of the available memory space to Runtime. After receiving the address, Runtime fills the prepared command into the command queue memory space, and calls the driver's dvCommandSend interface to update the current Tail information and Credit information of the command queue. After the queue receives a new command, a doorbell interrupt is generated and Task Scheduler is notified that a new command has been added to the command queue in the device memory. After Task Scheduler gets the notification, it enters the device memory, transferring the commands into the cache of the scheduler, and updating the header information of the command queue in the DDR memory of the device. Finally, Task Scheduler sends the commands in the cache to AI CPU or AI Core for execution.

Similiar to the architecture of software stack in most accelerators, Runtime, Driver and Task Scheduler in Ascend AI processor cooperate closely to complete tasks orderly and distribute tasks to corresponding hardware resources for execution. The scheduling process provides the deep neural network computing process with a tight and orderly delivery of tasks, which ensures the continuity and efficiency of task execution.

4. Runtime

The context of Runtime in the software stack is shown in Fig. 6.17. The upper layer of Runtime is TBE standard operator library and Offline Model Executor. TBE standard operator library provides neural network operators for Ascend AI processor, and Offline Model Executor is specially used to load and execute

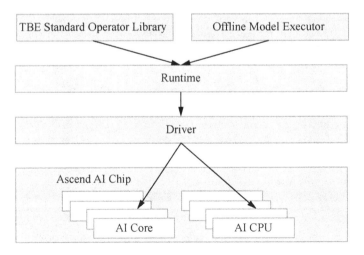

Fig. 6.17 The context of Runtime

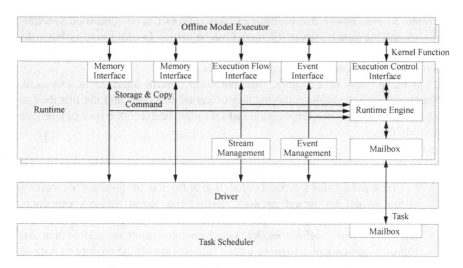

Fig. 6.18 Various calling interface provided by Runtime

offline model. The lower layer of Runtime is driver, which interacts with Ascend AI processor.

Runtime provides various call interfaces, such as memory interface, device interface, execution flow interface, event interface and execution control interface. Different interfaces are controlled by Runtime Engine to complete different functions, as shown in Fig. 6.18.

Memory interface provides the application, release and replication of High Bandwidth Memory (HBM) or Double Data Rate (DDR) Memory on the device, including device-to-host, from host-to-device, and from device-to-device data replication. These memory replication can be divided into synchronous and asynchronous modes. Synchronous replication means that memory replication is completed before the next operation is performed, while asynchronous replication means that other operations can be performed at the same time.

The device interface provides the query of the number and properties of the underlying devices, as well as the operation of selection and reset. After the offline model calls the device interface and selects a feature device, all tasks in the model will be executed on the selected device. If the task needs to be sent to other devices during the execution, the device interface needs to be called again for device selection.

The execution flow interface provides the creation, release, priority definition, callback function setting, event dependency definition and synchronization of execution flow. These functions are related to the task execution within the execution flow, and the tasks within a single execution flow must be executed in sequence.

If multiple execution flows need to be synchronized, the event interface needs to be called to create, release, record and define dependencies of synchronous events, so as to ensure that multiple execution flows can be completed synchronously and the final results of the model can be output. In addition to assign tasks or dependencies between execution flows, the event interface can also be used as a time mark to record the execution sequence.

In the process of execution, the execution control interface is also used. Runtime Engine completes the loading of kernel functions and the distribution of memory asynchronous replication tasks through the execution control interface and Mailbox.

5. Framework

(a) The Functional Outline of Framework

Framework works with Tensor Boost Engine to generate executable offline model for neural network. Before the neural network execution, Framework is tightly bounded with Ascend AI processor to generate a high-performance offline model with hardware matching, and Matrix and Runtime are connected to make a deep fusion of the offline model and Ascend AI processor. In the execution of the neural network, Framework combines Matrix, Runtime, Task Scheduler and the underlying hardware resources, with the integration of the offline model, data and Da Vinci Architecture, to optimize the execution process and obtain the application output of the neural network.

Framework consists of three parts: Offline Model Generator (OMG), Offline Model Executor (OME) and AI Model Manager, as shown in Fig. 6.19.

Developers use Offline Model Generator to generate the offline model and save it with a ". om" extension. Then, Matrix in the software stack calls AI

Fig. 6.19 Offline model functional framework

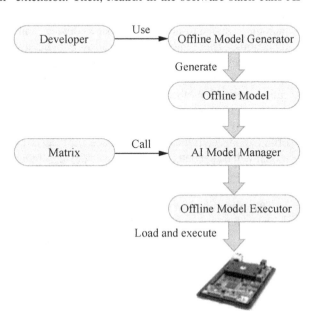

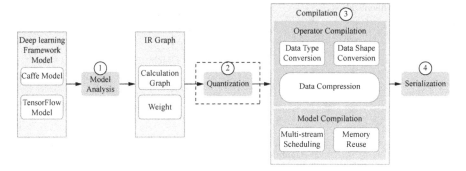

Fig. 6.20 The working principle of offline model generator

Model Manager in Framework, starts Offline Model Executor, loads the offline model onto Ascend AI processor, and finally completes the execution of the offline model through the whole software stack. From the birth of offline model, to the loading into the hardware of Ascend AI processor, until the final function runs, Offline Framework always plays an administrative role.

(b) The Offline Model Generated by Offline Model Generator

Taking Convolutional Neural Network (CNN) as an example, the corresponding network model is constructed under the deep learning framework, and the original data is well trained. Then Offline Model Generator is used to conduct operator scheduling optimization, weight data rearrangement and compression, memory optimization, etc., and finally the optimized offline model is generated. Offline Model Generator is mainly used to generate offline models that can be executed efficiently on Ascend AI processor.

The working principle of Offline Model Generator is shown in Fig. 6.20. After receiving the original model, Offline Model Generator conduct the process of Convolutional Neural Network model in four steps: model analysis, quantization, compilation and serialization.

• Model Analysis: In the process of analysis, Offline Model Generator supports the analysis of the original network model under different frameworks, extracts the network structure and weight parameters of the original model, and then the network structure is redefined by the unified intermediate graph (IR graph) through the graph representation. IR graph is composed of computing nodes and data nodes. The computing nodes are composed of TBE operators with different functions, while the data nodes receive different tensor data to provide all kinds of input data for the whole network. IR graph is composed of calculation graph and weight, covering all the information of the original model. IR graph builds a bridge between different deep learning frameworks and the software stack of Ascend AI, which makes the neural network model constructed by the external

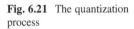

Fig. 6.21 The quantization
process

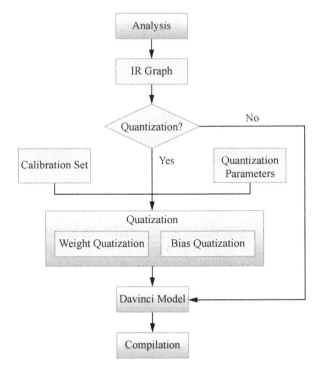

framework easily transformed into the offline model supported by Ascend
AI processor.

- Quantization: Quantization refers to low-bit quantization of high-precision
  data, so as to save network memory space, reduce transmission delay and
  improve operation efficiency. The quantization process is shown in
  Fig. 6.21.

  IR graph is generated when the analysis is completed. If the model still
  needs to be quantified, it can be quantified by automatic quantization tools
  based on the structure and weight of IR graph. In the operator, the weights
  and biases can be quantized. In the offline model generation process, the
  quantized weights and biases will be saved in the offline model. In the
  reasoning calculation, the quantized weights and biases can be used to
  calculate the input data, and the calibration set is used to train the quantization parameters in the quantization process to ensure the accuracy. If
  quantization is not needed, the offline model is compiled directly.

  Quantization is divided into two types, i.e., offset quantization and
  non-offset quantization, which need to output two parameters: Scale and
  Offset. In the process of data quantization, when the quantization method is
  specified as non-offset quantization, the data adopts the non-offset quantization to calculate the Scale of the quantized data; if the quantization
  method is specified as data offset quantization, the data adopts offset

quantization to calculate the Scale and Offset of the output data. In the process of weight quantization, due to the high accuracy of weight quantization, non-offset quantization is always used. For example, according to the quantization algorithm, INT8 type quantization of the weight file can output INT8 weight and Scale. In the process of offset quantization, according to the Scale of weight and date, the offset data of FP32 type can be quantized into INT32 type data output.

When there are higher requirements for model size and performance, one can choose to perform quantization operation. In the process of offline model generation, quantization will convert high-precision data to low-bit data, so that the final offline model is lightweight for the sake of saving network memory space, minimizing transmission delay and improving operation efficiency. In the process of quantization, the model storage size is greatly affected by parameters, so Offline Model Generator focuses on the quantization with parameters such as convolution operator, full connected operator and Convolution Depthwise.

• Compilation: After model quantization, the model needs to be compiled. The compilation is divided into two parts: operator compilation and model compilation. The operator compilation provides the specific implementation of the operator, and the model compilation aggregates the operator models to generate the offline model structure.

  – Operator Compilation: Operator Compilation is used to generate operators, mainly to generate operator specific offline structures. Operator Generation is divided into three processes: input tensor description, weight data conversion and output tensor description. In the process of input tensor description, the input dimension, memory size and other information of each operator are calculated, and the input data form of the operator is defined in Offline Model Generator. In the weight data conversion, the weight parameters used by the operator are processed by data format (such as FP32 to FP16 conversion), shape conversion (such as fractal rearrangement), data compression and so on. In output tensor description, the output dimension, memory size and other information of the operator are calculated.

    The process of operator generation is shown in Fig. 6.22. In the process of operator generation, the shape of output data needs to be analyzed, determined and described through the interface of TBE operator accelerator library. The data format conversion can also be realized through the interface of TBE operator acceleration library.

    Offline Model Generator receives IR graph generated by the neural network and describes each node in IR graph, analyzing the input and output of each operator one by one. Offline Model Generator analyzes the input data source of the current operator to obtain the operator types directly connected with the current operator in the upper layer, entering the operator library through the interface of TBE operator acceleration

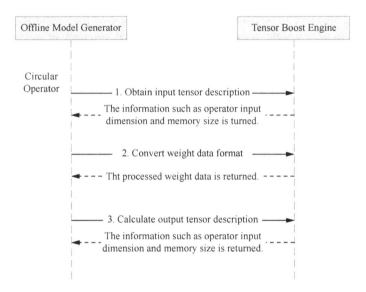

Fig. 6.22 The process of operator generation

library to find the output data description of the source operator. And then the output data information of the source operator is returned to Offline Model Generator as the specific input tensor description of the current operator. Therefore, the description of the input data of the current operator can be obtained by acquaintance of the output information of the source operator.

If the node in IR graph is not an operator but a data node, the input tensor description is not needed. If the operator has weight data, such as convolution operator and full connected operator, the description and processing of weight data are required. If the input weight data type is FP32, it needs to be converted to FP16 type by Offline Model Generator so as to meet the data type requirements of AI Core. After the type conversion, Offline Model Generator calls the ccTransFilter interface to rearrange the weight data, so that the weight input shape can meet the format requirements of AI Core. After obtaining the fixed format weights, Offline Model Generator calls the ccCompressWeight interface provided by TBE to compress and optimize the weights, so as to reduce the weight memory space and make the model lighter. After the weight data conversion is completed, the weight data meeting the calculation requirements is returned to Offline Model Generator.

After the weight data conversion is completed, Offline Model Generator also needs to describe the output data information of the operator and determine the output tensor form. For high-level complex operators, such as convolution operator and pooling operator, Offline Model Generator can directly obtain the output tensor information of the operator by combining the input tensor information and weight information of the operator through the calculation interface provided by TBE operator acceleration library. If it is a low-level simple operator, such as addition operator, the output tensor information can be directly determined by the input tensor information of the operator, and finally stored in Offline Model Generator. According to the above operation process, Offline Model Generator traverses all operators in IR Graph of the network, the steps of generating operators are executed in a circular way. Input-output tensors and weight data of all operators are described to complete the offline structure representation of operators, which provides the operator model for the next step of model generation.

– Model Compilation: After the operator generation is completed in the compilation process, Offline Model Generator also needs to generate the model to obtain the offline structure of the model. Offline Model Generator acquires IR Graph, conducts concurrent scheduling analysis on the operator, splits multiple IR Graph nodes into execution flows, obtaining multiple execution flows composed of operators and data input, which can be regarded as the execution sequence of operators. For nodes without interdependence, they are directly allocated to different execution flows. If the nodes in different execution flows have dependencies, the synchronization between multiple execution flows is carried out through rtEvent synchronization interface. In the case of surplus computing resources in AI Core, multi-execution flow splitting can provide multi-stream scheduling for AI Core, so as to improve the computing performance of network model. However, if there are many parallel processing tasks in AI Core, it will aggravate the degree of resource preemption and worsen the execution performance. By default, single execution flow is adopted to process the network, which can prevent the risk of blocking due to the concurrent execution of multiple tasks.

At the same time, based on the specific execution relationship of the execution sequence of multiple operators, Offline Model Generator can independently perform operator fusion optimization and memory multiplexing optimization. According to the input and output memory information of the operator, the computational memory multiplexing is carried out, and the related multiplexing information is written into the model and operator description to generate an efficient offline model. The optimization operations can reallocate the computing resources during the execution of multiple operators to minimize the memory occupation. At the same time, frequent memory allocation and release can also be avoided during operation, so that the execution of multiple operators with minimum memory usage and the lowest data migration frequency is implemented, with a better performance and a lower demand for hardware resources.

- Serialization: The complied offline model is stored in memory and needs to be serialized. The serialization process mainly provides the signature and encryption functions to the model files to further encapsulate and protect the integrity of the offline model. After the serialization process is completed, the offline model can be output from memory to an external file that can be called and executed by a remote Ascend AI processor chip.

6. Digital Vision Pre-processing

Digital Vision Pre-processing (DVPP) module, as the codec and image conversion module in Ascend AI software stack, plays the auxiliary function of pre-processing for neural network. When the video or image data from the system memory and network enter into the computing resources of Ascend AI processor for calculation, DVPP module needs to be called for format conversion prior to the subsequent neural network processing if the data does not meet the input format, resolution and other requirements specified by Da Vinci Architecture.

(a) The Function Architecture of DVPP

There are six modules for DVPP, i.e., Video Decoding (VDEC), Video Encoding (VENC), JPEG Decoding (JPEGD), JPEG Encoding (JPEG), PNG Decoding (PNGD) and Visual Pre-processing Core (VPC).

- VDEC provides the video decoding function of H.264/H.265, which can decode the input video stream and output the image. It is often used in the pre-processing of scenes such as video recognition.
- VNEC provides the output video coding function. For the output data of VPC or the original input YUV format data, VNEC can output the encoding into H.264/H.265 video, which is easy to play and display the video directly.
- JPEG can decode the JPEG format image, convert the original input JPEG image into YUV data, and pre-process the reasoning input data of neural network.
- After the completion of JPEG image processing, it is necessary to use JPEG to restore the processed data in JPEG format. JPEG Module is mostly used for neural network inference output data post-processing.
- When the input picture format is PNG, PNGD needs to be called to decode, for PNGD Module can output the PNG picture in RGB format for reasoning and calculation by Ascend AI processor.
- VPC provides other functions of image and video processing, such as format conversion (such as YUV/RGB format to YUV420 format conversion), size scaling, clipping and so on.

The execution flow of the digital vision processing modules is shown in Fig. 6.23, which needs to be completed by the cooperation of Matrix, DVPP, DVPP driver and DVPP dedicated hardware.

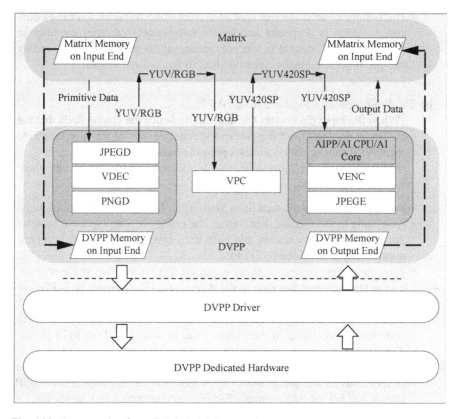

Fig. 6.23 The execution flow of digital vision processing modules

- At the top level of the framework is Matrix, which is responsible for scheduling the function modules in DVPP to process and manage the data flow.
- DVPP is located in the middle and upper layer of the functional architecture, which provides Matrix with programming interfaces to call the video graphics processing module. Through these interfaces, the relevant parameters of the encoding and decoding module and the visual pre-processing module can be configured.
- DVPP driver is located in the middle and lower layers of the functional architecture, which is the closest hardware module to DVPP. It is mainly responsible for device management, engine management and driver of engine module group. The driver will allocate the corresponding DVPP hardware engine according to the tasks issued by DVPP. At the same time, it also read and write the registers in the hardware module to complete some other hardware initialization work.

- The bottom layer is the real hardware computing resource, DVPP module group, which is a special accelerator independent of other modules in Ascend AI processor. It is specially designed for the encoding, decoding and pre-processing tasks corresponding to images and videos.

(b) The Pre-processing Mechanism of DVPP.

When the input data enters the data engine, once the engine finds that the data format does not meet the processing requirements of the subsequent AI Core, DVPP can be started for data pre-processing.

Taking image pre-processing as an example to describe the whole pre-processing process.

- First, Matrix moves the data from Memory to Buffer of DVPP for caching.
- According to the specific data format, the pre-processing engine completes the parameter configuration and data transmission through the programming interface provided by DVPP.
- After the programming interface is started, DVPP transfers the configuration parameters and raw data to the driver, and DVPP driver calls PNG or JPEG for initialization and task distribution.
- PNG or JPEG of DVPP special hardware starts the actual operation to complete the decoding of the picture so as to obtain YUV or RGB format data to meet the needs of subsequent processing.
- After decoding, Matrix continues to call VPC with the same mechanism to further convert the image into YUV420SP format. Because YUV420SP format has higher data storage efficiency and occupies less bandwidth, it can transmit more data under the same bandwidth to meet the demand of powerful computing throughput of AI Core. At the same time, DVPP can also complete the image clipping and scaling. Figure 6.24 shows a typical clipping and zeros-padding operation to change the image size. VPC takes out the part of the primitive image to be processed, and then performs zerofilling on this part, so as to retain the edge feature information in the calculation process of CVNN. The zeros-padding operation needs four filling sizes, i.e., top, bottom, left and right. The edge of the image is expanded in the filling area. Finally, the filled image can be calculated directly.
- After a series of pre-processing, the image data can be processed in the following two ways.

  – The image data can be further pre-processed by AIPP (AI Pre-processing) according to the requirements of the model (Optional. If the output data of DVPP meets the image requirements, it needn't be processed by AIPP), and then the image data that meets the requirements will enter the AI Core under the control of AI CPU for the required neural network calculation.
  – The output image data is encoded by JPEG, and the post-processing is completed. The data is put into the buffer of DVPP. Finally, Matrix takes

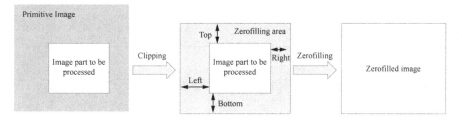

Fig. 6.24 Data flow of image pre-processing

out the data for subsequent operation. At the same time, the computing resources of DVPP are released and the cache is recovered.

In the whole pre-processing process, Matrix completes the function call of different modules. As a customized data supply module, DVPP uses heterogeneous or special processing methods to convert image data quickly, providing sufficient data sources for AI Core, thus meeting the needs of large amount of data and large bandwidth in neural network computing.

6.2.4 The Data Flow of Ascend AI Processor

Taking the reasoning application of face recognition as an example, the data flow of Ascend AI Processor (Ascend 310) is introduced. First, the data is collected and processed by Camera, then the data is reasoned, and finally the face recognition results are output, as shown in Fig. 6.25.

1. The data is collected and processed by Camera.

   Step 1: The compressed video stream is passed from Camera, and the data is stored in DDR through PCIe channel.
   Step 2: DVPP reads the compressed video stream into the cache.
   Step 3: After pre-processing, DVPP writes the decompressed frame into DDR Memory.

2. Reasoning on data.

   Step 4: Task Scheduler sends commands to Direct Memory Access (DMA) to preload AI resources from DDR to On-chip Buffer.
   Step 5: Task Scheduler configures AI Core to execute tasks.
   Step 6: When AI Core works, it reads feature graph and weight, and writes the result into DDR or On-chip Buffer.

3. The results of face recognition are output.

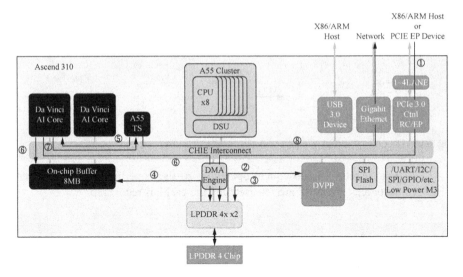

Fig. 6.25 The data flow of Ascend AI processor (Ascend 310)

Step 7: After AI Core completes the processing, it sends a signal to Task
Scheduler. Then Task Scheduler checks the result and assigns another task if
necessary, and returns to step 4.

Step 8: When the last AI task is completed, Task Scheduler reports the result
to Host.

6.3 Atlas AI Computing Solution

Based on Huawei Ascend AI processor, Huawei Atlas AI computing solution builds
a full-scene AI Infrastructure Solution oriented to end, edge and cloud through a
variety of product forms such as modules, boards, small stations, servers and
clusters. This section mainly introduces the corresponding products of Huawei
Atlas AI computing solution, including reasoning and training. Reasoning products
mainly include Atlas 200 AI acceleration module, Atlas 200 DK, Atlas 300I
reasoning card, Atlas 500 intelligent station and Atlas 800 reasoning server, all of
which use Ascend 310 AI processor. Training products mainly include Atlas 300T
training card, Atlas 800 training server and Atlas 900 AI cluster, all of which use
Ascend 910 AI processor. The landscape of Atlas AI computing solution is shown in
Fig. 6.26.

1. Atlas 200 AI Acceleration Module

   Atlas 200 AI Acceleration Module is an AI intelligent computing module with
high-performance and low-power consumption. It can be deployed on cameras,
UAV (unmanned aerial vehicles), robots and other devices for its size half of a

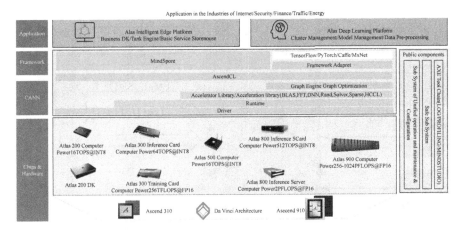

Fig. 6.26 The landscape of Atlas AI computing solution

credit card, with 9.5 W power consumption, supporting 16 channel real-time HD video analysis.

Atlas 200 is integrated with Ascend 310 AI processor, which can realize image, video and other data analysis and inference. It can be widely used in intelligent monitoring, robot, UAV, video server and other scenes. The system block diagram of Atlas 200 is shown in Fig. 6.27.

The following is the performance characteristics of Atlas 200.

(a) Powered by Huawei Ascend 310 AI processor, Atlas 200 can provide the multiplication and addition computing power of 16TOPS INT8 or 8TOPS FP16.

(b) With rich interfaces, Atlas 200 supports PCIe3.0x4, RGMII, USB2.0/USB3.0, I2C, SPI, UART and etc.

(c) Atlas 200 can achieve video access up to 16 channels of 1080p 30fps.

(d) Atlas 200 supports various specifications of H.264 and H.265 video codec, which can meet different video processing requirements of users.

2. Atlas 200 DK

Atlas 200 Developer Kit (Atlas 200 DK) is a kind of product with the core of Atlas 200 AI acceleration module.

Atlas 200 DK can help AI application developers get familiar with the development environment quickly. Its main function is to open up the core functions of Ascend 310 AI processor through the peripheral interface on the board, so that users can quickly and easily access to the powerful processing power of Ascend 310 AI processor.

Atlas 200 DK mainly includes Atlas 200 AI acceleration module, image/audio interface chip (Hi3559C) and LAN Switch. The system architecture is shown in Fig. 6.28.

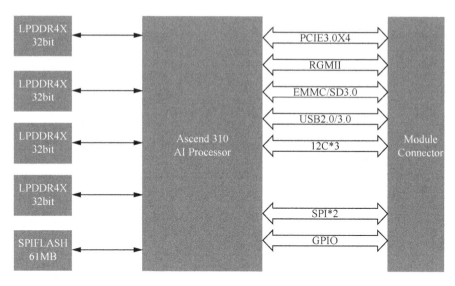

Fig. 6.27 The system block diagram of Atlas 200

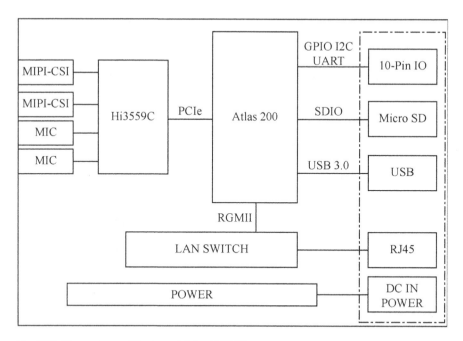

Fig. 6.28 The system architecture of Atlas 200 DK

The performance characteristics of Atlas 200 DK are as follows.

(a) Atlas 200 DK provides peak computing power of 16TOPS (INT8).
(b) Atlas 200 DK supports two camera inputs, two ISP image processing, and HDR10 high dynamic range technical standard.
(c) Atlas 200 DK, matched with strong computing power, supports 1000 MB Ethernet, providing high-speed internet access.
(d) Atlas 200 DK provides a universal 40 pin extension interface (reserved) to facilitate product prototype design.
(e) Atlas 200 DK supports a wide range DC power input from 5 to 28 V.

The product specifications of Atlas 200 DK are shown in Table 6.1.

Advantages of Atlas 200 DK: For developers, a development environment can be built by using a laptop computer, for the cost of a local independent environment is extremely low, and the multi-function and multi-interface can meet the basic requirements. For researchers, the collaborative mode of local development plus cloud training is adopted to build the environment, for Huawei Cloud and Atlas 200 DK adopt a set of protocol stack, cloud training and local deployment without any modification. For entrepreneurs, it provides a code-level prototype (Demo), based on the reference architecture, and modifies 10% of the code to

Table 6.1 The product specifications of Atlas 200 DK

Item	Specification
AI Processor	2 DaVinci AI Cores CPU: 8-core A55, max 1.6 GHz
AI Computing Power	The Multiplication and Addition Computing Power: 8TFLOPS/FP16, 16TOPS/INT8
Memory	LPDDR4X, 128 bit Volume: 8 GB/4 GB Interface Rate: 3200 Mbit/s
Storage	1 Micro SD Card, supporting SD3.0, Max Supporting Rate: SDR50, Max Capacity: 2 TB
Network Interface	1 GE RJ45
USB Interface	1 USB3.0 Type C interface, Only Used as a Slave Device, Compatible with USB2.0
Other Interfaces	1 40pin IO Connector 2 22pin MIPI Connectors 2 On-board Microphones
Power	5 V ~ 28 V DC, Default Setting: 12 V 3A Adapter
Dimension	137.8 mm × 93.0 mm × 32.9 mm
Power Consumption	20 W
Quality	234 g
Operating Temperature	0 °C ~ 35 °C (32 °F ~ 95 °F)
Storage Temperature	0 °C ~ 85 °C (32 °F ~ 185 °F)

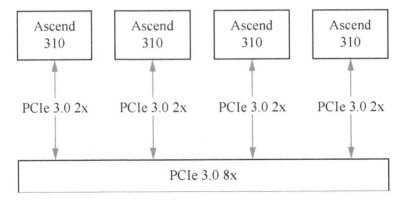

Fig. 6.29 The system Architecture of Huawei Atlas 300 AI accelerator card (Model 3000)

complete the algorithm function. Not only interaction between developers but also community and seamless migration of commercial products can be achieved.

3. Atlas 300I Inference Card

Huawei Atlas 300I Inference Card is the highest density 64 channel video inference AI accelerator card in the industry, including 3000 and 3010 models, namely Huawei Atlas 300 AI accelerator card of model 3000 and Huawei Atlas 300 AI accelerator card of Model 3010. The difference between the two models is mainly for different architectures (such as x86, ARM, etc.). Here only Huawei Atlas 300 AI accelerator card (Model 3000) is introduced. Huawei Atlas 300 AI accelerator card (Model 3000) is designed and developed based on Ascend 310 AI processor, which adopts four PCI HHHL card of Ascend 310 AI processor, and cooperates with main equipment (such as Huawei Taishan Server) to achieve fast and efficient inference, such as image classification, target detection, etc. The system architecture of Huawei Atlas 300 AI accelerator card (Model 3000) is shown in Fig. 6.29.

Atlas 300 AI accelerator card (Model 3000) is used in video analysis, OCR, speech recognition, precision marketing, medical image analysis and other scenes.

Atlas 300 AI accelerator card (Model 3000) is typically used in face recognition system. The system mainly uses face detection algorithm, face tracking algorithm, face quality scoring algorithm and high-speed face contrast recognition algorithm to achieve real-time face snapshot modeling, real-time blacklist contrast alarm and face background retrieval and other functions.

The architecture of face recognition system is shown in Fig. 6.30. The main components include front-end HD webcam or face snapshot machine, media stream memory server (optional), face intelligent analysis server, face comparison search server, central management server, client management software, etc. Atlas 300 AI accelerator card (Model 3000) is deployed in face intelligent analysis server, mainly to achieve video decoding/pre-processing, face detection, face alignment (correction) and face feature extraction and inference.

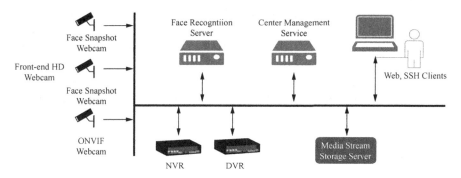

Fig. 6.30 The architecture of face recognition system

The product specifications of Atlas 300 AI accelerator card (Model 3000) are shown in Table 6.2.

The key features of Atlas 300 AI accelerator card (Model 3000): supporting the standard interface of half height and half length (single slot) of PCIe 3.0 × 16 HHHL; with maximum power consumption of 67 W; supporting power consumption monitoring and out-of-band management functions; supporting hardware H.264 and H.265 video compression and decompression.

4. Atlas 500 Intelligent Edge Station

Table 6.2 The product specifications of Atlas 300 AI Accelerator Card (Model 3000)

Item	Specification
Form	PCIe Card of half height and half length
Memory	LPDDR4 × 32 GB, 3200 Mbit/s
AI Computing Power	64 TOPS INT8
Codec	Supporting H.264 Hardware Decoding, 64-channel 1080P 30FPS (2-channel 3840 × 2160 60FPS) Supporting H.265 Hardware Decoding, 64-channel 1080P 30FPS (2-channel 3840 × 2160 60FPS) Supporting H.264 Hardware Decoding, 4-channel 1080P 30FPS Supporting H.265 Hardware Decoding, 4-channel 1080P 30FPS JPEG Decoding 4 × 1080P 256FPS, Encoding 4 × 1080P 64FPS PNG Decoding 4 × 1080P 48FPS
PCIe Interface	PCIe Gen3.0, Compatible with 2.0/1.0 ×16 Lanes, Compatible with ×8/×4/×2/×1
Power Consumption	67 W
Dimension	169.5 mm × 68.9 mm
Quality	319 g
Operating Temperature	0 °C ~ 55 °C (32 °F ~ 131 °F)

Atlas 500 Intelligent Edge Station is divided into two models, Model 3000 and Model 3010, which are designed for different CPU architectures. Here are some common features of Atlas 500 Intelligent Edge Station. It is Huawei's lightweight edge device for a wide range of edge application scenarios, which is characterized with super computing performance, large capacity storage, flexible configuration, small size, wide temperature ranges, strong fitness to surroundings, easy maintenance and management, etc.

Atlas 500 Intelligent Edge Station is a powerful edge computing product that can perform real-time processing on edge devices. A single Atlas 500 Intelligent Edge Station can provide 16 TOPS INT8 processing power with extremely low power consumption. Atlas 500 Intelligent Edge Station integrates Wi-i and LTE wireless data interfaces to provide flexible network access and data transmission solutions.

Atlas 500 Intelligent Edge Station is the pioneer in the industry to apply Thermo-electric Cooling (TEC) semiconductor cooling technology in large-scale edge computing products, adaptive to harsh The logical architecture of Atlas 500 Intelligent Edge Station is shown in Fig. 6.31.

Atlas 500 Intelligent Edge Station features the ease of use of edge scenes and 16-channel video analysis and storage capacity.

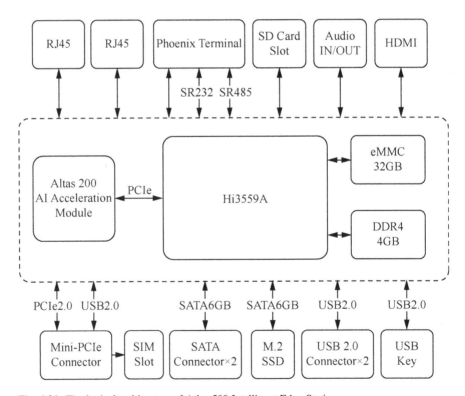

Fig. 6.31 The logical architecture of Atlas 500 Intelligent Edge Station

(a) The usability of edge scene mainly includes the following aspects.

  • Real-time: It provides real-time responses in the process of data.
  • Low bandwidth: Only the necessary information is sent to Cloud.
  • Privacy protection: Customers can decide what information they want to send to Cloud and keep locally. All information sent to Cloud can be encrypted.
  • It supports standard container engine, third-party algorithm and application rapid deployment.

(b) The 16-channel video analysis and storage capacity mainly includes the following aspects.

  • It supports 16-channel video analysis capability (maximum 16-channel 1080P decoding, 16T INT8 computing power).
  • It supports 12 TB memory capacity, and the video of 16-channels 1080P@4 MB Data Rate can be cached for 7 days while the video of 8-channel 1080P@4 MB Data Rate can be cached for 30 days.

Atlas 500 Intelligent Edge Station is mainly applied in intelligent video monitoring, analysis, data storage and other scenes, including safe city, intelligent transportation, intelligent community, environmental monitoring, intelligent manufacturing, intelligent care, self-service retail, intelligent buildings, etc. It can be widely deployed in various edge devices and central computer rooms to meet the needs of public security, communities, parks, shopping malls, supermarkets and other complex environmental areas Use, as shown in Fig. 6.32. In these application scenarios, the typical architecture of atlas 500 Intelligent Edge Station is as follows: Terminal, which is connected to IPC (IP Camera) or other front-end devices through wireless or wired; Edge, which achieves value

Safe City
Face Recognition
Driving License Plate Recognition

Intelligent Transportation
Traffic Signal Optimization
Smart Traffic Management

Intelligent Community
Resident Recognition
Stranger Identification

Environmental Monitoring
Pollution Detection

Intelligent Manufacturing
Intelligent Quality Inspection
Flexible Manufacturing

Intelligent Care
Kindergarten
Nursing Home

Self-service Retail
Self-service Counter
Smart Stores

Intelligent buildings
Checking-in
Security

Fig. 6.32 Application scenarios of ATLAS 500 Intelligent Edge Station

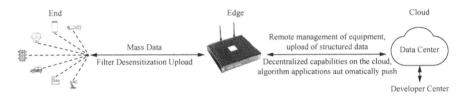

Fig. 6.33 Typical architecture of ATLAS 500 Intelligent Edge Station

information extraction, storage and upload; Cloud, via which data center model is push, managed, developed and applied, as shown in Fig. 6.33.

The product specifications of Atlas 500 Intelligent Edge Station are shown in Table 6.3.

5. Atlas 800 Inference Server

Atlas 800 Inference Server is divided into two models: Model 3000 and Model 3010.

(a) Atlas 800 Inference Server (Model 3000)

Atlas 800 Inference Server (Model 3000) is a data center inference server based on Huawei Kunpeng 920 processor. It can support eight atlas 300 AI accelerator cards (Model 3000), providing powerful real-time reasoning ability, and is widely used in AI inference scenarios. The server is oriented to the Internet, distributed storage, cloud computing, big data, enterprise business and other fields, with the advantages of high-performance computing, large capacity storage, low energy consumption, easy management, easy deployment and so on.

The performance characteristics of Atlas 800 Inference Server (Model 3000) are as follows.

- Atlas 800 Inference Server (Model 3000) supports the 64 bits high-performance multi-core Kunpeng 920 processor developed by Huawei

Table 6.3 The product specifications of Atlas 500 Intelligent Edge Station

Item	Specification
AI Processor	Built- in 1 Atlas 200 AI Acceleration Module, Providing 16 TOPS INT8 Computing Power; Supporting 16-channel HD Video Decoding
Internet	2 × 100 MB/1000 MB Adaptive Ethernet Port
Wireless Module	Optional support 3 GB/4 GB or Wi-Fi Module, Alternative, Dual Antenna
Display	One-channel HDMI Interface
Audio	One-channel Input and Output, 3.5 mm Audio Connector, Double-channel Output
Power	DC 12 V, External Power Adapter
Temperature	−40 ~ 70, Dependent on Configuration

and oriented to the server field. It integrates DDR4, PCIe4.0, 25GE, 10GE, GE and other interfaces, and provides complete SOC functions.

- It can most support Atlas 300 AI accelerator cards (Model 3000), providing powerful real-time reasoning capability.
- It can most support 64 cores and 3.0 GHz frequency. It also supports a variety of core number and frequency models.
- It is compatible with ARMv8-A architecture features, supporting ARMv8.1 and ARMv8.2 extension.
- Core is a self-developed 64 bits-TaiShan core.

The performance characteristics of Atlas 800 Inference Server (Model 3000) are as follows.

• Atlas 800 Inference Server (Model 3000) supports the 64 bits high-performance multi-core Kunpeng 920 processor developed by Huawei and oriented to the server field. It integrates DDR4, PCIe4.0, 25GE, 10GE, GE and other interfaces, and provides complete SOC functions.

- It can most support Atlas 300 AI accelerator cards (Model 3000), providing powerful real-time reasoning capability.
- It can most support 64 cores and 3.0 GHz frequency. It also supports a variety of core number and frequency models.
- It is compatible with ARMv8-A architecture features, supporting ARMv8.1 and ARMv8.2 extension.
- Core is a self-developed 64 bits-TaiShan core.
- Each core integrates 64 KB L1 ICache, 64 KB L1 DCache and 512 KB L2 DCache.
- It can most support L3 cache capacity of 45.5 MB ~ 46 Mb.
- It supports superscalar, variable length, pipeline out of order.
- It supports ECC 1 bit error correction and ECC 2 bit error reporting.
- It supports high-speed inter chip Hydra interface with the maximum channel speed of 30 Gbit/s.
- It supports eight DDR controllers.
- It supports up to eight physical Ethernet ports.
- It supports three PCIe controllers, GNE4 (16 Gbit/s) and downward compatibility.
- It supports IMU maintenance engine to collect CPU status.

• A single Atlas 800 Inference Server (Model 3000) supports two processors and a maximum of 128 cores, which maximizes the concurrent execution of multi-threaded applications.
• Atlas 800 Inference Server can most support 32 pieces of 2933 MHZ DDR4 ECC memory, as memory can support RDIMM with the maximum of 4096 GB.

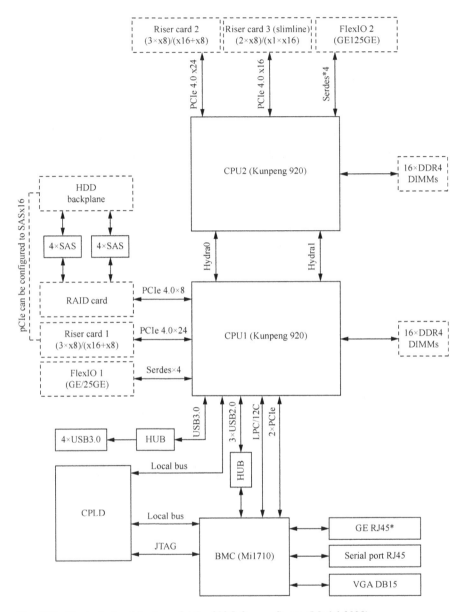

Fig. 6.34 The logical architecture of Atlas 800 Inference Server (Model 3000)

The logical architecture of Atlas 800 Inference Server (Model 3000) is shown in Fig. 6.34, and its features are as follows.

- It supports two Huawei self-developed Kunpeng 920 processors, and each processor supports 16 DDR4 DIMMs.

- CPU1 and CPU2 are interconnected by two Hydra buses, and the transmission rate can reach the maximum of 30 Gbit/s.
- It supports two kinds of flexible Ethernet interface cards, including $4 \times GE$ and $4 \times 25GE$, through the high-speed Serdes interface of CPU.
- Raid control card is connected with CPU1 through the PCIe bus, and connected with the hard disk backplane through SAS signal cable. It can support a variety of local storage specifications through different hard disk backplanes.
- Baseboard Manager Controller (BMC) uses Hi1710, a management chip developed by Huawei. It can be used for management interfaces such as Video Graphic Array (VGA), management network port and debugging serial port.

Atlas 800 Inference Server (Model 3000) is an efficient inference platform based on Kunpeng processor. The product specifications are shown in Table 6.4.

(b) Atlas 800 Inference Server (Model 3010)

Atlas 800 Inference Server (Model 3010) is a inference platform based on Intel processor, which is widely used in AI inference scenarios. It supports up to seven Atlas 300 or Nvidia T4 AI accelerators and up to 448 channels of HD video real-time analysis.

Atlas 800 Inference Server (Model 3010) has many advantages such as low power consumption, great extendibility, high reliability, easy management and deployment, etc.

The logical architecture of Atlas 800 Inference Server (Model 3010) is shown in Fig. 6.35.

The features of the Atlas 800 Inference Server (Model 3010) are as follows.

- It supports one or two Intel xtreme extensible processors.
- It supports 24 memories.
- The processors are interconnected by two UltraPath Interconnect (UPI) buses, and the transmission rate can reach the maximum of 10.4 GT/s.
- The processor is connected with three PCIe Riser cards through the PCIe bus, and supports different specifications of PCIe slots through different PCIe Riser cards.
- Raid Controller card is connected with CPU1 through the PCIe bus, and connected with the hard disk backplane through the SAS signal cable. It can support a variety of local storage specifications through different hard disk backplanes.
- Lbg-2 Platform Controller Hub (PCH) is used to support the following two interfaces.

  – It supports two on-board 10GE optical interfaces or two on-board 10GE electrical interfaces through X557 (PHY).
  – It supports two on-board GE interfaces.

Table 6.4 The product specifications of Atlas 800 Inference Server (Model 3000)

Item	Specification
Form	2U AI Server
Processor Model	• Supporting 2 channels of Kunpeng 920 Processor, Available in 3 Configurations of 64 cores, 48 cores and 32 cores, with the Frequency of 2.6 GHz; • 2 Hydra Interconnected Links, the Maximum Speed of a Single Link is 30 gbit/s; • The Volume of L3 Cache is 45.5 MB ~ 46 MB; • CPU Thermal Design TDP Power is 138 W ~ 195 W
AI Accelerator Card	Supporting 8 Atlas 300 AI Accelerator Cards at most
Memory Slot	• The maximum of 32 pieces of DDR4 Memory Slots, Supporting RDIMM; • The Maximum Memory Speed of 2933 MT/s; • Memory Protection Supporting the Function of ECC, SEC/DED, SDDC, Patrol scrubbing • Single Memory Chip Supporting 16 GB/32 GB/64 GB/128 GB
Local Storage	• 25 × 2.5 in. Hard Disk Configuration; • 12 × 3.5 in. Hard Disk Configuration; • 8 × 2.5 SAS/SATA+12 × 2.5 NVMe inch Hard Disk Configuration
Supported RAID Level	RAID 0, RAID 1, RAID 5, RAID 6, RAID 10, RAID 50, RAID 60; Power Failure Protection of Super Capacitor
Flexible IO Card	The single board supports two flexible IO cards at most. A single flexible IO card provides the following network interfaces: • 4 GE Electrical Interfaces, Supporting the Function of PXE; • 4 25GE/10GE Optical Interfaces, Supporting the Function of PXE
PCIe Extension	Up to 9 PCIe4.0 PCIe interfaces are supported, one of which is dedicated for RAID card, and the other 8 are standard PCIe extension slots. The specification of standard PCIE 4.0 extension slot is as follows. IO module 1 and IO module 2 support the following PCIe specifications: • It supports two PCIe4.0 × 16 standard slots of full height and full length (signal is PCIe4.0 × 8) and one standard slot of full height and half length (signal is pcie4.0 × 8) • It supports one PCIe4.0 × 16 standard slot of full height and full length, and one standard slot of full height half and length (the signal is pcie4.0 × 8) IO module 3 supports the following specifications. • It supports two 16 PCIe4.0 × 16 standard slots of half height and half length (the signal is pcie4.0 × 8); • It supports one PCIe4.0 × 16 standard slot of half height and half length; The PCIe extension slot supports the PCI SSD memory card, which is independently developed by Huawei, greatly improving the I/O performance in searching, cache, downloading and other application fields; Through the special Riser card, the PCI slot can support Atlas 300 AI Accelerator (Model 3000), which is independently

(continued)

Table 6.4 (continued)

Item	Specification
	developed by Huawei, carrying out the tasks of inference, image recognition and processing quickly and efficiently.
Power	2 hot swap 1500 W or 2000 W AC power modules, support 1 + 1 redundancy
Power Supply	In support of 100 V ~ 240 V AC, 240 V DC
Fan	Supporting 4 hot swap fan modules and N + 1 redundancy
Temperature	5 °C ~ 40 °C
Dimension (Width × Depth × Height)	447 mm × 790 mm × 86.1 mm

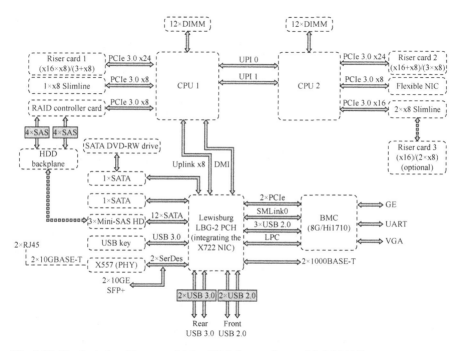

Fig. 6.35 The logical architecture of Atlas 800 Inference Server (Model 3010)

- Hi1710 management chip is used to support outgoing VGA, management network port, debugging serial port and other management interfaces.

Atlas 800 Inference Server (Model 3010) is a flexible inference platform based on Intel processor, and its product specifications are shown in Table 6.5.

Table 6.5 The product specifications of Atlas 800 Inference Server (Model 3010)

Item	Specification
Form	2U AI Processors
Processor	1/2 Intel® Xeon® SP Skylake or Cascade Lake Processor, with the maximum of 205 W
AI Accelerator	Up to 7 atlas 300 or NVIDIA T4 AI accelerators
Memory	24 pieces of DDR4 Memory slots, with the maximum Memory speed of 2933 MT/s
Local Storage	Supported hard disk configuration: • 8 × 2.5 in. Hard Disk Configuration; • 12 × 3.5 in. Hard Disk Configuration; • 20 × 2.5 in. Hard Disk Configuration; • 24 × 2.5 in. Hard Disk Configuration; • 25 × 2.5 in. Hard Disk Configuration. Supported Flash Storage: • Double M.2 SSDs
Supported RAID Level	Optionally support RAID0, RAID1, RAID10, RAID1E, RAID5, RAID50, RAID6, RAI0, support Cache super capacitor protection, provide RAID level migration, disk roaming, self-diagnosis, Web remote setting and other functions
Internet	On-board plug-in cards: two 10GE interfaces and two GE interfaces Flexible Cards: It can be optionally equipped with 2 × GE or 4 × GE or 2 × 10GE or 2 × 25GE or 1/2 56G FDR IB interfaces
PCIe Extension	Up to 10 PCIe3.0 extension slots, including one PCIe extension card for RAID card and one flexible LOM card
Fan	4 hot-swappable fans, N + 1 redundancy is supported
Power	2 redundant hot-swappable power supplies can be configured to support 1 + 1 redundancy. Optional specifications are as follows (Note1): 550 W AC platinum power supply, 900 W AC platinum/titanium power supply, 1500 W AC platinum power supply; • 1500 W 380 V high voltage DC power supply 1200 W-48 V ~ −60 V DC power supply
Operating Temperature	5 °C ~ 45 °C
Dimension (Width × Depth × Height)	Box dimension of 3.5-in. hard disk: 86.1 mm × 447 mm × 748 mm Box dimension of 2.5-in. hard disk: 86.1 mm × 447 mm × 708 mm

6.3.1   Atlas for AI Training Acceleration

1. Atlas 300T Training Card: The Most Powerful AI Training Card
   Huawei Atlas 300T Training Card, namely Huawei Atlas 300 Accelerator (Model 9000), is designed and developed based on Ascend 910 AI processor. It provides a single card up to 256TOPS FP16 AI computing power for data center training scenarios, which is the most powerful AI accelerator in the industry. It can be widely used in various general servers in data centers, providing customers with AI solutions of super performance, high efficiency and low TCO.

Table 6.6 The product specifications of Huawei Atlas 300 Accelerator (Model 9000)

Item	Specification
Form	Standard full-height and 3/4 long PCIe卡
Memory	Built-in 32 GB HBM + 16 GB Two-level Large Memory
AI Computing Power	256T FLOPSa@FP16
PCIe Interface	PCIe 4.0 × 16

Based on Ascend 910 AI processor, Huawei Atlas 300 Accelerator (Model 9000) has many features as follows.

(a) It supports PCIe 4.0 × 16 full-height and 3/4 long standard interface (double slots).
(b) The maximum power consumption is 350 W.
(c) It supports power consumption monitoring and out-of-band management.
(d) It supports video compression or decompression of hardware H.264/H.265.
(e) It supports the training framework of Huawei MindSpore and TensorFlow.
(f) It supports Linux OS on x86 platform.
(g) It supports Linux OS on ARM platform.

The product specifications of Huawei Atlas 300 Accelerator (Model 9000) are shown in Table 6.6.

The computing power of Atlas 300 (Model 9000) single card is increased by two times, and the gradient synchronization delay is reduced by 70%. Figure 6.36 shows the speed comparison between the frameworks of mainstream training card + TensorFlow and Huawei Ascend 910 + MindSpore, by using ResNet 50 V1.5 to compare the results on ImageNet 2012 dataset via "Optimal batch size respectively". It can be seen that the training speed of Huawei Ascend 910 + MindSpore is much faster than the other.

2. Atlas 800 Training Server: The Most Powerful AI Training Server

Atlas 800 Training Server (Model 9000) is mainly used in AI training scenes with super performance to build an AI computing platform of high efficiency and low power consumption for training scenes. It supports multiple Atlas 300 Accelerators or Acceleration modules, adapting to various video image analysis scenes.

Fig. 6.36 The speed comparison between Huawei Ascend 910 + MindSpore and the other

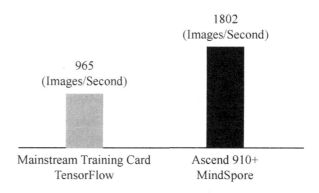

1802
(Images/Second)

965
(Images/Second)

Mainstream Training Card
TensorFlow

Ascend 910+
MindSpore

Table 6.7 The product specifications of Atlas 800 Training Server (Model 9000)

Item	Specification
Form	4U AI Server
Processor	4 Kunpeng 920 processor
AI Computing Power	2P FLOPS@FP16
Codec Capability	Built-in 32 hardware decoders It can be processed in parallel with training
Heat Dissipation	Two kinds of heat dissipation are supported, air cooling and liquid cooling
Power Consumption	2P FLOPS/5.6 KW

It is mainly used in video analysis, deep learning training and other training scenes.

Atlas 800 Training Server (Model 9000) is based on Ascend 910 processor. Its computing power density is increased by 2.5 times, the hardware decoding capacity is increased by 25 times, and the energy efficiency ratio is increased by 1.8 times.

Atlas 800 Training Server (Model 9000) has the strongest computing power density, up to 2P FLOPS@FP16/4U Super computing power.

Atlas 800 Training Server (Model 9000) has flexible configuration and adapts to multiple loads. It supports the flexible configuration of SAS/SATA/NVMe/M.2 SSD combination. It supports on-board network card and flexible IO card, providing a variety of network interfaces.

The product specifications of Atlas 800 Training Server (Model 9000) are shown in Table 6.7.

3. Atlas 900 AI Cluster: The Fastest AI Training Cluster in the World

Atlas 900 AI Cluster represents the peak computing power in the world, which is composed of thousands of Ascend 910 AI processors. Through Huawei cluster communication library and job scheduling platform, it integrates three high-speed interfaces, i.e., HCCS, PCIe4.0 and 100 g RoCE, to fully release the powerful performance of Ascend 910 AI processor. The total computing power achieves 256p ~ 1024p FLOPS @FP16, which is equivalent to the computing power of 500,000 PCs. According to the actual measurement, Atlas 900 AI Cluster can complete the training based on ResNet-50 model in 60 s, which is 15% faster than the second place, as shown in Fig. 6.37. It allows researchers to train AI models with images and voices more quickly, so that human beings can more efficiently explore the mysteries of the universe, predict the weather, explore for oil, and accelerate the commercial process of automatic driving.

The following are key features of Atlas 900 AI Cluster.

(a) Leader of the computing power industry: 256–1024 PFLOPS@FP16, thousands of Ascend 910 AI processors are interconnected, providing the fastest ResNet-50@ImageNet performance in the industry.

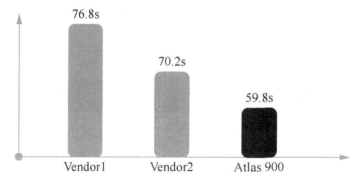

- Testing Benchmark
  □ Benchmark: ResNet-50 V1.5 Model, ImageNet-1k Data Set
  □ Cluster: 1024 Ascend 910 AI processors
  □ Accuracy: 75.9%

Fig. 6.37 Speed comparison of Atlas 900 AI Cluster and other training clusters

(b) Best cluster network: Three kind of high-speed interfaces, HCCS, PCIe and 100 GB RoCEs, are integrated to vertically integrate communication library, topology and low delay network with its linearity greater than 80%.

(c) Super heat dissipation system: Single cabinet 50 KW mixed liquid cooling system supports more than 95% liquid cooling, PUE less than 1.1, saving 79% room space.

In order to allow all industries to obtain super computing power, Huawei is going to deploy Atlas 900 AI Cluster to Cloud, launch Huawei Cloud EI cluster service, and open its application for global scientific research institutions and universities at a very favorable price.

6.3.2 Atlas Device-Edge-Cloud Collaboration

Huawei Atlas AI computing solution has three advantages over general industry solutions, i.e., unified development, unified operation and maintenance, and security upgrade. Generally, different development architectures are used in the edge side and the center side of the industry, so the models need secondary development for they cannot flow freely. Huawei Atlas, based on the unified development architecture of Da Vinci Architecture and Compute Architecture for Neural Networks (CANN), can be used in the terminal, edge and cloud for primary development. Generally, there is no operation and maintenance management tool in the industry, while only API is open, so that customers need to develop it by themselves. However, FusionDirector of Huawei Atlas can manage up to 50,000 nodes to achieve a unified management of central and edge devices, and either model push or device upgrade can be done remotely. The industry generally has no encryption

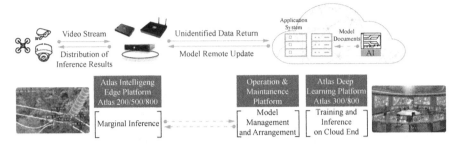

Fig. 6.38 AtlasDevice-Edge-Cloud Collaboration

and decryption engine and does not encrypt the model, while Huawei Atlas encrypts both the security of the transmission channel and the model for double protection. AtlasDevice-Edge-Cloud Collaboration, the consistent training of central side, and the remote update of modes are shown in Fig. 6.38.

6.4 Industrial Implementation of Atlas

This section mainly introduces the industry application scenarios of Atlas AI computing solutions, such as applications in power, finance, manufacturing, transportation, supercomputing and other fields.

6.4.1 Electricity: One-Stop ICT Smart Grid Solution

With the increasing dependence of modern society on electricity, the traditional extensive and inefficient way of power utilization can not meet the current demand, and more efficient and reasonable power supply is needed. How to achieve reliable, economic, efficient and green power grid is the biggest challenge for the power industry.

Relying on its leading ICT technology, Huawei, together with its partners, has launched a full range of intelligent business solutions covering all aspects including power generation, transmission, transformation, distribution and utilization. The traditional power system is deeply integrated with cloud computing, big data, Internet of things and mobile technology to achieve the comprehensive perception, interconnection and business intelligence of various power terminals.

For example, the pioneer intelligent unmanned patrol inspection (see Fig. 6.39) replaces the traditional manual patrol inspection, which boosts the operation efficiency by five times and reduces the system cost by 30%. The front-end camera of the intelligent unmanned patrol inspection system is equipped with Huawei Atlas 200 acceleration module, which can quickly analyze problems and send back alarms.

Fig. 6.39 Intelligent unmanned patrol inspection

At the same time, the remote monitoring and management platform is equipped with Atlas 300 AI training card or Atlas 800 AI server, used for training model, can realize the remote upgrade operation of the model.

6.4.2   Intelligent Finance: Holistic Digital Transformation

Financial technology and digital financial services have become an integral part of the overall lifestyle of residents, which is not limited to payment, but also investment, deposits and loans.

One of Huawei Atlas AI computing solutions for the financial industry is the smart banking outlets, which adopts advanced access solutions, security and all-in-one technology to help customers build a new generation of smart banking outlets.

Huawei Atlas AI computing solution uses AI to change finance, helping banking outlets carry out intelligent transformation. Through the accurate identification of VIP customers, the conversion rate of potential customers increased by 60%; Through the intelligent face-scanning authentication, the business processing time dropped by 70%; Through the analysis of customer queuing time, the customer complaints dropped by 50%, as shown in Fig. 6.40.

6.4.3   Intelligent Manufacturing: Digital Integration of Machines and Thoughts

In the era of industry 4.0, the deep integration of the new generation of information technology and manufacturing industry has brought far-reaching industrial changes. Mass customization, global collaborative design, intelligent factories based on Cyber Physical System (CPS) and Internet of Vehicles are reshaping the industrial value chain, forming new production modes, industrial forms, business models and economic growth points. Based on cloud computing, big data, Internet of Things (IoT) and other technologies, Huawei joins hands with global partners to help customers in the manufacturing industry reshape the value chain of manufacturing industry, innovate business models and achieve new value creation.

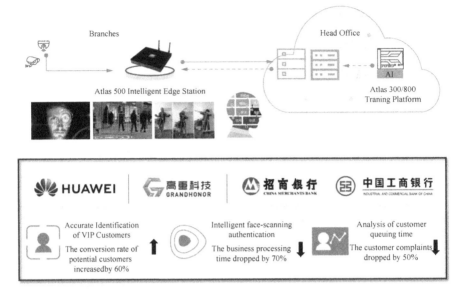

Fig. 6.40 Intelligent finance—intelligent transformation of bank branches

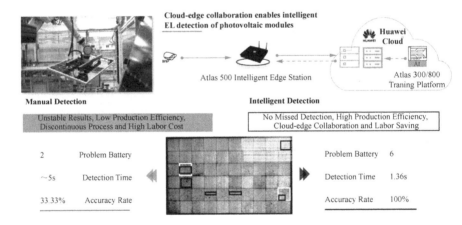

Fig. 6.41 Cloud-edge collaboration, intelligent detection

Huawei Atlas AI computing solution helps upgrade the intelligence of production line, using machine vision technology for intelligent detection instead of traditional manual detection. The "unstable results, low production efficiency, discontinuous process and high labor cost" of manual detection is transformed into "no missed detection, high production efficiency, cloud-edge collaboration and labor saving" of intelligent detection, as shown in Fig. 6.41.

6.4.4   Intelligent Transportation: Easier Travel and Improved Logistics

With the acceleration of globalization and urbanization, the demand for transportation is growing day by day, which greatly drives the construction demand of green, safe, efficient and smooth modern integrated transportation system. Adheres to the concept of "Easier Travel and Improved Logistics", Huawei is committed to providing customers with innovative solutions such as digital railway, digital urban rail transit and smart airport. Through new ICT technologies such as cloud computing, big data, Internet of things, agile network, BYOD, eLTE and GSM-R, Huawei improves the information level of the industry and helps industry customers to raise transportation service level, ensuring an easier travel, an improved logistics, a smoother and safer traffic. Huawei Atlas AI computing solution helps to upgrade the national expressway network, so that the traffic efficiency increased by five times though cooperative vehicle infrastructure, as shown in Fig. 6.42.

6.4.5   Super Computer: Building State-Level AI Platform

Pengcheng Yunnao II is mainly built on Atlas 900, the fastest training cluster in the world, with the strongest computing power (E-level AI computing power), the best cluster network (HCCL collective communication supports 100 TB non-blocking parameter area network), and the ultimate energy efficiency (AI cluster PUE < 1.1).

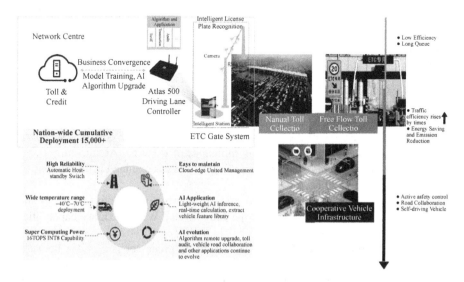

Fig. 6.42   Cooperative vehicle infrastructure, improved traffic efficiency

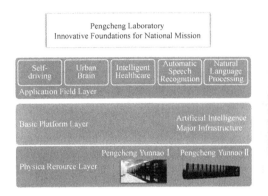

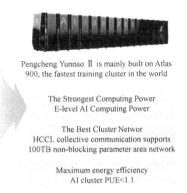

Pengcheng Yunnao Ⅱ is mainly built on Atlas 900, the fastest training cluster in the world

The Strongest Computing Power
E-level AI Computing Power

The Best Cluster Networ
HCCL collective communication supports
100TB non-blocking parameter area network

Maximum energy efficiency
AI cluster PUE<1.1

Fig. 6.43 Pengcheng laboratory

Atlas helps Pengcheng Yunnao II to set up Pengcheng laboratory, which is the basic innovation platform to realize the national mission, as shown in Fig. 6.43.

6.5 Chapter Summary

This chapter focuses on Huawei Ascend AI processor and Atlas AI computing solution. Firstly, the hardware structure and software structure of Ascend AI processor are introduced, and then the related inference products and training products of Atlas AI computing solution are introduced. Finally, the industry application scenarios of Atlas is introduced.

6.6 Exercises

1. As two processors for AI computing, what is the difference between CPU and GPU?
2. Da Vinci Architecture is specially developed for boosting AI computing power. It is not only the engine of Ascend AI computing, but also the core of Ascend AI processor. What are the three main components of Da Vinci Architecture?
3. What are the three kinds of basic computing resources contained in the computing unit of Da Vinci Architecture?
4. The software stack of Ascend AI processor is mainly divided into four levels and one auxiliary tool chain. What are the four levels? What auxiliary capabilities does the tool chain provide?
5. The neural network software flow of Ascend AI processor is a bridge between deep learning framework and Ascend AI processor. It provides a shortcut for neural network to transform from original model, to intermediate computing

graph representation, and then to independent offline model. The neural network software flow of Ascend AI processor mainly completes the generation, loading and execution of the neural network application offline model. What are the main function modules contained in it?

6. Ascend AI processors are divided into two types, i.e., Ascend 310 and Ascend 910, which are both based on Da Vinci Architecture. But they are different in precision, power consumption and process. What are the differences in their application fields?

7. The corresponding products of Atlas AI computing solutions mainly include inference and training. What are the reasoning and training products?

8. Illustrate the application scenario of Atlas AI computing solution.

Chapter 7
HUAWEI AI Open Platform

This chapter is an introduction to HUAWEI HiAI, an open AI capability platform for smart devices. Firstly, Architecture of HUAWEI HiAI Platform, a three-layer open architecture based on "Service, Engine and Foundation" that provides capabilities at chip, application and service, as well as its three sub modules, is introduced. Then the development of Apps based on HUAWEI HiAI and some solutions of HUAWEI HiAI are briefly introduced too.

7.1 Introduction to HUAWEI HiAI Platform

Currently most consumers are exposed to such AI Apps as voice assistant, AI photography, image beautifying, whose application scenarios are relatively single and limited. In fact, with the evolution of on-engine AI to distributed AI and the sharing of resources and computing power among multiple terminals, the application scenarios of on-engine AI will be greatly broadened, which will further empower developers to achieve more intelligent innovation and bring the marvelous experience to consumers.

Based on the above background, Huawei launched HUAWEI HiAI 3.0. The evolution of HUAWEI HiAI platform has experienced single-device version 1.0, multi-device version 2.0 and current distributed scenario version 3.0, as shown in Fig. 7.1.

AWEI HiAI 3.0 was officially released at Software Green Alliance Developer Conference on November 19, 2019, marking that on-engine AI is officially moving towards distributed AI. HUAWEI HiAI 3.0 will bring users the marvelous full-scene intelligent life experience.

HUAWEI HiAI 3.0 provides one-access service and multi-terminal adaptive operation. Users can enjoy convenient services such as voice assistant and HiBoard on mobile phones, tablets, smart screens, smart speakers and other devices, so that

Huawei Technologies Co., Ltd., *Artificial Intelligence Technology*,
https://doi.org/10.1007/978-981-19-2879-6_7

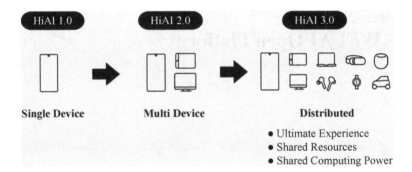

Fig. 7.1 Evolution of HUAWEI HiAI platform

the same service can be realized on different devices. Here are two cases: private coaching and driving experience.

Case 1: Private coaching. HUAWEI HiAI 3.0 opens its distributed Computer Vision (CV) and Automatic Speech Recognition (ASR), which are designed to enable users to exercise at home as effectively as being guided by a gym private coach. Distributed Computer Vision can recognize 3D human body key points so that users can capture multiple angles of motion posture in real time through multiple cameras at home, and correct posture through multiple screen displays. In addition, Automatic Speech Recognition assists users to control their motional rhythm and further helps them to enjoy private coaching at home.

Case 2: Driving experience. Combined with distributed technology, HUAWEI HiAI 3.0 enables users to connect smart phones with cars, so that safety detection of users' driving behavior is carried out through the in-car camera, and the AI chip computing power provides safety reminders for dangerous behaviors such as fatigue driving. Through the in-car network environment and local data operation with lower delay, drivers can better protect themselves from accidents.

7.1.1 Architecture of HUAWEI HiAI Platform

HUAWEI HiAI platform builds a three-layer ecosystem of "Service, Engine and Foundation". Service supports a rich front-end mainstream framework while Engine provides various upper functional business APIs, which can run efficiently on mobile devices, and Foundation flexibly schedules heterogeneous resources to meet the needs of developers so as to accelerate neural network model calculation and operator calculation. Moreover, HUAWEI HiAI provides a systematic tool chain, complete documents, various APIs and quick-start source code, which can enable rapid application development. The architecture of HUAWEI HiAI mobile computing platform is shown in Fig. 7.2.

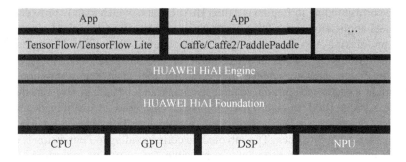

Fig. 7.2   The architecture of HUAWEI HiAI mobile computing platform

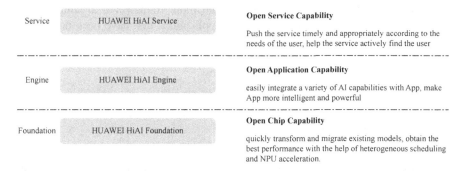

Fig. 7.3   The three-layer AI ecology of HiAI

HUAWEI HiAI is a mobile terminal oriented AI computing platform. Compared with on-service AI, on-engine AI has three core advantages: more security, lower cost and less delay. HUAWEI HiAI constructs three layers of AI Ecology: open service capability, open application capability and open chip capability. The three-layer open platform of "Service, Engine and Foundation" brings more marvelous experience to users and developers. Each layer features as follows.

1. Service: Create once, reuse many times.
2. Engine: Distributed, full scenario.
3. Foundation: Greater computing power, more operators; more frames, smaller models.

The three-layer AI ecology of HiAI is shown in Fig. 7.3.

HUAWEI HiAI enables App to have the following values: real-time, timeliness, stability, security and cost.

The biggest feature of HUAWEI HiAI 3.0 platform is that AI enables distributed full scenarios. The architecture of HUAWEI HiAI consists of three layers: Service, Engine and Foundation. The corresponding sub module of Device is Service, which is mainly to open the service capability. It will push the service timely and appropriately according to the needs of the user, so that the service can actively find the user. What it brings to the user is to create once and reuse many times. The sub module corresponding to Engine is called HiAI Engine, which mainly provides API to open AI application capabilities. It can easily integrate a variety of AI capabilities with App, making App more intelligent and powerful. Through HiAI engine, you can call various algorithms in HiAI platform and integrate them in App. For example, if you want to achieve image recognition, character recognition, face recognition, speech recognition, natural language understanding, you can directly call the API in HiAI Engine. HiAI engine can be used in distributed and full scenarios. Foundation is a batch of chips, mainly based on Huawei's Kirin chip, with the chip capability open. The sub module corresponding to Foundation is called HiAI Foundation, which is mainly responsible for providing operators. It can quickly transform and migrate existing models, and obtain the best performance with the help of heterogeneous scheduling and NPU acceleration. The chip provides more operators, greater computing power, and more frameworks to simplify the model. If you want to migrate some of AI applications that have been developed locally to terminal devices, you can use HiAI Foundation to transform the model to fit the terminal devices.

The three sub-modules are highlighted below.

7.1.2 HUAWEI HiAI Foundation

HiAI Foundation AP is an Artificial Intelligence Computing Library in mobile computing platform, which is designed for developers of artificial intelligence applications. It allows developers to easily and efficiently write artificial intelligence applications running on mobile devices. It features as follows.

1. Based on the constant improvement of high performance and high precision of Kirin chip, it provides better AI performance with greater computing power.
2. The number of supported operators exceeds 300, which is the largest in the industry, and more frameworks are supported, so the flexibility and compatibility have been greatly improved.
3. Honghu chip, Kirin chip, AI Camera chip and full scene chip enable more AI capabilities of devices.

HiAI Foundation API is going to be released as a unified binary file. The set of API aims to accelerate the calculation of neural network through HiAI heterogeneous computing platform. Currently, it only supports running on Kirin SoC.

By using HiAI Foundation API, developers can focus on novel AI application development rather than computing performance optimization.

HiAI Foundation API is integrated on Kirin SoC chip, which provides developers with running environment and debugging tools based on mobile devices. Developers can run neural network model in mobile devices and call HiAI Foundation API to accelerate computing. HiAI Foundation API does not need to be installed, for it supports relevant integration, development and verification by using the default image of mobile devices.

The following two main function are provided for AI application developers by HiAI Foundation API.

1. It provides a common AI business API, which can run efficiently on mobile devices.
2. It provides an acceleration API, independent of processor hardware, so that application manufacturers and developers can accelerate model computing and operator computing on HiAI heterogeneous acceleration system.

The following basic functions are supported by HiAI Foundation API.

1. It supports AI model management interfaces such as model compilation, model loading, model running and model destruction.
2. It supports basic operator computing interfaces, including convolution, pooling, full link.

HiAI Foundation supports special AI instruction set for neural network model operation, so that more neural network operators can be executed efficiently and in parallel with the least clock cycle.

HiAI Foundation does the offline compilation of various neural network operators, such as convolution, pooling, activation, full link into the special AI instruction sequence of NPU through tools. At the same time, it rearranges the data and weight, and fuse the instruction and data to generate the offline execution model. When compiling offline, the operators that can be fused between the front and back layers (convolution, activation function Relu, pooling) can be fused between layers. This method reduces the read-write bandwidth of DDR and improves the performance.

HiAI Foundation rearranges the relevant data (Batch, Channel, Height, Width) in the neural network model in an efficient way, especially the channel data of characteristic graph. During the convolution operation, the calculation efficiency of associated with the channel is greatly improved.

HiAI Foundation supports sparse model acceleration. Under the premise of no loss of calculation accuracy, the weight is set to zero and sparse optimization is carried out. NPU skips the multiplication and addition operation with zero coefficient, which greatly improves the calculation efficiency and reduces the bandwidth.

Figure 7.4 shows that the trained neural network model is generated by the compiler tool, which is executed efficiently on HiAI Foundation, and saved as a binary file offline model.

The standard neural network model, such as Caffe, is compiled and converted into an offline model. The purpose of compilation is to optimize the network configuration and generate the optimized object file, which is the offline model. The offline model is serially stored on the disk. When the neural network is used for forward calculation, the optimized object file is used for calculation directly, and the speed is faster.

Figure 7.5 shows that in offline model calculation, the offline model is loaded from the file, and the user's input data (such as pictures) is copied to the NPU of HiAI for calculation. In the process of calculation, each inference only needs to import and export user data from DDR to NPU once.

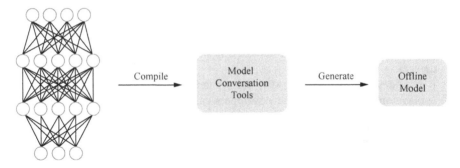

Fig. 7.4 Neural network model compiled into offline model

Fig. 7.5 Loading calculation of offline model

HUAWEI HiAI Foundation supports a variety of intelligent platform frameworks, including Caffe and TensorFlow, and different intelligent platform frameworks are used. The third party needs to indicate the specific intelligent platform framework to be used in this calculation in the interface, and other interfaces and parameters need no modification.

HUAWEI HiAI Foundation supports most models and neural network operators, and continues to optimize and improve them.

7.1.3 HUAWEI HiAI Engine

HUAWEI HiAI Engine, as an open platform of application capabilities, easily integrates a variety of AI capabilities with Apps, making Apps more intelligent and powerful. HUAWEI HiAI Engine 3.0 adds some API recognition capabilities on the basis of the previous one, so that the number of underlying APIs exceeds 40. HUAWEI HiAI Engine not just allows users to directly call the existing API, but helps developers to focus on business development. To achieve image recognition, voice processing and other functions, users just need to put the integrated API into App. Moreover, in HUAWEI HiAI 3.0, APIs such as computer vision and speech recognition are distributed, which helps developers develop more full scene intelligent life experiences.

HiAI's open application engines include CV engine, ASR engine, NLU engine, etc. According to the survey results of developers' demands for HiAI's capabilities, more than 60% of the respondents focused on CV, ASR, NLU.

1. Computer Vision (CV) features the capability of computer to simulate human visual system to perceive the surrounding environment, which is composed of judgment, recognition and understanding space. It includes image super resolution, face recognition, object recognition and so on.
2. Automatic Speech Recognition (ASR) designates the capability of converting human voice into text for further analysis and understanding by computer. It includes speech recognition, speech conversion and so on.
3. Natural Language Understanding (NLU) indicates the capability of computer to understand human voice or text, communicate or act naturally in combination with ASR. It includes word segmentation, text entity recognition, sentiment bias analysis, machine translation and so on.

The application scenarios and open engines of HUAWEI HiAI Engine are shown in Table 7.1, and the specific API introduction is shown in Appendix 1 in Chap. 8.

7.1.4 HUAWEI HiAI Service

HUAWEI HiAI Service API achieves intelligent distribution of Pan terminal, so that developers only need to access the service once before they reuse it in mobile phones, tablet computers and other terminals to complete the distribution efficiently. HiAI Service API can timely and appropriately recommend AI applications or services to users, so that users quickly gets what they need in massive services. At the same time, AI applications also accurately connects users. With the help of HiAI Service API, each function or content in the application is split into individual atomic services for push. HiAI Service API has the function of multi-scene and multi-entry precise distribution. HiAI Service API is used in multiple portals such as HiBoard intelligent assistant, global search, HiVoice, HiTouch and HiVison to recommend and display relevant applications according to users' habits or search contents, voice instructions and other operations, making the corresponding applications reach users more intelligently and accurately. HiAI Service API connects man and services intelligently, realizing the experience upgrading from "man hunting for services" to "services hunting for man".

7.2 Application Development Based on HUAWEI HiAI Platform

HUAWEI HiAI also provides IDE, a development tool for rapid integration of HiAI capabilities, aiming to help developers use Huawei EMUI open capabilities quickly, conveniently and efficiently. Based on Android Studio function extension (provided in plug-in form), IDE supports HiAI Engine, HiAI Foundation (AI model analysis, AI model transformation, business class generation, AI model market), etc. IDE

Table 7.1 The application scenarios and open engines of HUAWEI HiAI engine

Short video, Live video	Social platform	AR	Photograph, image post-processing	Shopping	Translation Word processing
Face Recognition Gesture Recognition Portrait Segmentation Posture Recognition Video Stylization Speech Control Intelligent Depth-of-filed Control Image Scene Recognition	Photo Classification Image Recognition Image Super Resolution Sensitive Information Identification	Situational Awareness Speech Control Depth Estimation Ray Estimation	Makeup Mode Image Intensification Aesthetic Scoring Photo Album Generation Speech Control Camera Gesture Control Camera	QR Code Scanning Direct Service and Recommendation ID Card Identification Bank Card Identification Picture-reading Shopping	Photo translation OCR Word Segmentation Named Entity Recognition Text Emotion Recognition Text Intelligent Reply Text Image Super Resolution
CV, ASR	CV, NLU	ASR, CV	CV	CV	NLU, CV, ASR

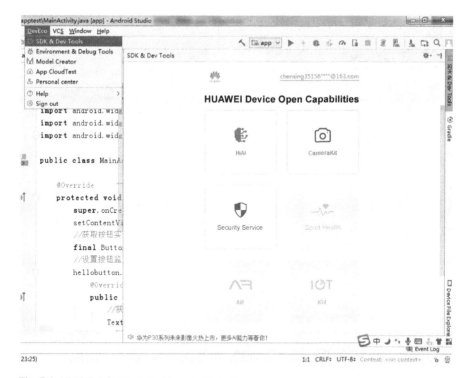

Fig. 7.6 HiAI IDE integrated with android studio

supports drag operation, fast and efficient integration, and provides free remote real machine service (3000 + AI real machine, 7 × 24 h remote one-click debugging).

IDE supports operating systems such as Android studio 2.3. X and above, Windows 7, Windows 10, Mac OS 10.12/10.13. If the operating system does not meet the requirements, it only affects the AI local model conversion function.

IDE selects corresponding functions according to actual scenarios: HUAWEI HiAI Engine is selected when using EMUI AI API, while HUAWEI HiAI Foundation is selected to convert TensorFlow/Caffe model into HUAWEI HiAI model, and then integrate model into App. And HUAWEI HiAI Service is used as a service provider for ordinary App.

HiAI is perfectly integrated with Android Studio, that is, HiAI is used as a plug-in of Android Studio, as shown in Fig. 7.6.

HiAI platform plug-in provides the functions of HiAI Engine and HiAI Foundation. HiAI Engine mainly provides API integrated with App, which can be called directly. HiAI Foundation integrates the trained models, which can be downloaded and used directly, as shown in Fig. 7.7.

After the development of APP is completed, it will enter the real machine debugging phase. Huawei provides a full range of Huawei remote real machine debugging services for developers. Developers can access the real machine of Huawei remote terminal laboratory with one click, conducting real-time remote

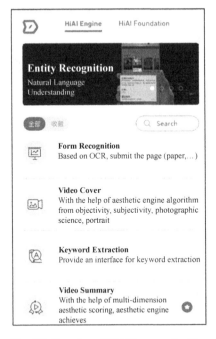

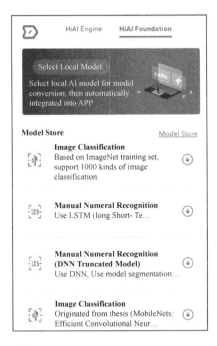

Fig. 7.7 Function of HiAI integrated with android studio

Fig. 7.8 Huawei models supported by HiAI

control and single-step debugging, with provided profiling and log. Some Huawei models supported by HiAI are shown in Fig. 7.8.

The steps of App integrated into HiAI DDK are as follows: Firstly, we get the framework models such as trained Caffe/TensorFlow, and then use the provided OMG model conversion tool to convert the original open source framework model into OM model, which contains 8-bit quantization function, suitable for DaVinci platform. Finally App integration is carried out, which includes model preprocessing, model inference and other parts, as shown in Fig. 7.9.

Fig. 7.9 Procedure of App
integrated into HiAI DDK

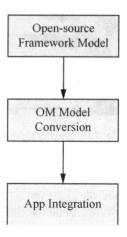

The integration process of App is as follows.

1. Step 1: Create a project.

   (a) Create an Android Studio project and check the "Include C++ support" option.
   (b) C++ Standard select C++ 11, check "Exceptions Support (-fexceptions)" option, check "Runtime Type Information Support(-frtti)" option.

2. Step 2: Compile JNI.

   (a) Realize JNI, write Android.mk Documents.
   (b) rite Application.mk File, copy sdk so to the resource library.
   (c) In build.gradle File, specify NDK to compile C++ files.

3. Step 3: Model integration.

   (a) Model preprocessing: application layer model preprocessing, JNI layer model preprocessing.
   (b) Model Inference.

7.3 Part of the HUAWEI HiAI Solutions

7.3.1 HUAWEI HiAI Helping the Deaf and Dumb

Hearing-impaired children cannot enjoy normal good time because of their physical handicaps. They cannot hear the greetings from their family and friends. For them, the world is silent and lonely. According to the statistics, there are about 32 million hearing-impaired children in the world. They can neither hear beautiful voices nor speak out their inner thoughts i, so their way of communicating with the world is fraught with obstacles.

Fig. 7.10   Huawei HiAI animating the text

The cruel reality is that the parents of 90% of hearing-impaired children are able-bodied. However, 78% of them are unable to communicate with their children. Hearing impaired children have great difficulties in language learning and reading.

Language is the basis of listening, speaking, reading and writing, and listening is the only way to language learning. For example, when encountering a new word, normal children can understand its meaning by listening to the explanation of adults, and then they can master it through continuous listening, speaking, reading and writing. Hearing-impaired children, however, cannot do it, as for them language learning is carried out through sign language. Without the help of professional sign language teachers, they can not communicate with ordinary people.

Therefore, together with European Union for the Deaf (a non-profit organization), Penguin Group and Aardman (an animation master), Huawei has developed an application StorysSign. With the aid of Huawei HiAI platform's some capabilities such as Image Recognition and Optical Character Recognition (OCR), if you use your mobile phone to face the text on the book, Huawei HiAI will animate the text immediately. Sister Xingxing uses sign language to express the text on the book, as shown in Fig. 7.10.

7.3.2   HUAWEI HiAI Enhancing the Visual Effects of Yuanbei Driving Test Application

Yuanbei driving test is a tailor-made driving learning application for beginners. It provides illustrated driving test services, including enrollment for driving school, booking learning, and simulation driving test. It is committed to establishing a convenient and practical one-stop driving test platform.

Simulation driving test, one of the main features of Yuanbei driving test, combines graphics, video, voice and other forms of the built-in installation package. It effectively helps learners quickly get familiar with the test content and specifications, so that they can pass the driving test quickly.

Simulation test contains a large number of pictures to assist learners to practice, but the practice might be impacted due to some low-quality pictures' poor display and clarity lack on the ordinary mobile phones.

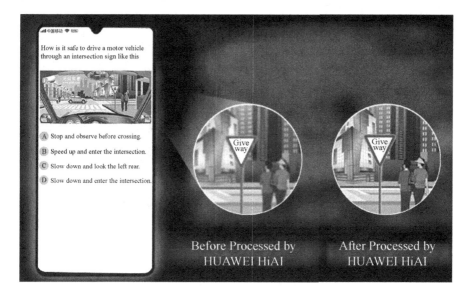

Fig. 7.11 HUAWEI HiAI enhancing the visual effects of Yuanbei driving test application

On most devices, image optimization program of simulation driving test relies on the Internet. Therefore, in the case of weak network signal or no network, the improvement of picture quality will be significantly hindered.

HUAWEI HiAI adopts intelligent noise reduction and 9× resolution amplification, which significantly improves the image quality, bringing users more clear image details, and comprehensively enhancing the user's visual experience.

Relying on HUAWEI HiAI on-device learning model, Yuanbei driving test achieves the optimization and amplification of on-device pictures, and the same pictures are displayed more clearly on Huawei NPU models. Meanwhile, free from network dependence, users can still view high-quality amplified pictures when the network is unstable or disconnected, as shown in Fig. 7.11.

7.3.3   HUAWEI HiAI Empowering Ctrip Travel

Ctrip mobile app provides users with comprehensive travel services, including hotel reservation, air tickets, train tickets, travel guides, admission ticket discounts, travel insurance, etc.

During the journey, users often take many photos, hoping to capture the beautiful scenery for memory. But due to the lack of professional photography knowledge, most people cannot judge accurately whether the photos are good or not, and they always doubt whether the photos have taken the best effect. At the same time, the pictures taken by users are not clear enough, and the rendering effect is poor. Therefore, improving the image quality has become the appeal of many users.

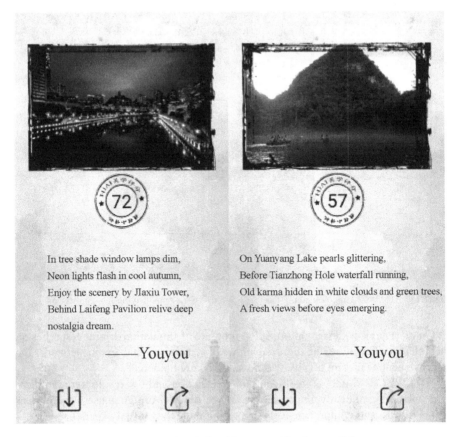

In tree shade window lamps dim,
Neon lights flash in cool autumn,
Enjoy the scenery by JIaxiu Tower,
Behind Laifeng Pavilion relive deep
nostalgia dream.

——Youyou

On Yuanyang Lake pearls glittering,
Before Tianzhong Hole waterfall running,
Old karma hidden in white clouds and green trees,
A fresh views before eyes emerging.

——Youyou

Fig. 7.12 HUAWEI HiAI empowering Ctrip with poem writing in one-click

By accessing the aesthetic scoring capability of HUAWEI HiAI Engine, it automatically integrates the technical factors such as defocus and jitter of the image, and the subjective aesthetic feeling such as skew, color and composition, evaluate and score the image. Users can quickly understand the photo quality through the score level, solve their doubts, and adjust accordingly, so as to take the most beautiful scenery.

In addition, with the help of HUAWEI HiAI, the application also realizes the functions of voice wake-up and poem writing in one-click, which provides users with a lot of conveniences, as shown in Fig. 7.12.

7.3.4 HUAWEI HiAI Empowering WPS Document Error Detection and Correction

WPS App is an office software, which can edit and view common office documents such as text, forms, presentation. Meanwhile, users can use free cloud space and document templates.

With the rise and development of mobile devices, mobile phones are increasingly used in editing documents, sending and receiving e-mails. However, without the assistance of keyboard or mouse, only through the fingers on the screen to complete the operation, mobile phone office efficiency is extremely low. For example, when attending a class or attending a meeting or training, we see the key points and "essences" on the presentation, we will take out our mobile phone immediately to take photos and record them. However, the photos often need clipping on the computer before sorted into presentation, which is quite cumbersome and time-consuming.

1. Surroundings interference: In addition to the presentation, there are surrounding interference such as the screen, walls, desks and chairs in the pictures taken by users, which need to be cropped.
2. Distorted document image: When the shooting angle is not directly facing the document, the document imaging will be distorted to varying degrees, and the stretched or compressed image will affect the subsequent use.
3. Blur image: Restricted in light, distance and other factors, the images taken by users may be blur, which will subsequently affect the perception and information recognition.
4. Non-editable content: Many users want to edit or modify the content of the presentation when viewing the captured presentation pictures. However, the image content cannot be edited directly.

WPS can easily solve the above problems by accessing to HUAWEI HiAI ecology and the powerful performance of Huawei Kirin 970 processor. It only takes 3 s to generate a presentation from multiple pictures with one click.

1. Document perception for automatic identification of document valid area: By accessing to HUAWEI HiAI Engine document detection and correction capability, WPS accurately perceives the area where the document is located, and automatically clip the surroundings such as the screen, walls, desks and chairs, as shown in Fig. 7.13.
2. Document correction for quick adjustment to center view: It is an auxiliary enhancement in the process of document remaking, which automatically adjusts the camera angle directly to the document, with the maximum correction angle of 45°, as shown in Fig. 7.14.
3. Text super-resolution for clearer text in the document: HUAWEI HiAI magnifies the image that contains the text content by nine times of resolution (three times of height and width), as a result, the quality of the picture is significantly improved and the text is legible, as shown in Fig. 7.15.

Fig. 7.13 WPS document perception

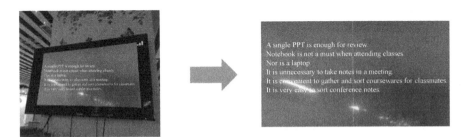

Fig. 7.14 WPS document correction

Fig. 7.15 Text super-resolution

4. OCR recognition for free editing of text content in pictures: By accessing to general OCR, WPS automatically recognizes and extracts text information in pictures, achieving free modification, clipping, copying and deleting of text content in presentation pictures, as shown in Fig. 7.16.

For more solutions, please pay attention to the official website of HiAI.

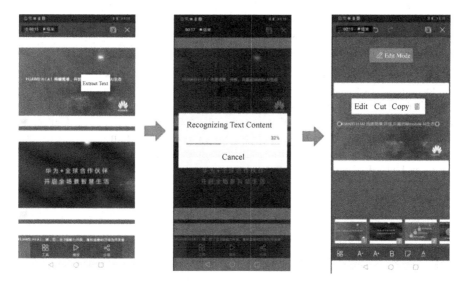

Fig. 7.16 WPS OCR recognition

7.4 Chapter Summary

This chapter mainly introduces the three-layer ecological structure of HUAWEI HiAI platform: HUAWEI HiAI Foundation, HUAWEI HiAI Engine, and HUAWEI HiAI Service API. The relevant capabilities of each layer, and some HiAI solutions are introduced as well.

Finally, in order to connect developers in an all-round way, HUAWEI HiAI has adopted the following activities to encourage innovation and achieve ecological win-win.

1. HUAWEI HiAI has organized the following profound communication activities of offline connection.

   (a) HUAWEI Developer Day salons.
   (b) HUAWEI HiAI open classes.
   (c) HUAWEI HiAI special technical meetings.

2. HUAWEI HiAI has organized the following activities worth of $1 billion to spur full scene innovation.

   (a) Open innovation of terminal capability.
   (b) Digital service innovation of full scene.
   (c) Ecological co-construction of Cloud service.

3. HUAWEI HiAI has organized the following innovation contests.

(a) AI application innovation contest.
(b) Future application creativity contest.
(c) AR application innovation contest.

Huawei believes that AI can make users' lives better. Whether it is the back-end or the terminal, AI can break through the imagination and bring users with unprecedented convenience. But all of these need to have practical application scenarios, in which more enterprises and developers can participate so that users can get substantial experience improvement. Huawei is willing to cooperate with more talents and enterprises, so as to jointly promote the implementation of industry intelligence based on HUAWEI HiAI 3.0 platform.

7.5   Exercises

1. HUAWEI HiAI 3.0 was officially released at Software Green Alliance Developer Conference on November 19, 2019, marking that on-engine AI is officially moving towards distributed, which will bring the ultimate full scene intelligent life experience. What is the three-layer AI ecology of HUAWEI HiAI?
2. Which layer of HUAWEI HiAI can compile the standard neural network model into offline model?
3. Which layer of HUAWEI HiAI can easily integrate multiple AI capabilities with App to make App more intelligent and powerful?
4. Which tool can HiAI integrate with perfectly?
5. What is the integration process of APP?

Chapter 8
Huawei CLOUD Enterprise Intelligence Application Platform

This chapter mainly introduces Huawei CLOUD Enterprise Intelligence (EI), including Huawei CLOUD EI service family. It focuses on Huawei ModelArts platform and Huawei EI solutions.

8.1 Huawei CLOUD EI Service Family

Huawei CLOUD EI service family is composed of EI big data, EI basic platform, conversational bot, natural language processing (NLP), speech interaction, speech analysis, image recognition, content review, image search, face recognition, Optical Character Recognition (OCR) and EI agent, as shown in Fig. 8.1.

1. EI big data provides such services as data access, CLOUD data migration, real-time streaming computing, MapReduce, Data Lake Insight, table store.
2. EI basic platform provides such services as ModelArts platform, deep learning, machine learning, HiLens, graph engine service and video access.
3. Conversational bot provides intelligent QABot, TaskBot, intelligent quality inspection bot and customized conventional bot services.
4. Natural language processing provides natural language processing fundamentals, content review—text and language understanding, language generation, NLP Customization, machine translation.
5. Speech interaction provides speech recognition, speech synthesis and real-time speech transcription.
6. Video analysis provides video content analysis, video editing, video quality detection and video tagging.
7. Image recognition provides the services of image tagging and celebrity recognition.
8. Content review provides the review of text, image and video.

© The Author(s) 2023
Huawei Technologies Co., Ltd., *Artificial Intelligence Technology*,
https://doi.org/10.1007/978-981-19-2879-6_8

Fig. 8.1 Huawei CLOUD EI service family

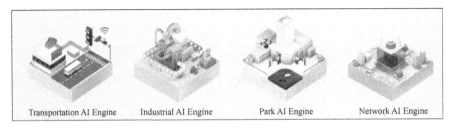

Fig. 8.2 EI agent

9. Image search indicates searching images with images, assisting customers to search the same or similar images from the designated image library.
10. Face recognition provides face recognition and body analysis.
11. OCR provides character recognition of general class, certificate class, bill class, industry class and customized template class.
12. EI agent is composed of transportation AI agent, industrial AI agent, park AI agent, network AI agent, auto AI agent, medical AI engine and geographic AI agent.

8.1.1 Huawei CLOUD EI Agent

EI agent integrates AI technology into the application scenarios of all walks of life. Combined with various technologies, it deeply excavates data value and makes full use of AI technology, and thus a scenario based solution is developed to improve its efficiency and users' experience. EI agent is composed of transportation AI engine, industrial AI engine, park AI engine and network AI engine, as shown in Fig. 8.2. In

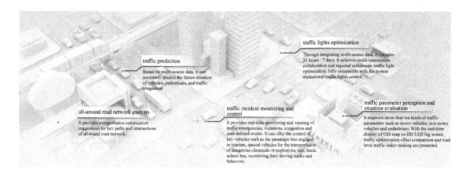

Fig. 8.3 Transportation AI engine

addition, vehicle AI engine, medical AI engine and geographic AI engine are launched by Huawei as well.

1. Transportation AI Engine

   Transportation AI engine realizes the products and solutions such as all-around road network analysis, traffic prediction, traffic incident monitoring and control, traffic lights optimization, traffic parameter perception and situation evaluation to ensure efficient, green and safe travelling. Transportation AI engine is shown in Fig. 8.3.

   Transportation AI engine has the following advantages.

   (a) It realizes comprehensive and in-depth data mining, with fully integrated Internet and transportation big data, and deeply excavated big data value.
   (b) It provides all-around collaboration and pedestrian-vehicle collaboration, which maximizes the traffic flow of the whole region and minimizes the waiting time of vehicles in the region. It also coordinate the traffic demand of vehicles and pedestrians, so as realize the orderly passage of vehicles and pedestrians.
   (c) It provides real-time traffic light scheduling, which is the first in the industry to achieve the standard formulation for safe communication interface between transportation AI agent and traffic light control platform.
   (d) It can accurately predict the driving path demand so as to plan the route in advance.

   Transportation AI engine is characterized as follows.

   (a) Full time: It realizes the 7×24 h whole-area and full-time perception of traffic incidents.
   (b) Intelligence: It achieves regional traffic light optimization.
   (c) Completeness: It can identify key congestion points and key congestion paths, making an analysis of congestion diffusion.
   (d) Prediction: It predicts the crowd density, obtaining the traffic regularity of crowd migration.

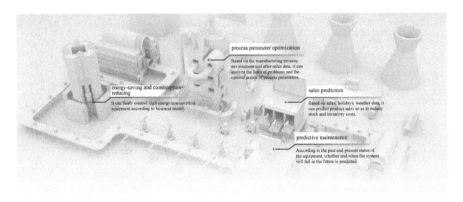

Fig. 8.4 Industrial AI engine

(e) Accuracy: It achieves the comprehensive and accurate control of traffic conditions in 7 × 24 h.
(f) Convenience: It realizes real-time traffic light scheduling and traffic clearance on demand.
(g) Visuality: It displays live traffic situation on large screen.
(h) Finess: It realizes key vehicle control and fine management.

2. Industrial AI Engine

Relying on big data and artificial intelligence, industrial AI engine provides full-chain services in the fields of design, production, logistics, sales and service. It excavates data value, assisting enterprises to take a lead with new technologies. Industrial AI engine is shown in Fig. 8.4.

Industrial AI engine causes the three major changes of the existing industry.

(a) Transformation from artificial experience to data intelligence: Based on data mining analysis, new experience of efficiency promotion and product quality improvement can be obtained from data.
(b) Transition from digital to intelligent: The ability of intelligent analysis has become the new driving force of enterprise digitization.
(c) Transition from product manufacturing to product innovation: Data collaboration from product design to sales in enterprises, as well as data collaboration between upstream and downstream of industrial chain, brings to new competitive advantages.

The application of industrial AI engine is as follows.

(a) Product quality optimization and improvement: Based on customer feedback, Internet comment analysis, competitor analysis, maintenance records and after-sales historical data, a classified analysis is carried out in order to find out key problems of products, so as to guide new product improvement and product quality promotion.

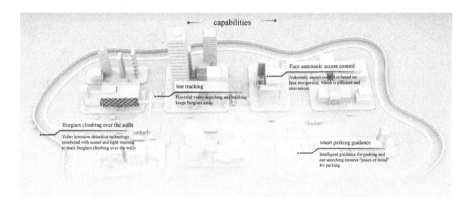

Fig. 8.5 Park AI engine

(b) Intelligent equipment maintenance: According to the past and present status of the system, predictive maintenance is taken through the predictive inference methods such as time series prediction, neural network prediction, regression analysis. It can predict whether the system will fail in the future, when it will fail, and the type of failure, so as to improve the efficiency of service operation and maintenance, reduce the unplanned downtime of the equipment, and save the labor cost on-site service.

(c) Production material estimation: Based on the historical material data, the materials needed for production are accurately predicted so as to reduce the storage cycle and improve the efficiency. Deep algorithm optimization is based on the industry time series algorithm model, combined with Huawei supply chain deep optimization.

3. Park AI Engine

Park AI engine applies artificial intelligence to the management and monitoring of industrial park, residential park and commercial park, so as to provide a convenient and efficient environment through the technologies such as video analysis, data mining. Park AI engine is shown in Fig. 8.5.

Park AI engine brings the following three changes.

(a) From manual defense to intelligent defense: Intelligent security based on artificial intelligence can relieve the pressure on security personnel.

(b) From card swiping to face scanning: Face-scanning automatically clocks in, so it is no longer necessary to bring the entrance card.

(c) From worry to reassurance: With powerful lost tracking and analysis ability, artificial intelligence makes employees and property owners feel more at ease.

The application of park AI engine is as follows.

(a) Park entrance control: Face recognition technology can accurately identify the identity of visitors and quickly return the results. Therefore, a high

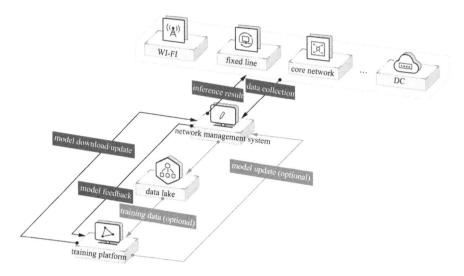

Fig. 8.6 Network AI engine

throughput of entrance control and automatic park management can be achieved.

(b) Safety Monitoring: Through the intelligent technologies such as intrusion detection, loitering detection, abandoned object detection, the area can be monitored to ensure its safety.

(c) Smart parking: Through vehicle license plate recognition and track trajectory, the services such as vehicle access control, driving line control, illegal parking management, parking space management can be realized.

4. Network AI Engine

Network AI engine (NAIE) introduces AI into the network field to solve the problems of network business prediction, repeatability and complexity. It improves the utilization of network resources, operation and maintenance efficiency, energy efficiency and business experience, making it possible to realize automatic driving network. Network AI Engine is shown in Fig. 8.6.

Network AI engine has the following commercial values.

(a) The utilization rate of resources has been improved. AI is introduced to predict the network traffic, according to the prediction results, so that network resources are managed in a balanced way to improve the utilization rate of network resources.

(b) Improve the efficiency of operation and maintenance. AI is introduced to compress a lot of repetitive work, predict faults and carry out preventive maintenance, so as to improve the operation and maintenance efficiency of the network.

(c) Improve the efficiency of energy utilization. AI technology is used to predict the business status in real time, automatically making dynamic adjustment of energy consumption according to the business volume, so as to improve the efficiency of energy utilization.

The technical advantages of network AI engine are as follows.

(a) Data safely entering lake. It supports the rapid collection of various types of data such as network parameters, performance and alarm into the lake. On the one hand, a large number of tools are provided to improve the efficiency of data governance. At the same time, multi tenant isolation, encryption and storage are applied to ensure the whole life cycle security of data entering lake.
(b) Network experience embedding. It uses the guided model development environment and presets multiple AI model development templates in network domain. It provides different services for different developers such as training service, model generation service, communication model service, aiming to help developers quickly complete model/application development.
(c) Rich application services. It provides application services for various network business scenarios such as wireless access, fixed network access, transmission load, core network, DC, energy. It can effectively solve the specific problems of operation and maintenance efficiency, energy consumption efficiency and resource utilization rate in network services.

8.1.2   EI Basic Platform: Huawei HiLens

Huawei HiLens is a multi-modal AI development and application platform of End-Cloud collaboration, which is composed of end-side computing devices and Cloud platform. It provides a simple development framework, an out-of-the-box development environment, a rich AI skill market and Cloud management platform. It connects with a variety of end-side computing devices, supporting visual and auditory AI application development, AI application online deployment, and massive device management. HiLens help users develop multi-modal AI applications and distribute them to end-side devices to realize intelligent solutions for multiple scenarios. HiLens is shown in Fig. 8.7.

HiLens products feature as follows.

1. End-Cloud collaborative inference, balancing low computing delay and high accuracy.
2. End-side analysis of data, minimizing the cost of cloud storage.
3. One-stop skill development, shortening the development cycle.
4. Skills market presets rich skills, online training, one-click deployment.

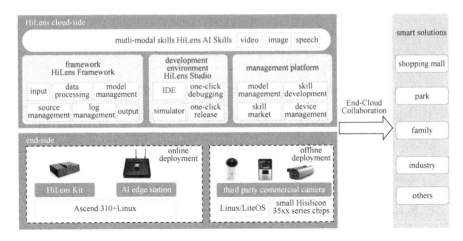

Fig. 8.7 Huawei Hilens End-Cloud collaboration

1. HiLens Product Advantage

(a) End-Cloud collaborative inference.

- End-Cloud collaboration can work in the scenario of unstable network and save user bandwidth.
- End-side device can cooperate with Cloud-side device to update the model online, and quickly improve the accuracy of end-side.
- End-side can analyze the local data, greatly minimizing cloud data flow and saving the storage cost.

(b) Unified skills development platform.

With a collaborative optimization of software and hardware, HiLens products use a unified skill development framework, encapsulate basic components, and support common deep learning models.

(c) Cross platform design.

- HiLens products support Ascend AI processor, Hisilicon 35xx series chips and other mainstream chips in the market, which can cover the needs of mainstream monitoring scenarios.
- HiLens products provide model conversion and algorithm optimization for end-side chips.

(d) Rich skill market.

- A variety of skills are preset in HiLens skill market, such as human shape detection and crying detection. Users can select the required skills directly from the skill market and quickly deploy them on the end side without any development steps.
- HiLens has done a lot of algorithm optimization to solve the problems of small memory and low precision of end-to-end devices.

- Developers can also develop custom skills through the HiLens admin console and join the skill market.

2. HiLens Application

(a) From the perspective of users, Huawei HiLens mainly has three types of users: ordinary users, AI developers and camera manufacturers.

- Ordinary users: Ordinary users are skill users, who can be family members, supermarket owners, parking-lot attendant or site managers. HiLens Kit can achieve the functions such as family security improvement, customer flow counting, the identification of vehicle attribute and license plate, the detection of safety helmet wearing. And the users only need to register to HiLens management console, purchase or customize appropriate skills (such as license plate identification, safety helmet recognition, etc.) in platform skill market. One-click to install HiLens Kit can meet their needs.
- AI developers: AI developers are usually technicians or college students who are engaged in AI development. They can easily deploy to the device to see how those skills work in real time if they want to obtain certain income or knowledge from AI. These users can develop AI skills in HiLens management console.

  HiLens integrates HiLens framework on the end side, which encapsulates the basic components, simplifies the development process, and provides a unified API interface, by which developers easily complete the development of a skill. After the skill development is completed, users can deploy it to HiLens Kit with one click to view the running effect. At the same time, skills can also be released to the skill market for other users to buy and use, or skills can be shared as templates for other developers to learn.
- Camera manufacturers: Manufacturers of Hisilicon 35xx series chip camera products. For this series of cameras may have weak or even no AI capabilities, the manufacturers expect their products to be more competitive after obtaining stronger AI capabilities.

(b) In terms of application scenarios, Huawei HiLens can be applied in various fields such as home intelligent surveillance, park intelligent surveillance, supermarket intelligent surveillance, intelligent in-vehicle.

- Home intelligent surveillance: Home Intelligent cameras and smart home manufacturers, integrated with Huawei Hisilicon 35xx series chips, as well as high-performance HiLens Kit integrated with D chip, can be used to improve home video intelligent analysis ability. It can be applied to the following scenarios.

  – Human shape detection. It can detect the human figure in the family surveillance, record the time of appearance, or send an alert to the mobile phone after it is detected in some period of time when no one is at home.

- Fall detection. When it detects someone falls down, the alert is sent out. It is used mainly for elderly care.
- Cry detection. When it detects baby's crying, the alert is sent to the user's mobile phone. It is used for child care.
- Vocabulary recognition. It can customize a specific word, such as "help", and give an alert when the word is detected.
- Face attribute detection. The face attributes are detected, including gender, age, smiling face, which can be used for door security, video filtering and so on.
- Time album. The video clips of the detected children are combined into a time album to record the growth of children.

- Park intelligent surveillance: Through HiLens management console, AI skills are distributed to the intelligent small station with Ascend chip integrated, so that edge devices can handle certain data. It can be applied to the following scenarios.

  - Face recognition gate. Based on face recognition technology, face recognition can be realized for the entrance and exit gates of the park.
  - License plate/vehicle identification. In entrance and exit of the park or garage, vehicle license plate and vehicle type identification can be carried out to realize the license plate and vehicle type authorization certification.
  - Safety helmet detection. Workers without wearing safety helmet will be found from video surveillance and alert will be initiated on the specified equipment.
  - Track restore. The face of the same person or vehicle identified by multiple cameras is analyzed to restore the path of pedestrian or vehicle.
  - Face retrieval. In the surveillance, face recognition is used to identify the specified face, which can be used for blacklist recognition.
  - Abnormal sound detection. When abnormal sound such as glass breakage and explosion sound is detected, alert shall be reported.
  - Intrusion detection. An alert is sent when a human shape is detected in the specified surveillance area.

- Shopping mall intelligent surveillance: The terminal devices applicable to shopping mall include HiLens Kit, intelligent edge station and commercial cameras. Small supermarkets can integrate HiLens Kit, which supports 4–5 channels of video analysis scenes. With small size, it can be placed in the indoor environment. It can be applied to the following scenarios.

  - Customer flow statistics. Through the surveillance of stores and supermarkets, the intelligent custom flow statistics at the entrance and exit can be realized, which can be used to analyze the customer flow changes at different periods.
  - VIP identification. Through face recognition, VIP customers can be accurately identified to help formulate marketing strategies.

  - Statistics of new and old customers. Through face recognition, the number of new and old customers can be counted.
  - Pedestrian counting heat map. Through the analysis of pedestrian counting heat map, the density of crowd can be identified, which is beneficial for commodity popularity analysis.

- Intelligent in-vehicle: Intelligent in-vehicle equipment is based on Android system, which can realize real-time intelligent analysis of internal and external conditions. It is applicable to the scenarios such as driving behavior detection, "two kinds of passenger coaches and one kind of hazardous chemical truck" surveillance. It can be applied to the following scenarios.

  - Face recognition. By identifying whether the driver's face matches the owner's pre-stored photo library, the driver's authority is confirmed.
  - Fatigue driving. Real time surveillance of driver's driving state can be detected, and an intelligent warning is sent if fatigue driving is detected.
  - Posture analysis. Detect the driver's distracted behaviors, such as making a phone call, drinking water, gazing around, smoking.
  - Vehicle and pedestrian detection. It can be used for pedestrian detection in blind area.

8.1.3   EI Basic Platform: Graph Engine Service

Huawei Graph Engine Service (GES) is the first commercial distributed native graph engine with independent intellectual property rights in China. It is a service for query and analysis of graph structure data based on "relation".

Adopting EYWA, a high-performance graph engine developed by Huawei, as its core, GES has a number of independent patents. It is widely used in the scenarios with rich relational data such as social applications, enterprise relation analysis, logistics distribution, shuttle bus route planning, enterprise knowledge graph, risk control, recommendation, public opinion, fraud prevention.

Massive and complex associated data such as social relations, transaction records and transportation networks are naturally graph data, while Huawei GES is a service for storage, querying and analysis of graph-structured data based on relations. It plays an important role in many scenarios such as social App, enterprise relation analysis, logistics distribution, shuttle bus route planning, enterprise knowledge graph, risk control.

In individual analysis, GES conducts user portrait analysis on individual nodes according to the number and characteristics of their neighbors. It can also excavate and identify opinion leaders according to the characteristics and importance of the nodes. For example, considering the quantity factor, the more attention a user receives from others, the more important the user is. On the other hand, the quality

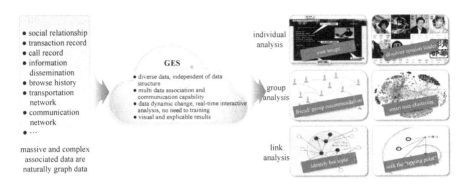

Fig. 8.8 Graph engine service

transfer factor is considered based on the transfer characteristics on the graph, the quality of fans is transferred to the concerned. When concerned by high-quality fans, the quality of the concerned increases.

In group analysis, with label propagation algorithm and community discovery algorithm, GES divides nodes with similar characteristics into one class, so that it can be applied to the node classification scenarios such as friend recommendation, group recommendation and user clustering. For example, in a social circle, if two people have a mutual friend, they will have the possibility of becoming friends in the future. The more mutual friends they have, the stronger their relationship will be. This allows to make friend recommendations based on the number of mutual friends.

In link analysis, GES can use link analysis algorithm and relationship prediction algorithm to predict and identify hot topics, so as to find "the tipping point", as shown in Fig. 8.8.

It can be seen that the application scenarios of GES in the real world are rich and extensive. There will be more industries and application scenarios in the future worthy of in-depth exploration.

The product advantages of GES are as follows.

1. Large scale: GES provides efficient data organization, which can more effectively query and analyze the data of 10 billion nodes and 100 billion edges.
2. High performance: GES provides deeply optimized distributed graph computing engine, through which users can obtain the real-time query capability of high concurrency, second-level and multi-hop.
3. Integration of query and analysis: GES provides a wealth of graph analysis algorithms, which a variety of analysis capabilities for business such as relationship analysis, route planning and precision marketing.
4. Ease of use: GES provides a guided, easy-to-use visual analysis interface, and what you see is what you get; GES supports Gremlin query language, which is compatible with user habits.

The functions provided by GES are as follows.

1. Rich domain algorithms: GES supports many algorithms such as PageRank, K-core, shortest path, label propagation algorithm, triangle count, interaction prediction.
2. Visual graphic analysis: GES provides a guided exploration environment, which supports visualization of query results.
3. Query analysis API: GES provides API for graph query, graph index statistics, Gremlin query, graph algorithm, graph management, backup management, etc.
4. Compatible with open source Ecology: GES is compatible with Apache TinkerPop Gremlin 3.3.0.
5. Graph management: GES provides graph engine services such as overview, graph management, graph backup, metadata management.

8.1.4 Introduction to Other Services Provided by EI Family

1. Conversational BOT
   Conversational BOT Service (CBS) is composed of QABot, TaskBot, Intelligent Quality Inspection Bot and Customized Conventional Bot. Conversational BOT is shown in Fig. 8.9.

   (a) QABot: It can help enterprises quickly build, release and manage intelligent question-answering robot system.
   (b) Taskbot: It can accurately understand the intention of the conversation, extract key information. It can be used for intelligent telephone traffic, intelligent hardware.
   (c) Intelligent quality inspection bot uses natural language algorithm and user-defined rules to analyze the conversation between customer service agents

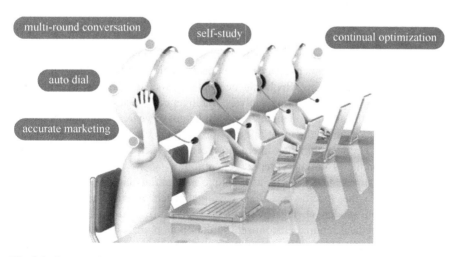

Fig. 8.9 Conversational bot

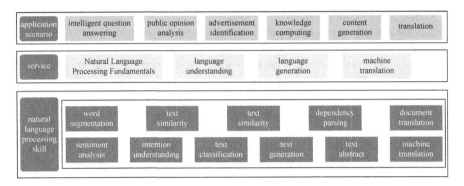

Fig. 8.10 Natural language processing service

and customers in call center scenarios, helping enterprises to improve the
service quality and customer satisfaction.

(d) Customized conversational bot can build AI bots with various capabilities
according to customer needs, including QA of knowledge base and knowledge graph, task-based conversation, reading comprehension, automatic text
generation, multimodality, serving customers in different industries.

2. Natural Language Processing

Natural language processing (NLP) provides the related services needed by
robots to realize semantic understanding, which is composed of four sub services:
NLP foundation, language understanding, language generation and machine
translation. NLP service is shown in Fig. 8.10.

Natural Language Processing Fundamentals provides users with natural language related APIs, including word segmentation, named entity recognition,
keyword extraction, text similarity, which can be applied to such scenarios as
intelligent question answering, conversational bot, public opinion analysis, content recommendation, e-commerce evaluation and analysis.

Language understanding provides users with APIs related to language understanding, such as sentiment analysis, opinion extraction, text classification, intention understanding, etc., which can be applied to such scenarios as comment
opinion mining, public opinion analysis, intelligent assistant, conversational bot.

Based on the advanced language model, language generation generates readable texts according to the input information, including text, data or image. It can
be applied to human-computer interaction scenarios such as intelligent Q&A and
conversation, news summary, report generation.

NLP Customization is to build a unique natural language processing model
according to the specific needs of customer, such as customized automatic
classification model of legal documents, customized automatic generation
model of medical reports, customized public opinion analysis model of specific
fields, which aims to provide unique competitiveness for enterprise applications.

3. Speech Interaction

one-sentence recognition/short speech recognition

real-time speech transcription

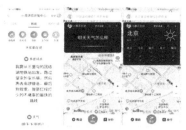

recording file recognition

audio book

Fig. 8.11   Speech interaction

Speech interaction is composed of speech recognition, speech synthesis and real-time voice transcription, as shown in Fig. 8.11.

The main applications of speech recognition are as follows.

(a) Speech search: Search content is directly entered by speech, which makes the search more efficient. Speech recognition supports speech search in various scenarios, such as map navigation, web search and so on.

(b) Human computer interaction: Through speech wake-up and speech recognition, speech commands is sent to terminal devices and real-time operation of devices is implemented to improve human-computer interaction experience.

The applications of speech synthesis are as follows.

(a) Speech navigation: Speech synthesis can convert on-board navigation data into speech material, providing users with accurate speech navigation service. Using the personalized customization ability of speech synthesis, it provides rich navigation speech service.

(b) Audio book: Speech synthesis can transform the text content of books, magazines and news into realistic human voice, so that people can fully free their eyes while obtaining information and having fun in such scenarios such as taking the subway, driving or physical training.

(c) Telephone follow-up: In the scene of customer service system, the follow-up content is converted into human voice through speech synthesis, and the user experience is improved by direct communication with customers in speech.

(d) Intelligent education: Speech synthesis can synthesize the text content in books into speech. The pronunciation close to the real person can simulate live teaching scenes, so as to realize the reading aloud and leading reading of texts, helping students better understand and master the teaching content.

The applications of real-time speech transcription are as follows.

(a) Live subtitle: Real-time speech transcription converts audio in live video or live broadcast into subtitles in real time, providing more efficient viewing experience for the audience and facilitating content monitoring.
(b) Real-time recording of conference: Real-time speech transcription converts audio in video or teleconference into text in real time, which can check, modify and retrieve transcribed conference content in real time, so as to improve conference efficiency.
(c) Instant text entry: Real-time speech transcription on mobile App can be used to record and provide transcribed text in real time, such as speech input method. It is convenient for post-processing and content archiving, saving manpower and time cost of recording, and thus the conversion efficiency is greatly promoted.

4. Video Analysis

Video analysis provides such services as video content analysis, video editing, video tagging.

The applications of video content analysis are as follows.

(a) Monitoring management: Video content analysis conducts a real-time analysis on all videos in the shopping mall or park, in order to extract key episodes, such as warehouse monitoring, cashier compliance troubles, fire exit blockage. It also conducts high security area intruder detection, loitering detection, abandoned object detection, etc.; Intelligent loss prevention can be conducted, such as portrait surveillance, theft detection, etc.
(b) Park pedestrian analysis: Through a real-time analysis on the active pedestrians in the park, video content analysis identifies and tracks the high-risk persons after configuring the pedestrian blacklist, sending a warning. It counts the pedestrian flow at key intersections to formulate park management strategies.
(c) Video character analysis: Through the analysis of the public figures in the media video, video content analysis accurately identifies the political figures, movie stars and other celebrities in the video.
(d) Motion recognition: Video content analysis detects and recognizes the motions in the video after an analysis of the front and back frame information, optical flow motion information, scene content information.

The applications of video editing are as follows.

(a) Highlight clip extraction: Based on the content relevance and highlight of video, video editing extracts scene segments to make video summary.

train   search

About14 results are found

Fig. 8.12   Video search

(b) News video splitting: Video editing splits the complete news into news segments of different themes based on the analysis of characters, scenes, voices and character recognition in the news.

The applications of video tagging are as follows.

(a) Video search: Based on the analysis of video scene classification, people recognition, voice recognition and character recognition, the video tagging forms hierarchical classification tags so as to support accurate and efficient video search and search experience improvement, as shown in Fig. 8.12.

(b) Video recommendation: Based on the analysis of scene classification, person recognition, speech recognition and OCR, video tagging forms hierarchical classification tags for personalized video recommendation.

5. Image Recognition

Image recognition, based on deep learning technology, can accurately identify the visual content in the image, providing tens of thousands of objects, scenes and concept tags. It has the ability of target detection and attribute recognition, so as to help customers accurately identify and understand the image content. Image recognition provides such functions as scene analysis, intelligent photo album, target detection, image search, as shown in Fig. 8.13.

(a) Scene analysis: The lack of content tag leads to low retrieval efficiency. Image tagging can accurately identify image content, improve retrieval efficiency and accuracy, so as to make personalized recommendation, content retrieval and distribution more effective.

scene analysis   smart photo album

target detection   image search

Fig. 8.13 Applications of image recognition

(b) Smart photo album: Based on tens of thousands of tags identified from images, smart photo album can be customized in categories, such as "plants", "food", "work", which is convenient for users to manage.

(c) Target detection: At the construction site, based on the customized image recognition, target detection system can real-time monitor whether the on-site staff wear safety helmet, in order to reduce the safety risk.

(d) Image search: The search of massive image database is troublesome. Image search technology, based on image tag, can quickly search for the desired image no matter whether the user inputs a keyword or an image.

6. Content Review

Content review is composed of text review, image review and video review. Based on the leading detection technology of text, image and video, it can automatically detect the contents concerning pornography, advertising, terrorism, politics, so as to help customers reduce the risk of business violations. Content review is shown in Fig. 8.14.

Content review includes the following applications.

(a) Pornography identification: Content review can judge the pornographic degree of a picture, give three confidence scores: pornographic, sexy and normal.

(b) Terrorism detection: Content review can quickly detect whether the picture contains the content concerning fire, guns, knives, bloodiness, flag of terrorism, etc.

Fig. 8.14 Content review

(c) Sensitive figures involved in politics: Content review can judge whether the content is involved in sensitive political figures.

(d) Text content detection: Content review can detect whether the text content concerns with pornography, politics, advertising, abuse, adding water and contraband.

(e) Video review: Content review can judge whether video has the risk of violation so as to provide violation information from the dimensions of screen, sound and subtitle.

7. Image Search

Image search is to search image with image. Based on deep learning and image recognition technology, it uses feature vectorization and search ability to help customers search for the same or similar pictures from the specified library.

The applications of image search are as follows.

(a) Commodity picture search: Image search can search the pictures taken by the user from the commodity library. By similar picture searching, the same or similar commodity are pushed to the user, so as to sell or recommend the related commodity, as shown in Fig. 8.15.

(b) Picture copyright search: Picture copyright is an important asset of photography and design websites. Image search can quickly locate tort pictures from massive image databases so as to defend the rights of image resource websites.

8. Face Recognition

Face recognition can quickly identify faces in images, analyzing the key information and obtaining face attributes, so that accurate face comparison and retrieval can be achieved.

The applications of face recognition are as follows.

Fig. 8.15 Commodity search

(a) Identity authentication: Face identification and comparison can be used for identity authentication, which is suitable for authentication scenes such as airport, customs.

(b) Electronic attendance: Face identification and comparison is applicable to the electronic attendance of employees in enterprises as well as security monitoring.

(c) Trajectory analysis: Face search can retrieve N face images and their similarity degree that are most similar to the input face in the image database. According to the time, place and behavior information of the return pictures, it can assist customers to realize trajectory analysis.

(d) Customer flow analysis: Customer flow analysis is of great value to shopping malls. Based on the technology of face recognition, comparison and search, it can accurately analyze the information of customers such as age and gender, so as to distinguish new and regular customers, helping customers with efficient marketing. Customer flow analysis is shown in Fig. 8.16.

9. Optical Character Recognition

Optical Character Recognition (OCR) is the recognition of text in a picture or scanned copy into editable text. OCR can replace manual input to improve business efficiency. It supports the character recognition of such scenarios as ID card, driver's license, driver's license, invoice, English customs documents, common forms, common characters, as shown in Fig. 8.17.

OCR supports the character recognition of general class, certificate class, bill class, industry class and customized template class.

Fig. 8.16 Customer flow analysis

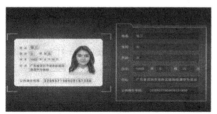

user authentication

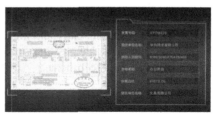

financial reimbursement audit

finance and insurance

electronic customs documents

Fig. 8.17 Optical character recognition

General OCR supports automatic recognition of text information on arbitrary format pictures, such as forms, documents, network pictures. It can analyze various layouts and forms, so as to quickly realize the electronization of various documents.

The applications of general OCR are as follows.

(a) Electronic filing of enterprise historical documents and reports: It can identify the character information in documents and reports and establish electronic files, and so as to facilitate rapid retrieval.
(b) Automatic filling in the sender information of express delivery: It can identify the contact information in the picture and automatically fill in the express delivery form, reducing manual input.
(c) Efficiency improvement of contract handling: It can automatically identify the structured information and extract the signature and seal area, which is helpful for rapid audit.
(d) Electronic customs documents: As many companies have overseas business. General OCR can realize the automatic structure and electronization of customs document data, so as to improve the efficiency and accuracy of information entry.

Certificate character recognition supports automatic identification of valid information and structured extraction of key fields on ID card, driving license, vehicle certificate, passport.

The applications of certificate character recognition are as follows.

(a) Fast authentication: It can quickly complete the real-name authentication of mobile phone account opening and other scenes, so as to reduce the cost of user identity verification.
(b) Automatic information entry: It can identify key information in certificates so as to save manual entry and improve efficiency.
(c) Verification of identity information: It can verify whether the user is the holder of a real certificate.

Bill type character recognition supports automatic recognition and structured extraction of valid information on various invoices and forms, such as VAT invoice, motor vehicle sales invoice, medical invoice, etc.

The applications of bill character recognition are as follows.

(a) Automatic entry of reimbursement document information: It can quickly identify the key information in the invoice and effectively shorten the reimbursement time.
(b) Automatic entry of document information: It can quickly enter motor vehicle sales invoice and contract information, so as to improve the efficiency of vehicle loan processing.
(c) Medical insurance: It can automatically identify key fields such as drug details, age and gender of medical documents before entering them into the system. Combined with ID card and bank card OCR, it can quickly complete insurance claims business.

Industry type character recognition supports the extraction and recognition of structured information of various industry-specific pictures, such as logistics sheets and medical test documents, which helps to improve the automation efficiency of the industry.

The applications of industry type character recognition are as follows.

(a) Automatic filling in the sender's information of express delivery: It can identify the contact information in the picture before automatically filling in the express delivery form so as to minimize manual input.
(b) Medical insurance: It can automatically identify key fields such as drug details, age and gender of medical documents and enter them into the system. Combined with ID card and bank card OCR, it can quickly complete insurance claims business.

Customized template type character recognition supports user-defined recognition templates. It can specify the key fields to be recognized, so as to realize the automatic recognition and structural extraction of user-specific format images.

(a) Identification of various certificates: For card images of various formats, it can be used to make templates to realize automatic identification and extraction of key fields.
(b) Recognition of various bills: For various bill images, it can be used to make templates to realize automatic recognition and extraction of key fields.

8.2 ModelArts

As EI basic platform in EI service family, ModelArts is a one-stop development platform for AI developers. It provides massive data preprocessing and semi-automatic annotation, large-scale distributed training, automatic model generation and on-demand deployment capabilities of End, Edge and Cloud model, helping users quickly create and deploy models and managing full cycle AI workflow.

"One-stop" means that all aspects of AI development, including data processing, algorithm development, model training and model deployment, can be completed on ModelArts. Technically, it supports various heterogeneous computing resources, so that developers can choose to use flexibly according to their needs, regardless of the underlying technologies. At the same time, ModelArts supports mainstream open source AI development frameworks such as TensorFlow and MXNet, as well as self-developed algorithm frameworks to match the usage habits of developers.

Aiming to make AI development easier and more convenient, ModelArts provides AI developers with a convenient and easy-to-use process. For example, business-oriented developers can use automatic learning process to quickly build AI applications without focusing on model or coding; AI beginners can use preset algorithms to build AI applications without much concern for model development; provided with a variety of development environments, operation processes and modes by ModelArts, AI engineers can easily code expansion and quickly build models and applications.

8.2.1 Functions of ModelArts

ModelArts enables developers to complete all tasks in one stop, from data preparation to algorithm development and model training, and finally to deploy models and
integrate them into the production environment. The function overview of
ModelArts is shown in Fig. 8.18.

ModelArts features as follows.

1. Data governance: ModelArts supports data processing such as data filtering and
   annotation, providing version management of data sets, especially large data sets
   for deep learning, so that training results can be reproduced.
2. Extremely "fast" and "simple" training: Moxing deep learning framework, developed by ModelArts, is more efficient and easier to use, greatly improving the
   training speed.
3. Multi-scenario deployment of end, edge and cloud: ModelArts supports the
   deployment of models to a variety of production environments, which can be
   deployed as cloud online reasoning and batch reasoning, or directly deployed to
   end and edge.
4. Automatic learning: ModelArts supports a variety of automatic learning capabilities. Through "automatic learning" training model, users can complete automatic
   modeling and one-click deployment without writing code.
5. Visual workflow: ModelArts uses GES to manage the metadata of development
   process and automatically visualize the relationship between workflow and
   version evolution, so as to realize model traceability.
6. AI Market: ModelArts preset common algorithms and data sets, supporting the
   sharing of models within the enterprise or publicly.

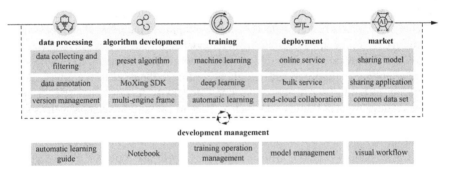

Fig. 8.18 Function overview of ModelArts

8.2.2 Product Structure and Application of ModelArts

As a one-stop development platform, ModelArts supports the whole development process of developers from data to AI application, including data processing, model training, model management, model deployment and other operations. It also provides AI market functions, and can share models with other developers in the market. The product structure of ModelArts is shown in Fig. 8.19.

Modelarts supports the whole process development from data preparation to model deployment AI, and a variety of AI application scenarios, as detailed below.

1. Image recognition: It can accurately identify the object classification information in the picture, such as animal identification, brand logo recognition, vehicle identification, etc.
2. Video analysis: It can accurately analyze key information in video, such as face recognition and vehicle feature recognition.
3. Speech recognition: It enables machines to understand speech signals, assisting in processing speech information, which is applicable to intelligent customer service QA, intelligent assistant, etc.
4. Product recommendation: It can provide personalized business recommendation for customers according to their own properties and behavior characteristics.
5. Anomaly detection: In the operation of network equipment, it can use an automated network detection system to make real-time analysis according to the traffic situation so as to predict suspicious traffic or equipment that may fail.
6. In the future, it will continue to exert its strength in data enhancement, model training speed and weak supervision learning, which will further improve the efficiency of AI model development.

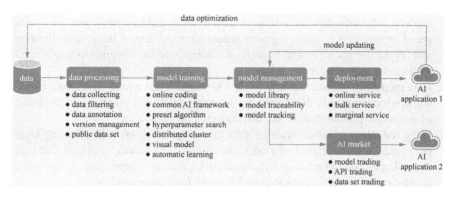

Fig. 8.19 Product structure of ModelArts

8.2.3 Product Advantages of ModelArts

The product advantages of ModelArts are reflected in the following four aspects.

1. One-stop: Out of the "box". It covers the whole process of AI development, including the functions of data processing, model development, training, management and deployment. One or more of these functions can be flexibly used.
2. Easy to use: It offers a variety of preset models, and open source models can be used whenever wanted; model super-parameters are automatically optimized, which is simple and fast; zero code development is simple to operate for training their own models; one-click deployment of models to end, edge and cloud is supported.
3. High performance: Moxing deep learning framework developed by ModelArts improves the efficiency of algorithm development and training speed; the utilization optimization of GPU in deep model reasoning can accelerate cloud online reasoning. As a result, models running on ascend chip can be generated to realize efficient end-side inference.
4. Flexibility: It supports a variety of mainstream open source frameworks (TensorFlow, Spark)_ MLlib, etc.). It supports mainstream GPU and self-developed ascend chip. It supports exclusive use of exclusive resources. It supports user-defined mirror image to meet the needs of user-defined framework and operator.

In addition, ModelArts has the following advantages.

1. Enterprise level: It supports massive data preprocessing and version management. It supports multi-scene model deployment of end, edge and cloud, to realize visual management of the whole process of AI development. It also provides AI sharing platform, assisting enterprises to build internal and external AI ecology.
2. Intellectualization: It supports automatic design of models, which can train models automatically according to deployment environment and reasoning speed requirements. It also supports automatic modeling of image classification and object detection scenes, as well as automatic feature engineering and automatic modeling of structured data.
3. Data preparation efficiency improved 100 times: It has a built-in AI data framework, which improves the efficiency of data preparation through the combination of automatic pre-annotation and difficult-case set annotation.
4. Great reduction of model training time consumption: It provides Moxing high-performance distributed framework developed by Huawei, adopting the core technologies such as cascade hybrid parallel, gradient compression, convolution acceleration, to greatly reduce model training time consumption.
5. The model can be deployed to the end, edge and cloud with one click.
6. AI model deployment: It provides edge reasoning, online reasoning and batch reasoning.
7. Accelerating AI development process with AI method—Automatic Learning: It provides UI guide and adaptive training.

8. Creating whole process management: It realizes automatic visualization of development process, restart training breakpoints, and easy comparison of training results.
9. AI Sharing—assisting developers to realize AI resource reuse: It realizes intra-enterprise sharing so as to improve efficiency.

8.2.4 Approaches of Visiting ModelArts

Huawei cloud service platform provides a web-based service management platform, namely management console and Application Programming Interface (API) management mode based on HTTPS request. ModelArts can be accessed in the following three ways.

1. Management Console Mode

   ModelArts provides a simple and easy-to-use management console, including the functions such as automatic learning, data management, development environment, model training, model management, deployment online, AI market, which can complete AI development end-to-end in the management console.

   To use ModelArts management console, you need to register a Huawei cloud account first. After registering the Huawei cloud account, you can click the hyperlink of "EI Enterprise Intelligence → AI Services → EI Basic Platform → AI Development Platform ModelArts" on the Huawei cloud home page, and click the "enter console" button in the page that appears to log in to the management console directly.

2. SDK Mode

   If you need to integrate ModelArts into a third-party system for secondary development, you can choose to call ModelArts SDK. ModelArts SDK is a Python encapsulation of REST API provided by ModelArts service, which simplifies the user's development work. For the specific operation of calling ModelArts SDK and the detailed description of SDK, please refer to the product help document "SDK Reference" on the official website of ModelArts.

   In addition, when writing code in the Notebook of the management console, you can directly call ModelArts SDK.

3. API Mode

   ModelArts can be integrated into a third-party system for secondary development. Modelarts can also be accessed by calling ModelArts API. For detailed operation and API description, please see the product help document "API overview" on the official website of ModelArts.

8.2.5   *How to Use ModelArts*

ModelArts is a one-stop development platform for AI developers. Through the whole process management of AI development, it helps developers create AI models intelligently and efficiently and deploy them to the end, edge and cloud with one click.

ModelArts not only supports automatic learning function, but also presets a variety of trained models, integrating Jupyter Notebook to provide online code development environment.

According to different groups of users, different use-patterns of ModelArts are to be selected.

For business developers without AI development experience, ModelArts provides automatic learning function, which can build AI model with zero foundation. Developers don't need to focus on development details such as model development, parameter adjustment. Just three steps (data annotation, automatic training, deployment online) are needed to complete an AI development project. The product help document "best practice" on the official website of ModelArts provides a sample of "Find Yunbao" (Yunbao is the mascot of Huawei Cloud), which is used to help business developers quickly get familiar with the use process of ModelArts automatic learning. This example is a scene project of "object detection". Through the preset Yunbao image data set, the detection model is automatically trained and generated, and the generated model is deployed as an online service. After the deployment, users can identify whether the input image contains Yunbao through the online service.

For AI beginners with certain AI foundation, ModelArts provides preset algorithm based on the mainstream engine in the industry. Learners do not need to pay attention to the model development process. They directly use preset algorithm to train existing data and quickly deploy it as a service. The preset algorithm provided by modelarts in AI market can be used for object detection, image classification and text classification.

The product help document "best practice" on the official website of ModelArts provides an example of flower image classification application, which helps AI beginners quickly get familiar with the process of using ModelArts preset algorithm to build models. This example uses the preset flower image data set to annotate the existing image data, and then uses the preset RESNET_ v1_50. Finally, the model is deployed as an online service. After the deployment, users can identify the flower species of the input image through the online service.

For AI engineers who are familiar with code writing and debugging, ModelArts provides one-stop management capability, through which AI engineers can complete the whole AI process in one stop from data preparation, model development, model training and model deployment. ModelArts is compatible with mainstream engines in the industry and user habits. At the same time, it provides a self-developed MoXing deep learning framework to improve the development efficiency and training speed of the algorithm.

The product help document "Best Practice" on the official website of ModelArts provides an example of using MXNet and NoteBook to realize the application of handwritten digital image recognition, which helps AI engineers quickly comb the whole process of AI development of ModelArts.

MNIST is a handwritten numeral recognition data set, which is often used as an example of deep learning. This example will use MXNet native interface or Note-Book model training script (provided by ModelArts by default) for MNIST dataset, deploying the model as an online service. After the deployment, users can identify the numbers entered in the picture through the online service.

8.3 Huawei CLOUD EI Solutions

This chapter mainly introduces the application cases and solutions of Huawei Cloud EI.

8.3.1 OCR Service Enabling Whole-Process Automated Reimbursement

Huawei Cloud OCR service can be applied to financial reimbursement scenarios. It automatically extracts the key information of bills, helping employees automatically fill in reimbursement forms. Meanwhile, combined with Robotic Process Automation (RPA) to it can greatly improve the work efficiency of financial reimbursement. Huawei Cloud Bill OCR recognition supports OCR recognition of various bills such as VAT invoice, taxi invoice, train ticket, itinerary sheet, shopping ticket. It can correct the skew and distortion of pictures, effectively removing the impact of seal on character recognition so as to improve the recognition accuracy.

In financial reimbursement, it is very common to have multiple bills in one image. Generally, OCR service can only identify one kind of bill. For example, VAT invoice service can only identify a single VAT invoice. However, Huawei Cloud OCR service, an online intelligent classification and identification service, supports multiple formats of invoice and card segmentation. It can recognize one image of multiple tickets, one image of multiple cards, mixed card and ticket, and realize total charging. Combined with each OCR service, it can realize the recognition of various kinds of invoices and cards including but not limited to air ticket, train ticket, medical invoice, driver's license, bank card, identity card, passport, business license, etc.

Financial personnel need to manually input the invoice information into the system after getting a batch of financial invoices. Even if you use OCR service of Huawei Cloud, you need to take photos of each financial invoice and upload it to the computer or server. Huawei Cloud can provide batch scanning OCR recognition solution, which only needs a scanner and a PC to scan invoices in batches through the scanner to generate color images. It can automatically call OCR service of Huawei Cloud in batch, to quickly complete the extraction process of invoice information, and visually compare the recognition results. It can also export the identification results to excel or financial system in batches, greatly simplifying the data entry process.

The solution has the following characteristics.

1. Multiple access methods: automatic connection scanner, batch acquisition of images; high camera, mobile phone photo acquisition of images.
2. Flexible deployment mode: supporting public cloud, HCS, all-in-one and other deployment modes, and unifying the standard API interface.
3. Applicable to all kinds of invoices: VAT general/special/electronic/ETC/voucher, taxi fare/train ticket/itinerary sheet/quota invoice/toll, etc.
4. Support one image of multiple invoices: automatic classification and recognition of multiple invoices.
5. Visual comparison: location information return, Excel format conversion, easy for statistics and analysis.

The invoice reimbursement solution is shown in Fig. 8.20. The advantages of the solution are list as the followings: improving efficiency and reducing cost, optimizing operation, simplifying process and enhancing compliance.

8.3.2 OCR Supporting Smart Logistics

Couriers can take pictures of ID card through mobile terminals (such as mobile App) when picking up the items. With Huawei Cloud ID identification service, the identity information is automatically recognized. When filling in the express information, you can complete the automatic entry of the express information by uploading the address screenshot, chat record screenshot and other pictures, for OCR can automatically extract the information such as name, telephone, address. In the process of express transportation, OCR can also extract the waybill information to complete the automatic sorting of express delivery, judging whether the information in the express face sheet is complete. OCR service of Huawei Cloud supports OCR recognition of complex pictures from any angle, uneven illumination, incomplete, with high recognition rate and good stability, which can greatly reduce labor costs and enhance user experience. The smart logistics solution is shown in Fig. 8.21.

8.3.3 Conversational Bot

Usually, a single function robot can not solve all the problems in the customer business scenario. By integrating multiple robots with different functions, a joint

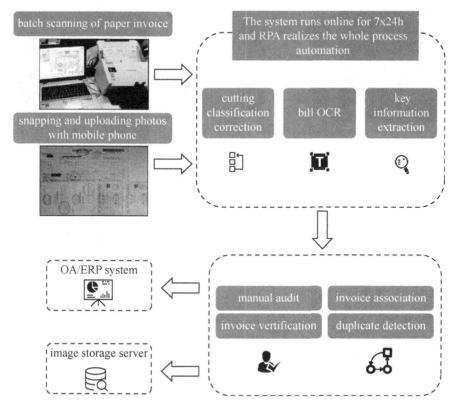

Fig. 8.20 Invoice reimbursement solution

solution of conversational bot is created, which is presented as a single service interface. Customers can only call a single interface to solve different business problems. The functional characteristics of each robot are as follows.

1. Applicable Scenarios of Intelligent QABot

   (a) Intelligent QABot can solve common types of problems such as consultation, help seeking in the fields of IT, e-commerce, finance, government. In these scenarios, users frequently consult or seek help.

   (b) Intelligent QABot has knowledge reserve, with QA knowledge base, FAQ or similar documents, as well as work order and customer service QA data.

2. Applicable Scenarios of TaskBot

   (a) TaskBot has clear conversational tasks. It can flexibly configure the conversational process (multi-round interaction) according to the actual business scenario. After loading the script template, TaskBot conducts multiple rounds

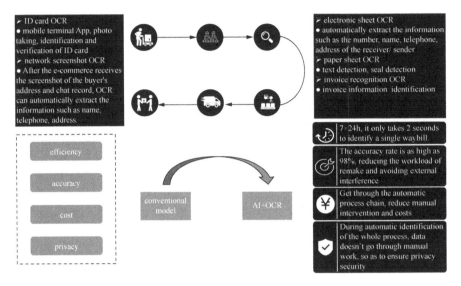

Fig. 8.21 Smart logistics solution

of dialogue with customers based on speech or text in the corresponding scene, understanding and recording customers' wishes at the same time.

(b) Outbound Bot: This kind of TaskBot can complete various tasks such as return visit of business satisfaction, verification of user information, recruitment appointment, express delivery notice, sales promotion, screening of high-quality customers.

(c) Customer Service: This kind of TaskBot can complete various tasks such as hotel reservation, air ticket reservation, credit card activation.

(d) Intelligent Hardware: This kind of TaskBot can serve in many fields such as speech assistant, smart home.

3. Applicable Scenarios of Knowledge Graph QABot

(a) Complex knowledge system.
(b) Answer requiring logical inference.
(c) Multiple rounds of interaction.
(d) A factual problem involving the value of an entity's attributes or the relationship between entities that cannot be exhausted by enumeration.

The features of dialogue robot are as follows.

(a) Multi robot intelligent integration, more comprehensive: a number of robots have their own strengths, self-learning and self optimization, so that the best answer can be recommended for customers.

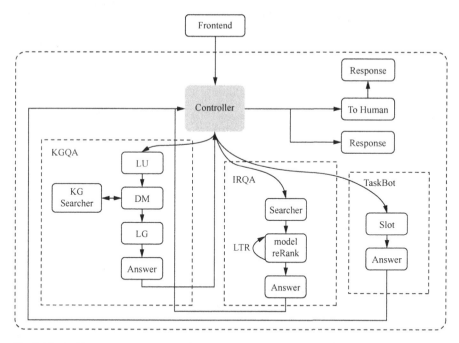

Fig. 8.22 Architecture of conversational bot

(b) Multiple rounds of intelligent guidance, better understanding: multiple rounds of dialogue, natural interaction, can accurately identify the user's intention, so that the user's potential semantics can be understood.

(c) Knowledge graph, smarter: general domain language model + domain knowledge graph; dynamic updating of map content; more intelligent robot based on graph. The architecture of conversational bot is shown in Fig. 8.22.

Intelligent QABot based on knowledge graph can conduct accurate knowledge Q&A. For example, vehicle conversational bot can be applied to query the price and configuration of a specific vehicle model. It can recommend vehicles according to price and level type. It can also conduct vehicle comparison, and offer the corresponding information such as text, table, picture. Vehicle conversational bot is shown in Fig. 8.23.

8.3.4   A Case of Enterprise Intelligent Q&A in a Certain District

Enterprise intelligent question answering system in a district of Shenzhen provides relevant business robots with automatic response. The question that are not directly answered by the robots will be automatically recorded, and then the follow-up

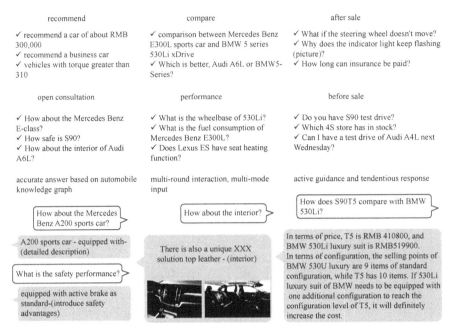

Fig. 8.23 Vehicle conversational bot

manual answering will be pushed to the questioner. The system provides a complete closed-loop solution for unsolved problems, which can realize the continuous optimization process of unsolved problems recording, artificial closed-loop knowledge formation, model annotation and optimization, making the robot more intelligent. Enterprise intelligent question answering system is shown in Fig. 8.24.

Business related to enterprise intelligent QA system mainly includes the following three categories.

1. Policy consultation (frequent policy changes).
2. Enterprise matters in office hall (more than 500 items).
3. Appeals (various types).

8.3.5   A Case in Genetic Knowledge Graph

Genetic knowledge graph includes various types of entities, such as gene, mutation, disease, drug, etc., as well as complex relationships between genes and mutation, variation and diseases, diseases and drugs. Based on this graph, the following functions can be realized.

1. Entity query: Based on genetic knowledge graph, the information of an entity (gene, mutation, disease, drug) can be quickly searched.

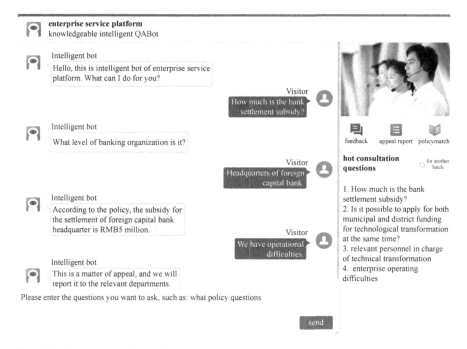

Fig. 8.24 Enterprise intelligent QA system

Fig. 8.25 Genetic knowledge graph

2. Auxiliary diagnosis: Based on the results of genetic testing, the possible variation or disease can be inferred by the graph so as to give diagnosis and treatment suggestions and recommend drugs.
3. Gene testing report: Based on the structured or semi-structured data of gene entity and its association knowledge with variation and disease, the readable gene testing report will be generated automatically.

Genetic knowledge graph is shown in Fig. 8.25.

8.3.6 Policy Query Based on Knowledge Graph

The state government often issues some incentive policies to enterprises, such as tax reduction and tax rebate policies. The contents of the policies are so professional, that ordinary people find it hard to understand and need professional interpretation.

There are many kinds of policies and reward categories. There are more than 300 conditions for enterprises to be recognized by policies, and there are logical relations between the conditions of the same policy, such as and, or, and not. Therefore, it is very difficult for enterprises to quickly obtain the policies they can enjoy.

Through policy knowledge map construction, all sorts of policy incentives and identification conditions are . In addition, we can build a knowledge map of enterprise information. Finally, we only need to input a enterprise name, and automatically obtain the value of various information (identification conditions) of the enterprise from the enterprise map, such as type, tax amount, scale and other identification conditions. Based on these identification conditions, we can Finally, all the policies and rewards that the enterprise can enjoy are obtained. The policy query based on knowledge map is shown in Fig. 8.26.

8.3.7 A Case in Smart Park

Tian'an Cloud Valley is located in Banxuegang Science and Technology City, the central area of Shenzhen, covering an area of 760,000 square meters, with a total area of 2.89 million square meters. It focuses on the new generation of information technology such as cloud computing and mobile Internet, as well as leading industries such as robot and intelligent device research and development. At the same time, the relevant modern service industry and productive service industry are developed around it. To meet the needs of leading industries, Tian'an Cloud Valley

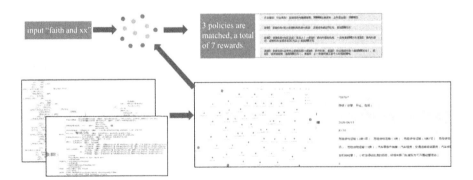

Fig. 8.26 Policy query based on knowledge graph

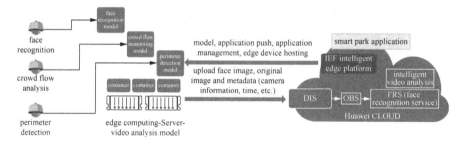

Fig. 8.27 Smart park

provides open and shared space and intelligent environment construction, so as to create a smart industry city ecosystem fully connected with enterprises and talents.

This project adopts the video analysis scheme of Edge-cloud collaboration. Video analysis models such as face recognition, vehicle recognition, intrusion detection are distributed to the local GPU inference server in the park. After the analysis of the real-time video stream is completed locally, the analysis results can be uploaded to the cloud or saved to the docking of the local upper application system.

By adopting the video analysis scheme of Edge-cloud collaboration, the park realizes intelligent analysis of surveillance video, real-time intruder perception, large flow of people and other abnormal events, so as to reduce the labor cost of the park. At the same time, the existing IPC cameras in the park can be used to change into intelligent cameras through edge cloud collaboration, which greatly protects users' stock assets. Smart park is shown in Fig. 8.27.

The end-side is an ordinary high-definition IPC camera, while the edge adopts a hardware GPU server. The competitiveness and value of edge video analysis are as follows.

1. Business value: The park conducts an intelligent analysis of surveillance video, with a real-time detection of abnormal events such as intrusion, large flow of people, so as to reduce the labor cost of the park.
2. Edge-cloud collaboration: The edge applies life-cycle management, with seamless upgrading.
3. Cloud model training: The model automatically conducts training, with good algorithm scalability, easy to update.
4. Good compatibility: The existing IPC cameras in the park can be used to change to intelligent cameras through edge cloud collaboration.

8.3.8 A Case in Pedestrian Counting and Heat Map

Pedestrian counting and heat map are mainly used to identify the crowd information in the screen, including the number of personnel information and the heat information of regional personnel. User-defined time setting and result sending interval

regional pedestrian counting

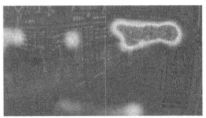
regional crowd heat map

Fig. 8.28 Pedestrian counting and heat map

setting are supported. It is mainly applied to pedestrian counting, visitor counting and heat identification in commercial areas, as shown in Fig. 8.28.

The following improvements can be achieved by using pedestrian counting and heat map.

1. Strong anti-interference: It supports pedestrian counting in complex scenes, such as face or body partially being covered.
2. High scalability: It supports the simultaneous sending of pedestrian crossing statistics, regional statistics and heat map statistics.
3. Usability improvement: It can be connected to the ordinary 1080P surveillance camera.

8.3.9 A Case in Vehicle Recognition

Vehicle recognition is shown in Fig. 8.29. With vehicle recognition, the following improvements can be achieved.

1. Comprehensive scene coverage: It supports various scenarios such as vehicle type, body color and license plate recognition in various scenes such as electric police, bayonet, etc.
2. High ease of use: Access to the ordinary 1080P surveillance camera, it can identify the vehicle information in the picture, including license plate and vehicle attribute information. It can recognize vehicle types such as cars, medium-sized

Fig. 8.29 Vehicle recognition

vehicles, and vehicle colors as well, including blue license plate and new energy license plate. It is mainly used in various scenarios such as park vehicle management, parking lot vehicle management and vehicle tracking.

8.3.10   A Case in Intrusion Identification

Intrusion identification is mainly used to identify the illegal intrusion behavior in the screen. It supports the extraction of the moving target in the camera field of vision. When the target crosses the designated area, an alarm will be triggered. It also supports the minimum number of people in the alarm area setting, alarm trigger time setting and algorithm detection cycle setting. Intrusion detection is mainly used for identification of illegal entry into key areas, illegal entry into dangerous areas or illegal climbing. Intrusion identification is shown in Fig. 8.30.

Using intrusion detection, the following improvements can be achieved.

1. High flexibility: It supports flexible alarm target sizes and category settings.
2. Low false alarm rate: It supports intrusion alarm based on person/vehicle, filtering interference from other objects.
3. Usability improvement: It can be accessed to the ordinary 1080P surveillance camera.

human over-line intrusion identification   human area intrusion identification

human climbing intrusion identification   vehicle crossing intrusion identification

Fig. 8.30 Intrusion identification

8.3.11 CNPC Cognitive Computing Platform: Reservoir Identification for Well Logging

With the completion and improvement of the integrated system, CNPC has accumulated a large amount of structured data and unstructured data. The structured data has been well used, but the unstructured data has not been fully applied. Moreover, the relevant knowledge accumulation and expert experience have not been fully exploited, and the intelligent analysis and application ability of data is insufficient.

The unstructured data features large data capacity, numerous varieties and low value density.

Cognitive computing represents a new computing mode, which is the advanced stage of artificial intelligence development. It contains a lot of technological innovation in the fields of information analysis, natural language processing and machine learning, which can help decision makers to obtain valuable information from a large number of unstructured data.

By using Huawei cloud knowledge map and NLP technology, CNPC has constructed the knowledge map of oil and gas industry. Based on the knowledge map, it constructs the upper business application (reservoir identification for well logging is identified as one of business scenarios, and other scenarios include seismic horizon interpretation, water content prediction, working condition diagnosis, etc.) Finally the following functions are realized.

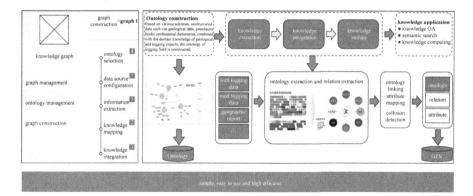

Fig. 8.31 CNPC cognitive computing platform—reservoir identification for well logging

1. Knowledge aggregation: The knowledge map of oil and gas industry can precipitate the professional knowledge of oil and gas industry.
2. Cost reduction and efficiency enhancement: Based on the knowledge map of oil and gas industry, the upper business application can simplify the business process and shortens the working time.
3. Reserve growth and production improvement: Based on the knowledge map of oil and gas industry, the upper business application can advance proved reserves and ensure energy security.

The solution of reservoir identification for well logging features as follows.

1. It can flexibly modify and manually intervene the key links such as ontology, data source, information extraction, knowledge mapping and knowledge fusion.
2. Simple knowledge reuse is simple: It can quickly create new pipeline tasks and build atlas based on existing ontology and data source.
3. Flexible modification and one-click effect: It can test frequently and quickly to improve efficiency. Finally, it can shorten the time by 70% and increase the coincidence rate by 5%. Reservoir identification for well logging is shown in Fig. 8.31.

8.4 Chapter Summary

This chapter first introduces Huawei Cloud EI ecology, and its related services are explained. Then, it focuses on the Huawei EI basic platform—ModelArts, and users can learn more about its services from the listed experiments. Finally, the relevant cases in the practical application of enterprise intelligence are discussed.

It is necessary to note that Huawei is committed to lowering the threshold of AI application. In order to assist AI lovers better understand Huawei cloud EI

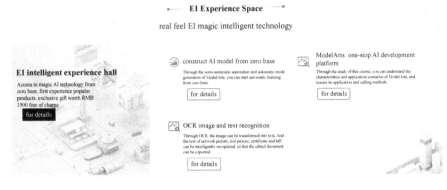

Fig. 8.32 EI experience space

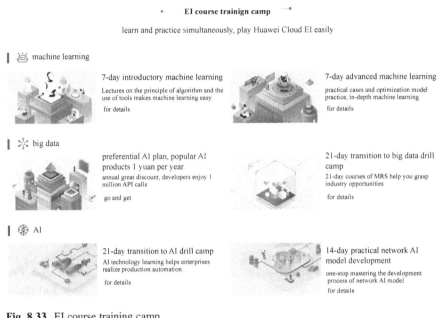

Fig. 8.33 EI course training camp

application platform, Huawei cloud official website has set up EI experience space and EI course training camp, as shown in Figs. 8.32 and 8.33.

8.5 Exercises

1. Huawei cloud EI is an enterprise intelligence enabling agent. Based on AI and big data technology, it provides an open, trusted and intelligent platform through cloud services (public cloud, dedicated cloud, etc.). What services does Huawei cloud EI service family currently include?
2. In Huawei cloud EI service family, the solutions for large-scale scenarios are called EI agents. What are they?
3. In Huawei cloud EI service family, what is EI basic platform consist of?
4. ModelArts belongs to EI basic platform in Huawei cloud EI service family. It is a one-stop development platform for AI developers. What functions does it have?
5. As a one-stop AI development platform, what are the advantages of ModelArts products?

Appendix 1: Introduction to the API of HiAI Engine

Face Recognition

1. Face Comparison

   Face comparison API performs a precise comparison of human images by recognizing and extracting face features, so that a confidence score is given to determine whether the figure is the same person. Face comparison technology can be applied to intelligent classification of photo gallery. Based on the advanced algorithm of end-side intelligent image recognition, it has high accuracy in face recognition and excellent application experience.

   The application scenarios of the algorithm are not recommended for authentication such as mobile phone unlocking and secure payment. It can be used in the scenes where face comparison function is needed in App, such as similarity comparison of between two people or between an average person and a star in entertainment App.

   When two photos of the same person are compared, the comparison result indicates that they are the same person, which has a high confidence score. When the two photos are not of the same person, the comparison result indicates they are not the same person, with a low confidence score.

   With this API, the time of algorithm development can be greatly saved. Rom space occupied by algorithm model can be saved too, so that the application is more portable. It can be used to realize local processing of data without network connection.

2. Face Detection

   Face detection API detects the face in the image before returning the high-precision rectangular coordinates of the face, which can be used as a key module to realize the functions of application and screen startup or shutdown. It can beautify the specific position of the face by locating facial features and position.

Face detection is widely used in various face recognition scenes, such as face unlocking, face clustering, beautification.

Adapting to common light, various head postures and occlusion, face detection supports multi-ethnic and multi face detection. Face detection achieves high detection rate and low false detection rate.

3. Face Analysis

Face analysis is to decompose the human head (including facial features) into different areas such as hair, facial skin, eyes, eyebrows, nose, mouth and ears. Its main function is to analyze the face in the input picture, providing the analysis results of various facial areas, including background, facial skin, left/right eyebrow, left/right eye, nose, upper lip/mouth interior/lower lip, left/right ear, neck, spectacles and sunglasses. Different parts are marked with different colors.

4. Face Attributes

Face attributes are a series of biological characteristics that represent face features. They have strong self stability and individual differences, which can identify human identity. Face attributes are composed of gender, skin color, age, facial expression.

The main function of this API is to recognize the face attributes in the input picture, identifying the gender. It supports seven facial expressions—— joy, grieve, astonishment, anger, pout, grimace and neutral facial expression, and three character attributes—— gender, age and wearing (wearing glasses, hat or beard). It also supports facial expression and attribute recognition of multiple faces.

5. Face Orientation Recognition

Face orientation recognition can check whether there is a person in the visual field of mobile phone camera, and identify the orientation of the face.It provides important information for the decision-making system of the smart phone. For example, face orientation recognition is applied to various scenes such as intelligent screen on, intelligent screen off, intelligent rotation, image rotation control. Face orientation means the direction of intermediate datum line (pointing to the top of the head) in facial plane, which can be divided into five scenarios, namely, no direction (unmanned), up, right, down and left.

Based on visible light image recognition technology, face orientation recognition uses image recognition technology to detect five categories of face up, face right, face down, face left and unmanned face in the plane. Through this API, we can get the specific category and confidence of the face orientation in the image.

The algorithm is used to check the face orientation information in the image. It can be applied to various scenes such as detecting the presence of person and judging the face orientation.

6. Facial Feature Detection

Facial feature detection API can detect facial features of input image before returning the coordinates of facial landmarks (the current number is 276) , which represent the contour position of facial features. It can provide input for subsequent processing such as beautification, face modeling, facial expression recognition.

Human Recognition

1. Pose Estimation

   Pose estimation is the basis of many computer vision tasks, such as motion classification, abnormal behavior detection and autonomous vehicle. It weighs a lot in posture description and behavior prediction. In recent years, with the development of deep learning technology, it has been widely used in the related fields of computer vision.

   Pose estimation mainly detects some key points of human body, such as joints, facial features, through which human bone information are stated.

2. Video Portrait Segmentation

   Video portrait segmentation API supports the real-time processing of real-time video streams (such as mobile camera). The developer transmits each frame image of the real-time video stream to HiAI Engine. Then the algorithm splits the portrait in the image, the mask result of byte array is returned to the user.

   Through video portrait segmentation, users can render the foreground (person), such as blurring and beautification. The background can also be processed such as background replacement and background removal.

Image Recognition

1. Aesthetic Score

   Implementing an advanced multi-dimensional scoring technology of video AI, the aesthetic engine comprehends complex subjective aspects in images, making high-level judgments related to the attractiveness, memorability and engaging nature of an image. It can be applied in various video intelligent scenarios, such as auxiliary photography, photo group auxiliary, auxiliary video editing and video splitting.

   This API can be used in photography or photo management apps, such as those for personal photo album management, automatic photo editing, and auxiliary photo shooting. The aesthetic engine's algorithms help realize the multi-dimensional evaluation of images, from aesthetic, technology, and compositional perspectives.

2. Picture Classification Tagging

   Based on deep learning method, picture classification tagging API identifies the information in the picture such as object, scene and behavior. The corresponding tag information, such as flowers, birds, fish, insects, cars and buildings can be returned. This API can be applied in various intelligent scenarios concerning picture content understanding, such as automatic classification and sorting of picture library, social picture recognition and sharing. Rich in tag information, this API supports the recognition of 100 kinds of common objects, scenes and behaviors. It creates a leading end-side intelligent image recognition algorithm, which has strong classification tag recognition and high accuracy.

3. Image Super-resolution

Image super-resolution is based on the extensive application of deep learning in computer vision, which can enlarge pictures intelligently or remove the compressed noise under the condition of constant resolution, so as to obtain clearer, sharper and cleaner photos than traditional image processing.

The algorithm, based on deep neural network and NPU chip of Huawei mobile phone, is nearly 50 times faster than pure CPU computing. This API is built into Huawei mobile phone, with less ROM and RAM consumption, which has a smaller-sized and lighter application.

4. Scene Detection

By identifying the scene of the image content, the scene detection API can quickly classify the input image, supporting multi types of scene recognition at present. The recognition scenes cover a variety of categories with high recognition accuracy, including animals, plants, food, buildings and cars. Through scene recognition, adding intelligent classification tags to images can be widely used in various scenarios such as creating intelligent photo albums and image classification management.

Generally, different scenes require different preferences or strategies for the photographic effect. This API can provide decision-making basis, so that the image rendering effect can choose a better strategy for each characteristic scene.

5. Document Detection and Correction

Document detection and correction can realize the auxiliary enhancement in the process of document reproduction. It can automatically identify the document in the picture, returning the position information of the document in the original picture. Documents here generally indicate square-shaped items, such as books, photos, and picture frames. This function contains two sub functions: document detection and document correction.

Document detection: It identifies the document in the picture and return the position information of the document in the original picture.

Document correction: According to the position information of the document in the original picture, it can correct the shooting angle of the document (the correction area can be customized), while automatically adjusting the shooting angle to the angle facing the document. This function works well in situations where old paper photos, letters, or paintings are reproduced into electronic versions.

6. Text Image Super-resolution

The text content in an image usually contains very important information. However, the text content may be blurred caused by shooting restriction, low resolution and remote subject. The text image super-resolution API can magnify the image containing text content by nine times (three times for height and three times for width), while significantly enhancing the clarity of the text in the image.

In the scene of text file reproduction, the identifiability of text is improved as a result of the boosted sharpness of images. At present, the algorithm is based on the deep neural network development, which makes full use of the NPU chip of

Huawei mobile phone to accelerate the neural network. The acceleration ratio can reach more than ten times.

7. Portrait Segmentation

Portrait segmentation refers to the separation of the portrait and background into different areas, with different tags to distinguish.

This API can implement portrait segmentation on the part of the input image containing the portrait, and the segmentation results are displayed as the portrait and background differentiation. It can be used to foreground replacement, background replacement and background blurring.

8. Image Semantic Segmentation

The image is recognized and segmented at the pixel level, so as to obtain the category information and accurate position information of the object in the image. As the basic information of image semantic understanding, these contents can be used for subsequent image enhancement processing. This API currently supports the recognition and segmentation of ten types of objects, i.e., human, sky, plants (including grass and trees), food, pets, buildings, flowers, water, beaches and mountains.

This API is used for pixel-level recognition and segmentation of photographic images, which can be applied to the scenarios such as app auxiliary photography and street scene recognition.

Code Recognition

Code recognition gets the information contained in the code by identifying QR code and bar code, providing service framework which can be integrated into its application.

This API covers the resolution of QR code/bar code image in 11 scenarios such as Wi-Fi and SMS. In addition to effective code detection, it also provides service capability based on detection results. It can be widely used in code scanning services of various applications, such as QR code and bar code recognition.

Video Technology

1. Video Summary

The aesthetic engine comprehends complex subjective aspects in images, making high-level judgments related to the attractiveness, memorability and engaging nature of an image, based on the multi-dimensional comprehensive aesthetic scoring technology of video AI. It can be applied in various video intelligent scenarios, such as auxiliary photography, photo group auxiliary, auxiliary video editing and video splitting.

This API can be used in photography or photo management apps, such as those for personal photo album management, automatic photo editing, and auxiliary photo shooting. The aesthetic engine's algorithms help realize the multi-dimensional evaluation of images, from aesthetic, technology, and compositional perspectives.

2. Video Cover

Implementing the multi-dimensional comprehensive aesthetic scoring technology based on video AI, the aesthetic engine can complex subjective aspects in images, making high-level judgments related to the attractiveness, memorability and engaging nature of an image. It can be applied in various video intelligent scenarios, such as auxiliary photography, photo group auxiliary, auxiliary video editing and video splitting.

The API can be used in photography or photo management apps, such as personal album management, automatic photo editing, auxiliary photo shooting. The algorithm of aesthetic engine help realize the multi-dimensional evaluation of images, from aesthetic, technology, and compositional perspectives, so as to obtain the static cover and dynamic cover with the highest aesthetic score.

Text Recognition

1. General Character Recognition

The core of general character recognition is optical character recognition (OCR) technology, which transforms the characters of various bills, newspapers, books, manuscripts and other printed matter into image information through optical input methods such as scanning. And then the image information is converted into usable computer input technology by OCR. It plays an increasingly important role in the process of smart mobile phone. In smart phones, OCR is used in more and more applications, such as the identification of documents, road signs, menus, business cards, certificates, scanning questions. The current end-side general character recognition interface is divided into focusing photography OCR and mobile phone screenshot OCR.

Focusing photography OCR API is applicable to various sources of image data such as cameras and galleries. It provides an open interface for automatic detection and recognition of text position and content in images. Focusing photography OCR API can support scenes such as text tilt, shooting angle tilt, complex lighting conditions and complex text background to a certain extent. It can be used for text detection and recognition of document reproduction and street view reproduction. It has such a wide range of applications and strong anti-interference ability that it can be integrated into other applications to provide text detection and recognition services, and related services based on the results.

Aiming at the characteristics of mobile phone screenshots, mobile phone screenshot OCR API provides light and fast text extraction function for mobile phone screenshot pictures on the end side, which is convenient for subsequent processing and service docking, such as copy, editing, word segmentation and semantic analysis. The API custom hierarchical result return, by which the text block, text line and text character coordinates in the screenshot can be returned according to the application needs. This API provides an optimized algorithm for text extraction. The average time of text extraction for simple background mobile phone screenshot API is less than 200 ms, while the average time of general mobile phone screenshot OCR API is less than 500 ms.

2. Table Recognition

Based on the ability of focusing photography OCR, table recognition can identify the text in the input picture and detect the structure information of the table, including the location information of the cell, the number of occupied rows and columns of the cell, and the text information in each cell. The table recognition API currently supports page scenarios (paper, printed pages, etc.) and projection scenarios (conference room presentation projection).

The table recognition API is applied to the content recognition of various table scenarios. The three-party app can use the results returned by the engine to generate Excel files so as to reduce the cost of manual input.

3. Passport Recognition

Passport recognition is based on OCR technology, which extracts the text information from a passport photo taken by mobile phones or in image gallery. With the help of the general OCR text detection and text recognition ability, it extracts the key information from the passport image before returning it to the user or the third-party application, which helps users to quickly enter the document information, and saves from the troubles of manual input. Passport recognition is applicable to various conditions such as the horizontal or vertical shot of mobile phone, complex lighting conditions. It can be integrated into a variety of applications, providing services for identification and identification of third-party applications.

Passport is a legal document issued by a country to prove the nationality and identity of a citizen when he or she enters or leaves the country and travels or resides abroad. The entry of passport information is currently involved in many apps. Due to the large amount of information on the passport, if the passport information is entered manually, it will bring a lot of problems such as low efficiency and poor users' experience. In order to improve the speed and accuracy of passport information input on mobile terminals, Huawei has developed passport recognition OCR technology to meet the application needs of various industries, offering better experience to users. Users only need to integrate the passport recognition SDK into the app to scan and recognize the passport information through the mobile phone camera.

4. ID Card Identification

ID card identification is an important application based on OCR technology. By calling the ability of focusing photography OCR, the mobile phone can directly take photos of the certificate and extract the key information on the certificate.

ID card identification can extract key information such as name, gender, birth, certificate number from ID card photos.

At present, the identity of customers requires to be verified in many apps such as payment apps (UnionPay, XX bank, Huawei pay), travel apps (Didi and 12306), and hotel apps (Huazhu). The customers are required to upload their ID card photos while using these apps. The ID card identification API assists such apps to automatically identify the user's ID card information.

Huawei's ID card recognition function extracts important information on the ID card by calling OCR ID card recognition ability, and outputs it in the form of JSON.

5. Driving License Identification

OCR driving license recognition API can be used to quickly identify key information on the license.

Through the identification of driving license, the information on the license is recognized in the form of JSON, which is convenient for the rapid information entry. The accuracy of identification is more than 97%, and the recalling rate is more than 97%.

6. Vehicle License Recognition

OCR vehicle license recognition API can be used to quickly identify the key information on the license.

Through vehicle license recognition, the license information is identified as JSON, which is convenient for the rapid entry of license information. The recognition accuracy is more than 97%, and the recall rate is more than 97%.

7. Document Conversion

Document conversion API can easily convert images to documents (such as presentations). This API can identify the document and the text of it as well, then return the identified document and text to the client-side, which can restore the information to the presentation format.

Only by calling one interface, developers can quickly obtain the document detection and correction, text supersession, OCR detection results.

8. Bank Card Identification

The function of the bank card identification API is to identify the bank card number in the input picture.

Through the identification of bank card, the card number information on the bank card is extracted and output in the form of corresponding card object.

The accuracy rate of bank card identification is more than 99%, and the recognition recall rate is more than 99%.

Speech Recognition

People have long dreamed to talk with the machine and let the machine understand what man says. SharKing IOT Circle vividly compared speech recognition to "machine hearing system". Speech recognition technology, also known as automatic speech recognition (ASR), is a technology that enables the machine to transform speech signals into corresponding text or commands through recognition and understanding process.

Huawei speech recognition engine is oriented to mobile terminals, providing developers with AI application layer API. It can transform speech files and real-time speech data streams into Chinese character sequences, with the recognition accuracy rate over 90% (the accuracy rate of local recognition is 95%, the accuracy of cloud recognition is 97%), giving users a lively application experience.

This API can be applied to develop the third-party applications with speech recognition requirements in various scenarios, such as speech input method, speech search, real-time subtitle, games, chatting, human-computer interaction, driving modes.

Natural Language Processing

1. Word Segmentation

    With the development of information technology, the rapid growth of network information, text information and the geometric growth of information dominates in today's society. In order to extract the key information of text, word segmentation becomes particularly important in search engine and other fields. As a basic research in the field of natural language processing, word segmentation has derived various applications related to text processing.

    The word segmentation API provides an interface for automatic word segmentation of text. For a piece of input text, the API can automatically segment words. At the same time, it provides different word segmentation granularity, which can be customized according to the needs.

2. Part-of-speech Tagging

    The part-of-peech tagging API provides an interface for text automatic word segmentation and part of speech. For a piece of input text, the API can automatically segment the word and give the corresponding part of speech. At the same time, it provides different word segmentation granularity, which can be customized according to the needs.

3. Assistant Intention Recognition

    With the popularity of human-computer interaction, the device needs to understand various instructions issued by users to facilitate the operation of users. Assistant intention recognition is to analyze and identify the text messages sent to the device by using machine learning technology. Based on semantic analysis, various intelligent application scenarios can be derived from assistant intention recognition, which makes smart devices more intelligent.

    This API can be applied to speech assistant. Through intelligent interaction between intelligent dialogue and instant question and answer, the API can help users solve problems quickly.

4. IM Intention Recognition

IM intention recognition indicates the use of machine learning technology to analyze and recognize the intention of text messages of user's SMS or chatting apps (such as wechat and QQ). Based on semantic analysis, machine learning technology is used to identify and understand the intention of user's message. Through IM intention recognition, a variety of intelligent application scenarios can be derived, making smart devices more intelligent.

This API provides an interface for identifying the intention of user's SMS or text messages on chatting apps. Through this API, the intention of text messages can be automatically analyzed and identified. At present, only three intentions of notification message are supported, namely, repayment reminder, successful repayment and missed calls.

5. Keyword Extraction

In our daily life, we are filled with all kinds of information, which is composed of ever-changing languages, integrating physics, mathematics, linguistics, computer and other disciplines into one. As a carrier of information, both useful information and useless information are contained in these languages. Keyword extraction is to quickly extract the key information and the core content from the vast information sea.

The keyword extraction API provides an interface to extract keywords. It can be used to extract the core content of the text from a large amount of information, which can be entities with specific meaning, such as person name, place, movie, etc., or some basic but key words in the text. Through the API, the extracted keywords can be sorted from high to low according to the weight in the text. The higher the ranking is, the more accurate the core content of the text is extracted.

6. Entity Recognition

The entity recognition API can extract entities with specific meaning from natural language, and then complete a series of related operations and functions such as search.

It covers a wide range, meeting the needs of entity recognition in daily development and offering a better application experience. It has a high accuracy for entity recognition, for it can accurately extract entity information, making a key impact on information-based follow-up services.

Appendix 2: Key to Exercises

Chapter 1

1. As long as the answer makes sense.
2. Among the three, machine learning is a way or subset of artificial intelligence, and deep learning is a special kind of machine learning. Artificial intelligence can be compared to brain. Machine learning is a process to master cognitive ability, and deep learning is a very efficient teaching system in this process. Artificial

intelligence is the purpose and the result, while deep learning and machine learning are methods and tools.

3. As long as the answer makes sense. Take smart medicine as an example. By using artificial intelligence technology, we can let AI "learn" professional medical knowledge, "memorize" a large number of historical cases, identify medical images with computer vision technology. And doctors can be equipped with reliable and efficient intelligent assistants. For example, in today's widely used medical imaging technology, researchers can establish models by using the past data to identify the existing medical images, so as to quickly determine the focus of patients and improve the efficiency of consultation.

4. Operator level fusion engine Fusionengine, CCE operator library, efficient and high-performance user-defined operator development tools, low-level compiler.

5. Answer according to individual understanding.

Chapter 2

1. For a certain kind of task T and performance measure P, the performance of a computer program measured by P on T improves with experience E, so we call the computer program learning from experience E.

2. Variance is the degree of deviation of the prediction results near the mean value, while deviation is the difference between the mean value and the correct value of the prediction results. Over-fitting model generally features low deviation and high variance.

3. The calculation of precision and recall in Figs. 8.2–8.25 is given in this chapter, which are 0.875 and 0.824 respectively. According to the formula, FF1 = 2 × 0.875 × 0.824/(0.875 + 0.824) = 0.848.

4. Validation sets can be used to help model search for hyperparameters, while test sets cannot participate in model training in any form. Validation sets are introduced for cross-validation.

5. New features can be constructed based on existing features, and then polynomial regression can be used. For example, the feature x of all samples is squared and x^2 is added to the dataset as a new feature.

6. There are many methods to extend the binary classification SVM to multi classification problems, One-against-one method is one of them. For each two categories in the data set, one-against-one method will build a binary classification SVM, so there are C_k^2 models that need to be trained , where k represents the number of categories. In the prediction, each model gives a classification result for the new sample, which is equivalent to a vote on the category to which the sample belongs. Finally, the category with the most votes is regarded as the classification result (one of them can be selected when there is tie).

7. Gaussian kernel function does not map vector to infinite dimensional space, and then calculate inner product, because this method is not feasible. In fact, it can be proved that the calculation of Gauss kernel function for the difference between

two vectors is equivalent to the above process. This is the principle of Gaussian kernel function.

8. Gradient descent algorithm is not the only way to train the model. Other methods such as genetic algorithm and Newton algorithm can be used to train the model. The disadvantages of gradient descent algorithm are as follows: easy to fall into local extreme value, only suitable for differentiable functions, and not considering the sensitivity of different parameters.

Chapter 3

1. There is little need for computer hardware in traditional machine learning , while deep learning needs a lot of matrix operations, and GPU for parallel computing. Traditional machine learning is suitable for small amount of data training, while deep learning can obtain high performance under massive training data. Traditional machine learning needs to decompose the problem layer by layer, while deep learning is an end-to-end learning. Traditional machine learning requires manual feature selection while deep learning uses algorithms to extract features automatically. The characteristics of traditional machine are highly interpretable, while the characteristics of deep learning are weak in interpretation.

2. The activation function introduces nonlinearity into neural network. Although the perceptron model is linear, the neural network with nonlinear activation function is no longer linear, so it can solve nonlinear problems, such as XOR problem.

3. The output of Sigmoid function is not centered on 0, easy to saturate. The tanh function corrects the function output so that it is centered on 0. But it does not solve the problem of easy saturation, which may cause the gradient to disappear.

4. The goal of regularization method is to reduce the generalization error of the model. Dropout is a kind of general regularization method with simple calculation. Its principle is to construct a series of sub networks with different structures and combine them in a certain way, which is equivalent to using the method of ensemble learning.

5. Compared with Adam optimizer, momentum optimizer is slower but not easy to over fit.

6. $\begin{bmatrix} 4 & 3 & 4 \\ 2 & 4 & 3 \\ 2 & 3 & 4 \end{bmatrix}$

7. The memory unit of recurrent neural network can realize the memory function by taking its own output as input. But the memory of recurrent neural network is very limited, and it can't deal with long sequence effectively. Alternative models are LSTM or GRU.

8. The result of the game is improved by generating the discriminator and generator of the alternate training of the counter network.

9. The problems of gradient vanishing and gradient explosion are caused by too deep network and unstable updating of network weight. The methods to deal with gradient vanishing problem are pre-training, the use of ReLU activation function, LSTM neural network, and residual module. The main scheme to deal with gradient explosion is gradient shear.

Chapter 4

1. The mainstream development framework of artificial intelligence is as follows.

   • Tensorflow: Based on graph operation, and the variables of each link in training can be controlled by the node variables on the graph. Especially in the low-level operation, TensorFlow is easier than other frameworks.
   • Keras: TensorFlow, CNTK, MXNet and other well-known frameworks all provide support for Keras call syntax, and the API call method of building model has gradually become the mainstream. The code written in Keras is much more portable.
   • Pytorch: Its framework is also fairly extensible, but some interfaces are not comprehensive enough. Its biggest drawback is that it needs the support of LuaJIT and uses Lua language to program. The general performance of Pytorch is poor as Python is prevailing today.

2. The main difference between TensorFlow 1.0 and TensorFlow 2.0 is that the former uses static diagram, which is more efficient, wheras the latter uses dynamic diagram, which is easier to debug. Meanwhile, TensorFlow version 2.0 has stronger cross platform capability so that it can be deployed on various platforms such as Android, JavaScript, Java.

3. tf.errors:The exception type of TensorFlow error.
   tf.data: Realize the operation of data set. Use the input pipeline created by tf.data. to read the training data. It also supports convenient data input from memory (such as NumPy).
      tf.distributions:Realize various distributions in statistics

4. Characteristics of Keras: Keras itself is not a framework, but an advanced API on top of other deep learning frameworks. At present, it supports TensorFlow, Theano and CNTK, with good scalability, simple API, user-friendliness and complete documents. Therefore, Keras is widely used.

5. Answer is omitted.

Chapter 5

1. The features of MindSprore architecture include friendly development state (AI algorithm is code), efficient running state (Ascend/GPU optimization is supported), flexible deployment state (full scene on-demand collaboration).

2. MindSprore proposed three technological innovations: new programming paradigm, new execution mode and new collaboration mode.
3. On-device implementation is adopted and the whole image is sunk to give full play to the computing power of Ascend AI processor. MindSprore maximizes the parallelism of "data computing communication" by using the chip-oriented depth map optimization technology, which minimizes synchronous waiting and sinks the entire data + computing graph into Ascend chip for optimal effect.
4. See Sect. 5.2.3.

Chapter 6

1. GPU is mainly faced with highly unified, interdependent large-scale data and pure computing environment that does not need to be interrupted: thousands of cores, design based on high throughput; speciality in computing intensive and parallel programs.
   CPU requires a strong generality to handle different data types. At the same time, logic judgment is needed too. A large number of branch jump and interrupt processing are introduced: only a few cores; low delay design; speciality in logic control and serial operation.
2. Computing unit, storage system and control unit.
3. Cube unit, vector unit and scalar unit.
4. The four layers are L3 application enabling layer, L2 execution framework layer, L1 chip enabling layer and L0 computing resource layer. The tool chain mainly provides auxiliary capabilities such as engineering management, compilation and debugging, matrix, log and profiling.
5. Matrix, DVPP module, tensor boost engine, framework, runtime and task scheduler.
6. Ascend 310 is used for inference, while Ascend 910 is mainly for training.
7. The inference products are mainly composed of Atlas 200 AI acceleration module, Atlas 200 DK, Atlas 300 inference card, Atlas 500 intelligent edge station and Atlas 800 AI inference server.
   The training products mainly include Atlas 300 AI training card, Atlas 800 AI server and Atlas 900 AI cluster.
8. See Sect. 6.4.

Chapter 7

1. HUAWEI HiAI platform builds a three-tier ecosystem of "Service, Engine and Foundation": HiAI Foundation, HiAI Engine and HiAI Service. It supports rich front-end mainstream frameworks on the service side. It provides rich upper layer functional business APIs on the engine side, which can run efficiently on mobile devices. It flexibly schedules heterogeneous resources on the foundation side,

which can meet the needs of developers to accelerate neural network model calculation and sub calculation.

2. HiAI Foundation.
3. HiAI Engine.
4. Android Studio.
5. The integration process of App is as follows.

- Step 1: Project creation.
  ① Create an Android studio project and check the "Include C++ support" option.
  ② Select C++ 11 in C++ Standard, check "Exceptions Support (-fexceptions)" option, check "Runtime Type Information Support(-frtti)" option.
- Step 2: JNI compilation.
  ① Realize JNI, write Android.mk document.
  ② Write Application.mk File, and copy sdk so to the repository.
  ③ Specify ndk to compile C++ document in build.gradle document.
- Step 3: Model integration.
  ① Model pre-processing: Application layer model pre-processing, JNI layer model pre-processing.
  ② Model inference.

Chapter 8

1. Huawei CLOUD EI service family is composed of EI big data, EI basic platform, conversational bot, natural language processing (NLP), speech interaction, speech analysis, image recognition, content review, image search, face recognition, Optical Character Recognition (OCR) and EI agent.
2. EI agent is composed of transportation AI agent, industrial AI agent, park AI agent, network AI agent, auto AI agent, medical AI agent and geographic AI agent.
3. EI basic platform provides such services as ModelArts platform, deep learning, machine learning, HiLens, graph engine service and video access.
4. The functions of ModelArts include data governance, extremely "fast" and "simple" model training, multi-scenario deployment of "end, edge and cloud", automatic learning, visual workflow and AI market.
5. The product advantages of ModelArts are reflected in four aspects: one-stop, user-friendliness, high performance and flexibility.

Index

© The Author(s) 2023
Huawei Technologies Co., Ltd., *Artificial Intelligence Technology*,
https://doi.org/10.1007/978-981-19-2879-6

Printed in the United States
by Baker & Taylor Publisher Services